LEGISLATIVE WOMEN

DATE DUE

LEGISLATIVE WOMEN

Getting Elected, Getting Ahead

edited by
Beth Reingold

LYNNE
RIENNER
PUBLISHERS

BOULDER
LONDON

Published in the United States of America in 2008 by
Lynne Rienner Publishers, Inc.
1800 30th Street, Boulder, Colorado 80301
www.rienner.com

and in the United Kingdom by
Lynne Rienner Publishers, Inc.
3 Henrietta Street, Covent Garden, London WC2E 8LU

Library of Congress Cataloging-in-Publication Data
Legislative women : getting elected, getting ahead / edited by Beth
Reingold.
      p. cm.
  Includes bibliographical references and index.
  ISBN-13: 978-1-58826-592-0 (hardcover : alk. paper)
  ISBN-13: 978-1-58826-567-8 (pbk. : alk. paper)
  1. Women politicians. 2. Women in politics. I. Reingold, Beth.
  HQ1236.L42 2008
  328.082—dc22

                                                        2008012823

British Cataloguing in Publication Data
A Cataloguing in Publication record for this book
is available from the British Library.

Printed and bound in the United States of America

  ♻   Printed on 30% postconsumer recycled paper

        The paper used in this publication meets the requirements
  ∞   of the American National Standard for Permanence of
        Paper for Printed Library Materials Z39.48-1992.

Contents

Tables and Figures

Tables

Figures

Acknowledgments

THIS BOOK WOULD not have been possible without the encouragement, support, and hard work of many people. When we set out to explore the current status of women in US politics, we as scholars were honored to engage in dialogue with some of today's most influential political women—current and former elected and appointed public officials, high-ranking advisers, and campaign professionals included. We thank them all.

The generous support of both the Institute of Governmental Studies (IGS) at the University of California at Berkeley and the Center for Politics at the University of Virginia facilitated the dialogue between scholars and practitioners. In addition to our appreciation for all the staff at the IGS and the Center for Politics, we are especially grateful to Jack Citrin, Larry Sabato, Ethan Rarick, and Holly Hatcher. Jack Citrin, director of the IGS, deserves additional credit for envisioning and promoting the full scholarly potential of our deliberations. Special thanks also go to Marrisa Martino Golden (Department of Political Science, Bryn Mawr College) for being so willing to share her research, wisdom, time, and good humor.

The process of transforming this manuscript into a published book proceeded at a rapid but calm and efficient pace thanks in large part to Jessica Harrell and Barry Hashimoto, PhD students at Emory University. Each promptly provided a great deal of conscientious and detailed editorial assistance. We also thank the anonymous reviewers who read our work so carefully and offered both encouragement and constructive criticism. Last but certainly not least, we are extremely grateful to Leanne Anderson, our editor at Lynne Rienner Publishers, who has shared and sustained our interest in and enthusiasm for this project. Every chapter—indeed, every page—in this book has benefited from her creative insight and professional judgment.

—*Beth Reingold*

1

Understanding the Complex World of Women in US Politics

BETH REINGOLD

AS I WRITE (in January of 2008), Senator Hillary Rodham Clinton is making a historic run for the Democratic presidential nomination as the first female front-runner. Her early lead in the polls as well as her upset victory in the New Hampshire primary have been attributed to her strong support among women.[1] All the other Democratic nominees have been scrambling to compete for women's votes and campaign contributions. Meanwhile, Nancy Pelosi (D-CA) is presiding over the US House of Representatives as the first female Speaker. Of the record 86 women serving in Congress, 20 members, or 23 percent, are women of color.[2] Eight women serve as governor of their state, 10 as lieutenant governor. Over 1,700 women, 20 percent of whom are women of color, serve in state legislatures across the nation; in 13 state legislatures, women make up over 30 percent of the membership. Are women truly "in" politics now? What does it mean and what does it take for women to be truly "in" elite political positions and institutions?

Offering new insight into the meaning of "women *in* politics," each chapter of *Legislative Women* contemplates the changing and increasingly complex array of opportunities and challenges facing women today—as voters, candidates, and public officials. The research presented here, like the research that preceded it, focuses primarily on *legislative* women—women getting elected to and getting ahead in Congress and state legislatures. Yet it speaks to the experiences of women in US politics more generally. At the very least, our studies of legislative women raise interesting and important questions about executive women, judicial women, and women active in local politics. We hope the chapters that follow will help inspire—and equip—a new, expanded wave of research on women in all their diversity, across all political institutions, and at every level of US politics.

1

To introduce and frame the research collected in this volume, this chapter offers a brief history of both the events and scholarly research surrounding and involving women in US politics in recent decades. Beginning with the heady days of the 1992 Year of the Woman, both the "real" world of political women and our understanding of that world have changed in similar ways. Women truly "in" politics and studies of women in politics have grown in number and complexity. As a result, the Year of the Woman moniker, in all its singularity, has grown increasingly problematic. As this volume demonstrates, there is no singular, quintessential, or universal woman in politics, and there is no singular, quintessential year, or political context, in which women seek and exercise power. The experiences of women in US politics no doubt are gendered—profoundly shaped by social, political, and institutional biases, norms, and practices that constitute our shared notions of what is or should be "feminine" and "female" or "masculine" and "male." But as political scientists explore the dynamics of gender and politics, we are becoming increasingly aware that women in politics experience gender in many different ways.

The Year of the Woman

The 1992 Year of the Woman campaign season was quite remarkable. That was the year when the task of getting women into political office seemed most pressing and most promising. Record numbers of women ran for and won elective office. Most notably, the percentage of women in Congress almost doubled (from 6% to 10%) as their numbers increased from 32 just prior to the 1992 elections to 54. Women contributed to women's election campaigns in record numbers (Wilcox 1994, 10–11). EMILY's List and other political action committees (PACs) devoted to supporting female candidates shattered records for campaign fund-raising (Nelson 1994). Women's representation, or the lack thereof, was a prominent campaign issue. Numerous problems, from the Clarence Thomas/Anita Hill sexual harassment debacle, to widespread political corruption, to the lack of affordable health care, seemed to be related to, or at least exacerbated by, the shortage of women in politics. "This is a year when the voters are very angry with the political establishment and politics as usual," Lynn Yeakel declared when she won the Democratic nomination for one of Pennsylvania's US Senate seats, "and women represent change."[3] Getting more—many more—women elected and appointed to high public office held much promise for a better future. Women in politics were going to change things; they were going to "make a difference"—for women, for women and children, for the entire country.

It turns out that 1992 also marked the beginning of a very optimistic and productive era for *research* on women in US politics. Of course, political scientists did not suddenly discover women in politics in 1992. Many of us had long been concerned about the limited opportunities and gendered biases confronting women trying to get their feet in the doors of political power. Many of us celebrated the few and slowly increasing numbers of women who managed to get in. But soon after 1992, we became increasingly confident that many of the hopes and achievements of the Year of the Woman were neither unfounded nor aberrant.

First, we were realizing that 1992 was not the only, or even the first, year in which female candidates enjoyed considerable—and equitable—success. Since at least the 1980s, women have managed to raise just as much money and garner just as many votes as their male counterparts (Burrell 1985, 1994, 2005; Seltzer, Newman, and Leighton 1997; Uhlaner and Schlozman 1986; see also, Chapter 2 in this volume).[4] Women running as incumbents, like men running as incumbents, hardly ever lose; women running against incumbents, like men running against incumbents, hardly ever win; and women running in open seat races are just as competitive as men running in open seat races. Thus, what was so remarkable about the Year of the Woman elections was not really the success of female candidates, but the unprecedented number of open seats available—thanks to redistricting and scandals—and the unprecedented number of qualified, experienced women who seized the opportunity to run for them (Wilcox 1994).

While political scientists were uncovering evidence of gender neutrality on the campaign trail, we were also accumulating evidence of significant gender gaps in the behavior of elected officials. By the end of the decade, we were confident that women in Congress and in state legislatures often do make a difference (Reingold 2008). They are more likely than their male colleagues to initiate, prioritize, and support policymaking that addresses a broad range of women's issues and interests, from feminist women's rights measures to more "traditional" social welfare legislation (e.g., Bratton and Haynie 1999; Burrell 1994; Diamond 1977; Dodson and Carroll 1991; J. Dolan 1997; Thomas 1994). Women even practice politics differently. They pay more attention to their constituents (e.g., Carey, Niemi, and Powell 1998; Richardson and Freeman 1995; Thomas 1992), and their leadership styles tend to be more inclusive, more cooperative, less hierarchical, and less authoritative (e.g., Dodson and Carroll 1991; Jewell and Whicker 1994; Kathlene 1994; Rosenthal 1998). In all these ways, we could see a strong link between women's descriptive and substantive representation (Pitkin 1967), that is, between being a woman in public office and acting on behalf of women and women's interests.

Beyond the Year of the Woman

Where do we stand today? What has happened since 1992? Overall, the numbers of women in public office have continued to increase (see Figure 1.1). Perhaps the most significant gains have been made in Congress, which has seen an increase of 10 women about every eight years since 1993. When the 110th Congress convened in January 2007, a total of 87 women were sworn in to the Senate and House, constituting 16 percent of all members of Congress. The percentage of statewide elective executive offices (e.g., governor, lieutenant governor, secretary of state) held by women increased from 18.5 percent in 1992 to a record high of 28.5 percent in 2000; since then, the numbers and proportions have decreased slightly. Today, only 23.5 percent of those positions are held by women. The number of women currently serving in state legislatures (1,741) is at an all-time high, but since the late 1990s, there has been very little change in those numbers. Between 1999 and 2006, the proportion of women in state legislative office hovered at about 22 percent.

In almost every election cycle since 1992, observers have speculated about the possibility of another Year of the Woman. We look for the same

Figure 1.1 Women in US Elective Office

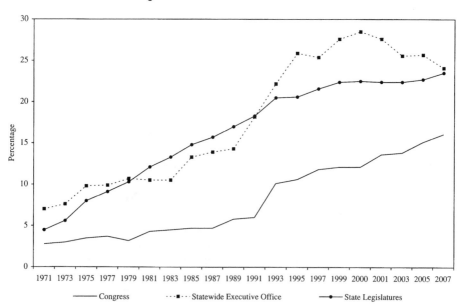

Source: CAWP, "National Information Bank on Women in Public Office" (New Brunswick, NJ: Eagleton Institute of Politics, Rutgers University, various years).

conditions that were so conducive in 1992: lots of opportunities for new-comers to run competitive campaigns in open-seat races, anti-incumbent sentiment, salient "women's" issues such as health care, education, and abortion. But each time, we seem to come up short. The 2002 election cycle, for example, was much anticipated for, like the 1992 elections, it coincided with the decennial redrawing of congressional and state legislative districts. But there were far fewer open seats available in 2002 than in 1992, and in the wake of the September 11 attacks, domestic women's issues were overshadowed and incumbent support was high. As a result, the 2002 elections brought an increase of only one woman in Congress and a decrease in the number of women in state legislatures (from 1,682 to 1,654). At best, 2002 could be called the Year of the Woman Governor, for the number of women elected to the top state executive position had increased from five to a record seven.[5] Again in 2006, conditions seemed ripe. In contrast to 2002, the "culture of corruption" in Washington, DC, was a regular news item; opposition to the Iraq war was growing rapidly, along with calls for more attention to domestic economic and social welfare issues; anti-incumbent sentiment was very strong; and Nancy Pelosi was poised to become the first female Speaker of the House. But because there were so few open seats available, 2006 was dubbed only a "mini" Year of the Woman (see Chapter 3 in this volume).[6]

It is not that the gains made in 1992 were not real or valuable. More women are in politics than ever before. And these women are here to stay, both literally and figuratively. In the words of one commentator, "Steady political gains by women are no longer big news. And that's the big news."[7] We are looking at years of women (lots of women!) in politics, not just a year of the woman.

Yet we are still a long way from gender parity. Immediately after 1992, the rate by which the numbers of women in politics increased returned to its previous, slow pace (see Figure 1.1). It did not take long for observers to note, as Celinda Lake (a prominent Democratic pollster) did in 1996, that "the year of the 20-seat pick-up has given way to the prospect of many years 'just slugging it out, seat by seat.'"[8] At the beginning of the twenty-first century, however, there were signs that we could not even count on steady, incremental progress. As noted above and as seen in Figure 1.1, the proportions of women in statewide elective office and in state legislatures stopped increasing altogether. The charts were beginning to look an awful lot like glass ceilings. "We're really kind of stuck," observed Debbie Walsh, director of the Center for American Women and Politics at Rutgers University.[9] Even with the slight uptake following the 2006 election, it looks like it is going to take many years of many women struggling to gain a foothold in politics, not just one silver-bullet year of one figurative woman beating the odds.

As the first decade of the twenty-first century unfolds, the view from the political science literature appears more guarded as well. We too are realizing that the status of women in politics is much more complicated and contingent than we had hoped. We are learning, for example, that while winning elections is important, it is not everything. Equitable electoral outcomes tend to obscure the fact that too few women are choosing or being encouraged to run for office in the first place (Lawless and Fox 2005). State party leaders, who play a large role in recruiting new candidates, often underestimate the electoral viability of women (Sanbonmatsu 2006b); and the advent of term limits in over a dozen states seems to have done little to help (Carroll and Jenkins 2001). Female incumbents may be just as likely as male incumbents to win reelection, but recent research suggests they have to work a lot harder and raise even more money to do so (Green 2003; Palmer and Simon 2006; see also Chapter 2 in this volume).

Researchers have known for quite some time that those women who do run for public office almost always have to confront powerful gender stereotypes, not only about their viability, but also about their issue expertise (e.g., soft on crime, strong on education), political ideology (more liberal), and their character (e.g., more honest and compassionate, not as tough, knowledgeable, or decisive) (Alexander and Andersen 1993; Burrell 1994; K. Dolan 2004; Huddy and Terkildsen 1993a; Kahn 1996; Koch 2000, 2002; Lawless 2004b; Leeper 1991; McDermott 1997; Sapiro 1981/1982; see also Chapter 4 in this volume). While it is not entirely clear whether these stereotypes help or hinder female candidates at the polls (K. Dolan 2008), there is some evidence suggesting that gender stereotypes may limit the kinds of offices women will pursue—channeling them toward positions that are either more "feminine" (e.g., state school superintendent) or less discretionary (e.g., county clerk) (Fox and Oxley 2003; Lublin and Brewer 2003).

Political scientists are also beginning to realize that "making a difference" for women and changing both the substance and style of policymaking may be a lot more difficult and complicated than we had hoped (Dodson 2006; Reingold 2000, 2008). Not all women in politics are able, or even willing, to act for women. Numerous studies of state legislators and members of Congress have found that liberal, Democratic women are more committed to women's substantive representation than are conservative, Republican women, especially when women's representation is defined as support for or advocacy of feminist policy initiatives (e.g., Evans 2005; Reingold 2000; Swers 2002; Wolbrecht 2002). A lot also depends on being in the right place at the right time—for example, being on relevant committees when your party, or the Democratic party, has majority control and when competition over women's votes is intense (Dodson 2006; Hawkesworth et al. 2001; Norton 2002; Swers 2002).[10] A women's caucus with organizational resources and institutional clout also helps (Carroll

2001; Hawkesworth et al. 2001; Thomas 1994). Yet bipartisan consensus on what constitutes important women's issues, which is needed to forge a strong women's caucus, is not always assured. Even those female policy-makers who see themselves as representing women often have very different ideas about what representing women actually entails (Carroll 2002; Dodson 2006; Reingold 2000). In short, although the links between women's descriptive and substantive representation are strong, they are by no means guaranteed, automatic, universal, or uniform.

Underlying all these recent revelations about the complexity of women's experiences in politics is an emerging appreciation for the great diversity among women, especially those running for and occupying public office in recent decades. Most of these women are Democrats; the vast majority of them are white. Yet sizeable numbers of these women are Republicans who, like their male counterparts, are growing increasingly more conservative. And a good many are African American or Latina, all or most of whom are Democrats. Today, 29 percent of the women in Congress are Republican, as are 36 percent of statewide elected executive women and 31 percent of women in state legislatures. As mentioned earlier, 23 percent of the women currently serving in Congress are African American, Latina, or Asian American, as are 5 percent of those serving in statewide elective executive office and 20 percent of those serving in state legislatures. Yet, until recently, the partisan and racial makeup of women in elite US politics has received little attention, scholarly or otherwise.

Some media commentators and scholars noticed that the 1992 Year of the Woman was more like the "Year of the Democratic Woman" or the "Year of the Liberal Democratic Woman" since those women were the primary beneficiaries (Wilcox 1994, 2).[11] Others noted that Republican women made considerable gains in the 1994 elections, especially conservative Republican women in Congress.[12] But political scientists have only recently called attention to the fact that Republican women have been enjoying significantly fewer gains in electoral politics than have Democratic women and, as a result, the ratio of Democratic to Republican women in public office has been increasing (Fox 2006; King and Matland 2003; Sanbonmatsu 2006a; Chapters 2 and 3 in this volume). Some are now uncovering evidence that gender *and* party interact in the processes of candidate recruitment and the patterns of candidate success such that the experiences of Democratic and Republican women may be fundamentally different (e.g., Koch 2002; Palmer and Simon 2006; Sanbonmatsu 2002a). As noted above, recent research also shows that, once in office, partisanship can play a significant role in determining whether and how women in office "make a difference" (see especially, Evans 2005).

Even fewer discussions of the Year of the Woman, or of women in US politics more generally, have noted the very significant increase in the number of African American women and Latinas running for and winning public office. Hardly anyone noticed, for example, that as a result of the 1992 elections, the number of women of color in Congress almost tripled, jumping from 5 in 1992 to 13 in 1993. Few noted that many of the 1992 open seat opportunities for women were in newly created majority-minority districts (Garcia Bedolla, Tate, and Wong 2005; Smooth 2006; Tate 2003). "For African American women," Wendy Smooth (2006, 137) writes, "1992 was also the 'Year of Redistricting.'" Since 1992 (and in some cases, even before), African American women and Latinas have continued to make dramatic gains in electoral politics, sometimes outpacing other women, African American men, and Latino men (Bositis 2001; Fraga et al. 2006). As a result, female legislators have become more racially and ethnically diverse, and gender diversity among African American and Latino legislators is higher than it is among white, Anglo legislators (at both the congressional and state levels) (Bratton, Haynie, and Reingold 2008; Fraga et al. 2006; Garcia Bedolla, Tate, and Wong 2005; Montoya, Hardy-Fanta, and Garcia 2000; Smooth 2006; Tate 2003).

Not surprisingly, political scientists are only beginning to consider how gender, race, and ethnicity may interact to determine and distinguish patterns of candidate recruitment, electoral success, and representative behavior. Nonetheless, we are learning that the relative success of women of color in electoral politics may be attributed to both favorable opportunity structures, such as new majority-minority districts, and a long history of women's activism and leadership in civil rights movements and community organizing (Darcy and Hadley 1988; Fraga et al. 2006; Garcia Bedolla, Tate, and Wong 2005; Moncrief, Thompson, and Schuhmann 1991; Montoya, Hardy-Fanta, and Garcia 2000; Smooth 2006; Takash 1997; Tate 2003). Recent research also suggests that, once in office, women of color may be uniquely situated to recognize and act upon demands for both racial/ethnic and gender representation, realizing that such diverse interests are more likely to be mutually reinforcing and interdependent than mutually exclusive and independent (Barrett 1995, 1997; Bratton, Haynie, and Reingold 2006; Carroll 2002; Garcia Bedolla, Tate, and Wong 2005).

Clearly we have a lot more to learn about this complex world of women in US politics. Thus, women-in-politics scholars have been digging deeper, so to speak, and contemplating somewhat different questions lately. In addition to asking whether gender matters, we have been asking: *How* does gender matter? Under what conditions might gender matter more or less than usual? And what else besides gender matters? And in addition to comparing the experiences of women to those of men in politics, more of us are wondering about the diversity *among* women and the varied experiences of women in politics. Of particular interest are the ways in which gender interacts with partisanship, ideology, race, and ethnicity to affect women's choices, goals, strategies, interactions, and accomplishments.

Outline of the Book

The chapters that follow address these very questions and speak to the very diverse experiences of women in US politics today. In doing so, they necessarily highlight the complexity of those experiences and the gender dynamics that shape them.

If women's prospects for winning elections look so good, why are there still so few women in public office?

Jennifer Lawless and Kathryn Pearson in Chapter 2 examine the possibility that the gender dynamics of primaries are partially to blame. As they point out, the research documenting women's electoral success has focused almost exclusively on their experiences as candidates in the *general* elections. What happens before that? Do the primaries, where multiple candidates compete for their party's nomination in the general election, weed out more than a fair share of female candidates?

Analyzing decades of congressional primary races and paying close attention to potential variation across parties, Lawless and Pearson are able to determine that Democratic and Republican women alike win primaries as often as their male counterparts do. Digging deeper, however, they also reveal that, despite these equitable outcomes, women's primary races are more competitive and, thus, more difficult than those involving only men. Whether they are incumbents, challengers, or open seat contestants, women running in congressional primaries face a more crowded field than their male counterparts do. Finally, Lawless and Pearson highlight yet another possible explanation for the continued shortage of female candidates in general elections: in recent years, women have become increasingly likely to challenge each other, both within their own party's primary and within the opposing party's primary.

The implications of all this are far-reaching, as Lawless and Pearson acknowledge. Faced with such a daunting task, many (more) women may opt out of the primary races altogether. Furthermore, if the women who compete in the general elections had to work harder and be stronger candidates to get there, then why aren't they *more* successful than the men who compete in general elections?

How do women candidates manage to raise so much money, and at what cost? To what degree and how do the political parties recruit and support women candidates?

In Chapter 3, Barbara Burrell takes a close, critical look at the fund-raising efforts of female candidates in the most recent (2006) congressional elections, as well as party activities on their behalf. As Burrell explains, party support and money often go hand-in-hand: "How good candidates are at raising money and how much they can obtain or give themselves are the top two criteria for national party leaders in promoting candidacies" (p. 48 in this volume). Moreover, prodigious fund-raisers often become the party gatekeepers themselves. Success breeds success. In the 2006 congressional elections, this was no less true for women than it was for men. From the earliest days of the campaign season on, within both parties, and among incumbents, challengers, and open-seat candidates alike, women raised just as much money as men did—sometimes more. In part because of their own fund-raising ability and in part because of their leadership within the party fund-raising organizations, women running for Congress also received a great deal of financial support from their parties—more, in fact, than their male counterparts did.

While she finds that female candidates continue to be formidable fund-raisers who gain substantial support from their national party organizations, Burrell poses some intriguing questions about the implications of the contemporary stress on fund-raising prowess for the recruitment of future women candidates. As Burrell's analysis of the 2006 congressional races shows, there remains a critical shortage of women running for even the most promising open seats available, especially among Republicans. Might the pressure to raise so much money be preventing (more) women from taking advantage of those opportunities? If so, Burrell argues, campaign finance reform is sorely needed. But the fact that women already in Congress have been so successfully integrated into the current campaign finance regime makes prospects for meaningful reform look even dimmer.

To what degree and how are campaigns gendered?
Are some female candidates more likely than others to
"run as women"? And if so, why? What sorts of gender stereo-
types do they still encounter, and how do they deal with them?

In Chapter 4, Dianne Bystrom reveals how female candidates in the most recent national and statewide elections are employing new media technologies and strategies to confront gender stereotypes and double standards still prevalent among voters and in the media. Her detailed analysis of candidates' television advertisements and websites reveals that many women are embracing the stereotypes and running "as women"—emphasizing such issues as education and health care, for example. At the same time, however, women are just as likely and sometimes more likely to adopt certain "masculine" approaches, like running negative ads, attacking their opponents' records, or emphasizing their own strength, toughness, and experience. Many candidates, female and male, seem to be taking a balanced approach, emphasizing both "feminine" and "masculine" issues, character traits, and media styles. This balanced approach is particularly popular among winning candidates.

In the end, Bystrom concludes, campaign media strategies—in recent years, at least—are shaped as much by the current political context (which issues are most salient) and the medium (TV vs. the Web) as by gender or gender stereotypes. The balanced approach, which combines feminine and masculine themes in various ways, may be a particularly adept response to all the competing demands of politics, media, and gender. Running as a woman, or emphasizing feminine issues, traits, or styles, therefore, is a very strategic move, which candidates most likely adopt when conditions are favorable. And it is one of several ways women running for public office—from Hillary Clinton on down—can and do deal with gender stereotypes.

Do women's candidacies energize women in the electorate? If so, are some women's candidacies more energizing than others?

Chapter 5 by Kathleen Dolan and Chapter 6 by Atiya Stokes-Brown and Melissa Neal examine whether the symbolic "signals" of democratic openness, equality, and legitimacy suggested by the increasing presence of women running for high office have a mobilizing effect on women in the electorate.

Dolan employs survey data from 1990 to 2004 to examine whether voters, particularly female voters, who live in states and districts with a woman running for the US Senate or House of Representatives are more politically active, efficacious, and interested than those who have no opportunity to vote for (or against) a woman running for Congress. Her analysis also considers whether such "symbolic mobilization" accompanies all women candidates, or is instead contingent upon the idiosyncrasies of particular election seasons, the visibility of the office, the competitiveness of the race, or the political party of the candidate. Using similar survey data for 2002 and 2004, Stokes-Brown and Neal take a closer look at "symbolic mobilization" and the conditions under which it is more or less likely to occur. In particular, they investigate the possibility that the mobilizing effect of female candidates is enhanced when their campaigns focus on issues of concern to women. Emphasizing women's issues may, in fact, be the mechanism by which female candidates mobilize women in the electorate.

Both studies offer unexpected results. Neither finds much evidence of widespread or systematic symbolic mobilization. In Dolan's analysis, there are a few instances in which certain types of female candidates mobilize some voters in some races, but there are no clear patterns that would allow us to identify any conditions that promote or inhibit symbolic mobilization in any consistent fashion. In other words, the impact of female candidates appears infrequent and idiosyncratic. In Stokes-Brown and Neal's analysis, female candidates who run on women's issues do not do much more to mobilize women in the electorate, except to stimulate more discussion of politics. Interestingly, both studies find, contrary to expectations, that female candidates are just as likely to affect the political engagement of men. According to Stokes-Brown and Neal, for example, when female congressional candidates "run as women," men are apt to discuss politics *less* frequently.

Both studies conclude, therefore, on a cautionary note: if candidate gender works in such mysterious, complicated ways, then simplistic assumptions about gender politics may find little empirical support. Instead, we need to think harder about the various ways gender may be, in Stokes-Brown and Neal's words, "conditioned by external forces" (p. 112 in this volume).

Once in politics, why are some women more likely than others to act for women and women's interests? What does acting for women entail? Does it extend beyond "women's" issues?

Michele Swers, in Chapter 7, takes a close look at the relationship between sex, gender, and legislative activity surrounding the quintessential "men's" issues, national security and defense policy, in what is perhaps the quintessential men's club, the US Senate. In the post-9/11 world, these issues are preeminent concerns among voters and senators alike. Yet women in the Senate must face another, potentially conflicting imperative: powerful gender stereotypes that assume women lack expertise and strength on just such issues. For Democratic women, this problem is compounded by widespread perceptions that their party is weak on defense.

According to Swers's analysis of defense policy and her interviews with staff, women in the Senate are well aware of such stereotypes and work hard to overcome them—so hard, in fact, that their level of participation and their effectiveness on such issues are equal to those of their male colleagues. Nonetheless, the nature of their defense policy activity is distinctive. While female senators are just as active as others on "hard" issues concerning war and weaponry, they are significantly more likely to take the lead on "soft" issues concerning the quality of life for military personnel and their families—an approach congruent with their presumed expertise in social welfare policy.

Like the other chapters, Swers's research demonstrates both the power and the complexity of gender in US politics. Gender stereotypes about candidates' and lawmakers' policy concerns and issue expertise have a profound effect on women in the Senate. But that effect does not always translate into sex differences in representative behavior. As Swers illustrates, gendered activity can result in just the opposite: policymaking that appears, on its face at least, no different for men and women. Once again, we have to dig deeper and think harder.

To what degree and under what conditions are women in public office able to "make a difference" and provide substantive rep-resentation for women?

Susan Carroll's study of state legislators in Chapter 8 highlights the important role of committees and, more precisely, committee assignments, in understanding women's policy-related behavior and their ability to pursue their policymaking goals. As Carroll points out, legislators may or may not get the committee assignments they really want. Given that "final decisions about committee assignments are made by legislative leaders, still predominantly men in most states, who can bring their own attitudes about gender differences to bear on their decisions," female legislators may find that their own policy interests are not well served by their committee assignments (p. 135 in this volume). For example, women may prefer to serve on prestigious and powerful "money" committees (e.g., appropriations, ways and means), but gender stereotyping by legislative leaders might channel them into education, health, and human services committees instead. Conversely, women may be over- or well-represented on committees like education and health by choice—precisely because they want to make a difference for women.

Relying on 1988 and 2001 national surveys of state legislators, Carroll provides strong evidence that committee assignments can and do facilitate women's efforts to make a difference on women's issues. Regardless of race/ethnicity, party, or state political culture, female state legislators are more likely than their male colleagues to seek and obtain positions on committees dealing with education, health, and human services. Moreover, the women appear quite content with and interested in their work on these committees, for they are able to use those positions to advocate on behalf of women's interests. Carroll's research also assures us that, over the years, there is increasingly little evidence that women are being barred from the most powerful committees, which see their share of women's interest legislation as well.

Who or what else do women in politics act for or on behalf of? How do they balance those interests? What sorts of coalitions do they bring together or join, and why?

In Chapter 9, Luis Fraga, Valerie Martinez-Ebers, Linda Lopez, and Ricardo Ramírez compare the attitudes and behavior of Latina and Latino state legislators to see how gender and ethnic representation interact. They theorize that Latina public officials "are uniquely positioned to leverage the intersectionality of their ethnicity and gender," effectively balance women's interests and Latino interests, and reach across gender, ethnic, and racial lines to forge meaningful coalitions (p. 158 in this volume).

Once again, the findings and conclusions underscore the complexity of gender—and ethnic—politics in the United States. Contrary to most other studies of women's political representation, Fraga and associates find almost no significant differences in the policy priorities of Latina and Latino state legislators. Both groups are equally concerned about education and health care. But when it comes to reaching out to others and building legislative coalitions, Latinas do exhibit a "multiple identity advantage" that allows them to work more frequently (than Latinos do) with members of other historically underrepresented groups. Most striking and interesting, though, are the choices Latina and Latino legislators make when confronted with hypothetical trade-offs between Latino interests, women's interests, and constituent interests. Such choices are undoubtedly difficult and complicated (and perhaps infrequent), but Latinas do demonstrate a greater willingness to balance such competing interests, giving more weight to the women's caucus position without neglecting the demands of either the Latino caucus or their constituents. In these ways, Fraga et al. conclude, Latina legislators may position themselves—strategically and intersectionally—as "the most effective advocates on behalf of working class communities of color" (p. 157 in this volume).

To what degree and under what conditions are women able to advance in their careers in politics? What enables some women to move up the ladder, exert leadership, and wield power and influence? And what prevents so many others from doing so?

The two chapters by Wendy Smooth (Chapter 10) and Cindy Simon Rosenthal (Chapter 11) illuminate both the new opportunities and old barriers women face as they seek power and influence within state legislatures and Congress (respectively). Legislative power, as Smooth explains, comes in many forms—formal and informal, positional and reputational. Regardless of which form it takes, power is key for any legislator who wants to make a difference. Yet, as Smooth's in-depth study of African American women (and their colleagues) serving in the Georgia, Maryland, and Mississippi state legislatures vividly illustrates, access to power and influence is contingent upon both gender and race. Through various mechanisms, African American women in these legislatures are effectively shut out from both formal and informal positions of influence, despite their relatively large numbers, their seniority, and their formidable efforts to represent their constituents. State legislatures, Smooth concludes, have not adapted very well to the growing gender and racial diversity of their members, and women of color may be paying the highest price for this failure.

Rosenthal's timely analysis of recent leadership elections in Congress uncovers a new era in women's political incorporation, but also reveals considerable apprehension and ambivalence about women assuming such powerful positions. As Rosenthal points out, 2007 and the beginning of the 110th Congress might well have been dubbed the Year of the Woman Leader. In one of the most historic of women's "firsts" in US politics, Nancy Pelosi was elected Speaker of the House, the very top leadership position in Congress and one of the most powerful positions in the nation. Overall, women in the 110th Congress have gained more party and committee leadership positions than ever before. Yet it is equally important to note that women have been contesting party leadership elections in Congress for quite some time. Rosenthal's analysis of those leadership elections shows just how important—and gendered—those elections are.

According to Rosenthal, when women run for congressional leadership positions, so do lots of other people. Since the 1990s, leadership races with women candidates have been more competitive than those involving only men; women candidates are less likely to run unopposed and, when running in contested elections, face more opponents on average. Moreover, until quite recently, women in Congress, like "tokens" in general, tended to gain only "less powerful or specially designated" leadership positions, especially within the Republican hierarchy (p. 208 in this volume). Finally, Rosenthal's gender analysis of the media coverage of three of the most recent contested leadership elections (two involving Pelosi, one to replace Tom DeLay [R-TX]) suggests that women vying for the most powerful political positions in the country may be greeted with fascination, skepticism, and confusion. Given the "unspoken masculinity of Congress and its past leaders," women like Pelosi remain oddities (p. 218 in this volume).

Like the preceding chapters, these two chapters illustrate the need for and value of digging deeper and thinking harder. Both studies of gender and power go well beyond a cursory analysis of who is in what position—and for good reason. Smooth's research shows that, even when African American women do gain access to "positions that *traditionally* convey power," they often find their access to real power is still denied (p. 194 in this volume). Rosenthal's detailed analysis of leadership races, like Lawless and Pearson's analysis of primary races, demonstrates that power is not simply about who wins and who loses. It is also very much about who has to work harder to obtain victory by competing in a more crowded field and addressing the fears and misgivings spawned by gender stereotypes.

*   *   *

These chapters offer students and scholars alike a wide-ranging collection of research on women in US politics that is both cutting-edge and accessible. Every contributor breaks new ground. Lawless and Pearson are one of the very few who have investigated women's fortunes in congressional primaries, and theirs is the most comprehensive and systematic analysis available. Burrell builds upon her path-breaking work on women's campaign fund-raising and party support in congressional elections by incorporating the most recent developments from the 2006 midterm elections. Similarly, Bystrom provides the most recent and thorough analysis of gendered political communication available, including insights into Hillary Clinton's historic run for the 2008 Democratic presidential nomination. Dolan's findings on the mobilizing effects of women's political campaigns, as well as those of Stokes-Brown and Neal, challenge the tentative conclusions of this emerging field of inquiry. Swers's is one of the very few studies of women in the US Senate, and the first to examine women's legislative activity on defense and foreign policy issues. Carroll's work on the politics of women's committee positions in state legislatures is definitive, especially given its unprecedented reach across states and time. Fraga and associates are the first to examine in-depth the perspectives, choices, behavior, and strategic positioning of Latinas in public office; to date, theirs is the only survey of Latino/a state legislators available. Smooth provides an extraordinarily candid, eye-opening study of the intersections of gender, race, and power among public officials—a long neglected yet extremely important area of research. Rosenthal is the first to study, or even consider, the very gendered dynamics of congressional leadership selection.

The chapters employ a variety of methodological tools, from statistical analysis of large quantities of electoral data to in-depth, personal interviews with elected officials. They therefore illustrate quite vividly the many benefits of methodological pluralism and creativity. At the same time, each and every chapter remains accessible to interested readers of all kinds, regardless of the type or extent of their training in social science research methods. This is by design; from the very beginning, our goal was to reach out to an inclusive mix of scholars, practitioners, activists, and students of politics who possess a wide variety of analytical skills. In doing so, we hope our research will stimulate much discussion and debate, and raise many new, interesting questions for future research. Indeed, Karen O'Connor's concluding chapter (Chapter 12) does just that. It takes stock of what we have—and have not—learned from this collection and offers new questions and strategies for further research, all the while challenging us to think harder and dig deeper. The complex world of women in US politics and the ever-changing gender dynamics they face deserve no less.

Notes

1. Anne E. Kornblut and Matthew Mosk, "Clinton Owes Lead in Poll to Support from Women," *Washington Post*, 12 June 2007, sec. A; Jonathan Weisman

and Alec MacGillis, "Clinton's Campaign in N.H. Touched Chord with Women," *Washington Post*, 10 January 2008, sec. A.

2. These figures do not include the three women who serve as Delegates to the House from Guam, the Virgin Islands, and Washington, DC; nor do they include Juanita Millender-McDonald (D-CA) who died on April 22, 2007. These and other statistics regarding the numbers and proportions of women in public office are provided by the Center for American Women and Politics (CAWP), National Information Bank on Women in Public Office, Eagleton Institute of Politics, Rutgers University.

3. Scott Shepard, "'We Embody Change': Angry Voters See Women as Their Salvation," *Atlanta Constitution*, 29 April 1992, sec. A.

4. There is even some evidence from the most recent congressional elections that female candidates are raising slightly *more* money than are similarly situated male candidates (Burrell 2005 and in this volume; Fox 2006).

5. Adam Clymer, "In 2002, Woman's Place May Be the Statehouse," *New York Times*, 15 April 2002; Liz Marlantes, "Year of the Woman Governor?" *Christian Science Monitor*, 5 August 2002, sec. USA.

6. Linda Feldmann, "Wave of Women Candidates for Hill," *Christian Science Monitor*, 19 May 2006, sec. Opinion.

7. E. J. Dionne Jr., "Women on the March," *Washington Post*, 16 October 1998, sec. A.

8. Adam Nagourney, "A Good Year for Running: More Women, Fewer Causes," *New York Times*, 28 April 1996, sec. 4.

9. Susan Milligan, "Regression After 'Year of the Woman,'" *Boston Globe*, 30 January 2005, sec. National/Foreign.

10. It remains unclear whether having a lot of female colleagues makes women any more (or less) willing or able to act for women (Cammisa and Reingold 2004; Reingold 2008). Scholars are, in fact, becoming increasingly skeptical and critical of the "critical mass" theories underlying such expectations.

11. Catherine S. Manegold, "Women Advance in Politics by Evolution, Not Revolution," *New York Times*, 21 October 1992, sec. A.

12. Editorial, "Women Across Party Lines," *Washington Post*, 6 August 1995, sec. C.

PART 1
Getting Elected

2

Competing in Congressional Primaries

JENNIFER L. LAWLESS AND KATHRYN PEARSON

A CENTRAL QUESTION in the study of women in politics is the relationship between gender and electoral success.[1] Although the first congresswoman, Jeanette Rankin (R-MT), was elected in 1916, as late as 1970, only 10 women served in the United States Congress. And up until the 1970s, nearly half of all congresswomen were elected following the deaths of their husbands (Gaddie and Bullock 2000). During the last decade, the numbers of women running for and attaining political office significantly increased. In 2008, 16 women serve in the US Senate and 71 women serve in the US House of Representatives, including the first female Speaker of the House, Nancy Pelosi (D-CA). These numbers represent an eightfold increase since World War II and a threefold increase in just the past few decades. The fact remains, however, that men comprise 84 percent of the US Congress, and the United States ranks 84th worldwide in the percentage of women in the national legislature (Inter-Parliamentary Union 2008). It comes as no surprise, therefore, that scholarly research and journalistic commentary focus not only on women's increasing electoral success, but also on the relative paucity of women elected to Congress.

Research shows that when women run for Congress, women win at the same rates as their male counterparts. What, then, explains the dearth of women candidates and elected officials? Discrimination, the incumbency advantage, the pool of potential candidates, and gender differences in political ambition have all been identified as likely suspects. And in this chapter, we will discuss the role each has played regarding women's numeric representation. But we also suggest an additional culprit—one that has received very little scholarly attention—for the paucity of women in US political institutions: the congressional primary process.

Analyses of women's electoral fortunes have focused almost exclusively on end-stage assessments of the electoral process. In other words, who wins and loses general elections? There are some notable exceptions. Burrell (1994) examines women's presence in primary elections from 1968 to 1992. Gaddie and Bullock (2000) analyze women's electoral success in open seat primaries from 1982 to 1992. Matland and King (2002) present data pertaining to women's performance in open-seat primaries from 1990 to 2000. And Palmer and Simon (2006) show the rise in the number of women running and winning primaries and offer excellent descriptive analyses of incumbent congresswomen and the primaries in their districts from 1956 to 2004. But even these exceptions tend either to present aggregate data with little sophisticated multivariate analysis, or limit themselves to certain types of races in selected cycles. Hence, even though winning a congressional primary is a prerequisite to running in the general election, the extant literature does not adequately assess the gender dynamics of the primary process.

Based on a rich, new data set that includes all House candidates in primary elections from 1958 to 2004, we offer the first systematic, multivariate assessment of how women fare in congressional primaries of all types over time. Our findings reveal a paradox of women's low entry rates and high victory rates in congressional primaries. Generally speaking, women in both major political parties win primaries as often as do their male colleagues. In fact, in some recent cycles, Democratic women win more often than their male counterparts. Although these results may seem encouraging for women's numeric representation, we offer additional evidence that primary competition is more difficult for women than it is for men. Thus, our analysis sheds new light on the large gender gap in men and women's political ambition and representation in our political institutions.

Theories for Women's Underrepresentation in Congress

Scholars of women and politics have devoted the past few decades to gaining a better understanding of why so few women occupy positions of political power in the United States. Initially, the scholarship attributed women's exclusion from the political sphere to discrimination and overt bias against women candidates. Over the course of the past twenty years, however, cultural attitudes toward women in politics have evolved and an increasing number of women have sought and won election to public office. Scholars, therefore, began to focus on structural barriers, most notably the incumbency advantage and the proportion of women in the "pipeline" professions that precede political careers, to explain the low number of women office holders. More recent studies indicate that lower levels of political ambition also account for the dearth of women candidates and elected officials.

Scholars have shown that in contemporary congressional politics, once we take into account a candidate's incumbency status and the demographics of the district, women do not face widespread bias at the polls (Burrell 1998; Carroll 1994; Cook 1998; Duerst-Lahti 1998; Fox 2000; Seltzer, Newman, and Leighton 1997; Smith and Fox 2001; Thomas and Wilcox 1998). Examining women's electoral success in the 1990s, Thomas and Wilcox conclude that "whereas women may once have lost their elections more often than their male counterparts, that is not the case today. . . . When party and incumbency status are taken into account, the evidence is clear that women win races as often as men" (1998, 3). Based on her analysis of a series of public opinion polls and election results, Dolan (2004, 50) echoes this claim: "Levels of bias are low enough to no longer provide significant impediments to women's chances of election." And in perhaps the most widely cited study in elite women's campaign circles, the National Women's Political Caucus (NWPC) analyzed every major party candidate in a general election from 1972 to 1992 by office, year, party, sex, and race status. The findings confirmed that women face obstacles to winning not because of their sex, but because they are not incumbents (NWPC 1994).

The contemporary literature on women in politics, therefore, shifts the focus from discrimination to institutional inertia (Carroll 1994; Darcy and Choike 1986; Darcy, Welch, and Clark 1994; Smith and Fox 2001; Thomas and Wilcox 1998, but see Bledsoe and Herring 1990). Carroll's (1994) landmark study of female candidates running for congressional, statewide, and state legislative office concluded that the scarcity of women in electoral office could largely be explained by limitations in "political opportunity variables," incumbency advantages in particular. After all, not only do incumbents seek reelection in more than 75 percent of congressional elections, but their reelection rates are also consistently well above 90 percent (Duerst-Lahti 1998, 19). Recent congressional election cycles have seen even fewer open seats than usual; only 31 incumbents chose not to seek reelection in 2004, and only 28 vacated their House seats in 2006 (less than 7 percent of the total House of Representatives membership).

Recent research indicates, however, that the dearth of women candidates cannot be explained entirely by the political opportunity structure. Based on data from the Citizen Political Ambition Study, a national survey of almost 3,800 "potential candidates," Lawless and Fox (2005) find that women, even in the highest tiers of professional accomplishment, are substantially less likely than men to demonstrate ambition to seek elected office. Women are less likely than men to be recruited to run for office. They are less likely than men to think they are qualified to run for office. And they are less likely than men to express a willingness to run for office in the future. This gender gap in political ambition persists across generations. Despite cultural evolution and society's changing attitudes toward women in politics, running for public office remains a much less attractive and feasible endeavor for women than men.

Cultural evolution, structural barriers, and political ambition certainly contribute, in varying degrees, to the gender disparities in our political institutions. But the power of these explanations, even combined, is limited, because none tackles the fundamental question of whether women meet success when they enter primary contests for congressional seats.

A Gendered Congressional Primary Process?
Background and Hypotheses

In US congressional elections, candidates must be entrepreneurs who build their own personal followings. Explicit linkages to political party organizations and platforms, as well as other support networks, are at the candidates' discretion. This "candidate-centered" model is particularly prominent in the organizational structure of contemporary congressional primaries (Jacobson 2004).[2] Indeed, party organizations tend not to choose nominees, and they rarely provide resources in primary campaigns.[3] To compete, candidates must raise money, build coalitions of support, create campaign organizations, and develop campaign strategies. Although all candidates, regardless of sex, face hurdles in emerging as viable candidates in this entrepreneurial environment, the candidate-centered system in the United States may pose greater challenges for women than for men.[4]

Foremost, navigating the candidate-centered congressional primary process involves relying on and utilizing the types of skills, experiences, and characteristics that have historically been impressed upon men but discouraged among women. Women, in essence, still tend not to be socialized to possess the qualities the modern political arena demands of its candidates and elected officials. Whereas men are taught to be confident, assertive, and self-promoting, cultural attitudes toward women as political leaders, expectations of women's family roles, and the overarching male exclusiveness of most political institutions leave an imprint that suggests to women that it is often inappropriate to possess these characteristics (see Lawless and Fox 2005). The degree to which traditional gender socialization manifests itself in the congressional primary process is unknown, although we speculate that it will be more evident at the primary stage of the electoral game, since candidates least able to adapt the qualities voters demand will not make it to the general election.

Even when women overcome some of these obstacles, they may still have a more difficult time than men building name recognition because they tend not to be as well known in political circles. In general, women are less likely than men to be recruited to participate in politics (Burns, Schlozman, and Verba 2001). And among politically active individuals who represent the top tier of professional accomplishment, they are less likely than men to receive encouragement and support to run for office from elected officials, community leaders, and political activists (Lawless and Fox 2005; see also Sanbonmatsu 2002a; Niven 1998). Certainly, technological changes, including mass mailing and the spread of television, allow candidates the possibility of spreading their message and building a following apart from the party or their links to the political establishment. But it is plausible that women candidates may have less name recognition and credibility than men when they announce their candidacies and, thus, more ground to cover over the course of the campaign.[5]

Finally, congressional primaries tend to be low-turnout, low-visibility affairs. We have long known that citizens tend to pay only passing attention to politics, retain only minimal amounts of political information, and oftentimes lack the ability to organize the limited amount of political information they do have (Bartels 1996; Delli Carpini and Keeter 1996). Accordingly, in order to assess candidates, individuals invoke myriad heuristics. In general elections, voters can rely on partisan cues to make their vote choice, particularly when they lack other information (Rahn 1993). In congressional primaries, all candidates provide the same party cue, so voters rely on other cues, of which gender is one of the most straightforward (McDermott 1998, 1997). Because women candidates and office holders are generally perceived as more liberal than men candidates of the same party (Koch 2000; McDermott 1998, 1997; Alexander and Andersen 1993), gender stereotyping may pose particular challenges for women in primaries. King and Matland (2003), relying on data from a national survey, show that both male and female Republican party identifiers are less likely (11 percent and 14 percent, respectively) to vote for a fictitious female Republican candidate than a fictitious male candidate.

For these reasons, we expect that women will be disadvantaged in the congressional primary process. More specifically, we expect that women's victory rates and vote margins will be lower than those of their male counterparts. Because the political landscape and opportunity structure for women have improved over time, though—the women's movement of the 1970s served as a critical catalyst in expanding opportunities for women, for example—we should see a decrease in the extent to which men outperform women over time. In addition, Republican women may disproportionately suffer in primaries, whereas Democratic women may not. After all, voters view women in both parties as more liberal than men. While Republican primary voters tend to overrepresent the party's conservative base, Democratic primary voters tend to overrepresent the party's liberal base.

We also expect that women will face more primary competition than will their male counterparts. We hypothesize that women run in more difficult electoral environments because potential competitors, recruiters, and gatekeepers consider women more vulnerable (Palmer and Simon 2006; Sanbonmatsu 2006b). This means that women will not only draw a larger crowd in their own primaries, but also that they will be more likely to draw a crowd in the other party's primaries when they run as incumbents. Women may also be more likely to challenge other women in all types of primary contests, so as to neutralize the disadvantages they may face associated with being a woman in a congressional primary.

Testing these hypotheses will allow us to assess the gender dynamics of the congressional primary process, an endeavor that is long overdue and key to understanding women's numeric underrepresentation and gauging prospects for women's full integration into US political institutions.

The Data Set

We base our analyses on primary election candidates and results for the US House of Representatives from 1958 to 2004. We rely on a new data set we created that includes 33,094 primary candidates running in 19,221 primary contests. We drew the name of every candidate and his/her vote total from each year's *America Votes*.[6] Perhaps the most laborious aspect of the data collection process entailed discerning each candidate's sex. In many cases, *America Votes* lists only a first initial, so we searched newspaper records of candidacies in each district in each year, as well as contacted various secretaries of state and boards of election. In the 302 cases in which, despite our best efforts, we were unable to determine the candidate's sex, we dropped the individual from the analysis.[7] We coded each candidate's state, district, party, sex, vote total, and incumbency status. We arranged the data so that we could analyze outcomes at both the candidate and district levels.[8]

From 1958 to 2004, a total of 2,648 women ran in primaries for the US House of Representatives; women comprised 8 percent of the total House primary candidates. Of the 19,221 primary contests we examine, 87 percent were composed only of men, 12 percent of the races included one woman, and 1 percent (195 races) included more than one woman.

Despite women's underrepresentation as candidates, the results presented in Figure 2.1 reveal that the number of women running in congressional primaries has increased markedly since 1958, when women comprised only 3 percent of primary candidates. The first substantive jump in women's candidacies happened in 1972, in concert with the rise of the women's movement. The biggest jump in the number of female candidates occurred in 1992's Year of the Woman, as has been well documented (see Cook, Thomas, and Wilcox 1994). That year, a total of 219 women ran in primaries, compared to 116 women in the previous cycle.[9] By 2004, the total number of women in primaries had dipped slightly to 198, although women comprised 16 percent of total candidates, and the number of women winning general elections continued to increase because of the incumbency advantage.

Figure 2.1 also illustrates that women running in congressional primar-

Figure 2.1 Women Running in Congressional Primaries, by Party, 1958–2004

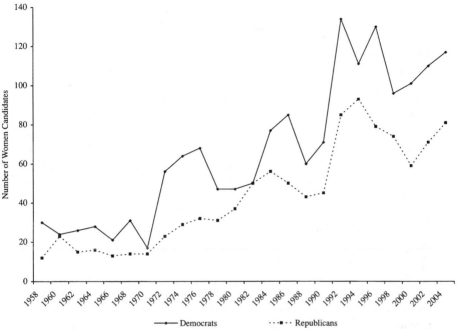

ies are disproportionately Democratic. This partisan primary gap predates the partisan gap inside Congress, which widened after the 1992 elections. From 1958 to 2004, Democratic women comprise 60 percent of the total pool of female candidates; and in every cycle except 1982, Democratic women outnumber Republican women. The gap begins to widen in 1972, as a handful of Democratic women, perhaps inspired by the women's movement, entered primaries. Although the partisan gap narrowed in the 1994 and 1998 cycles, it has widened since. Further, the *overall number* of Democratic primary candidates is higher than the number of Republican primary candidates. Of the total pool of 33,094 primary candidates, women represent 7 percent of the 14,878 Republicans; they comprise nearly 9 percent of the 18,095 Democrats. Even if national political parties tend to stay out of primary elections, it may be that local Democratic party leaders and activists are playing a stronger role than their Republican counterparts in recruiting and funding women candidates (see Sanbonmatsu 2006b and 2002a for a discussion of the role state party leaders play in recruiting women, especially in competitive elections). It may also be the case that Democratic political action committees and feminist organizations, including EMILY's List, give female Democratic candidates a boost that Republican women do not receive.

Results

Gender and Electoral Success:
Primary Victory Rates and Vote Margins

Contrary to our expectations, women's primary victory rates and vote margins are not significantly lower than those of their male counterparts. Table 2.1 presents the victory rates of female and male primary candidates by year and by party. These data include races in which primary candidates win without any opposition. Overall, women and men win at approximately the same rates (57 percent of the time for women, compared to 59 percent of the time for men). We identify minor variations across party: Republican men outperform Republican women (63 percent success rate, compared to 60), whereas Democratic women have a very small edge over their male counterparts (56% to 55%).

We do uncover larger differences when we turn to an analysis of victory rates over time. During the 1960s, 1970s, and 1980s, male candidates won their primaries more often than female candidates did, particularly among Democrats. In three election cycles during this time, Republican women were significantly less likely than men to win primaries. In six of these election cycles, Democratic women were significantly less likely than men to win their races. The data reveal a rather dramatic change throughout the course of the last decade, though. Democratic women have won more often than Democratic men in every primary election cycle since 1992, and Republican women have won more often than Republican men since 1996.

The data tell a similar story at the district level. Figure 2.2 illustrates the number of districts with at least one woman competing in a primary since 1958, and Tables 2.2 and 2.3 present female Republican and Democratic candidates' success by district. A Republican woman consistently won in districts with a woman in the primary at least 60 percent of the time beginning in 1996 (although Republican women began winning more than half the districts with a woman candidate as early as 1962). In Democratic primaries since 1990, a woman won in at least 60 percent of the districts in which at least one woman competed (see Table 2.3, column 1). The jagged rise in women's victory rates over time is propelled, in large part, by the increase in female incumbents. But there has also been an increase in the number of primaries sending nonincumbent women to the general election (as shown in the second and third columns of Tables 2.2 and 2.3).

These results are not an artifact of other predictors of primary election success. We find no systematic bias against women candidates, for example, after we control for incumbency status (Jacobson 2004) or whether the candidate ran in the previous election cycle, both of which increase the likelihood of victory. The results also hold after we take into account the total number of

Table 2.1   Primary Victory Rates (percentage), by Sex and Party, 1958–2004

Year	All		Republicans		Democrats	
	Women	Men	Women	Men	Women	Men
1958	57	57	58	63	57	54
1960	57	63	48#	66	67	60
1962	54	58	53	64	54	54
1964	34*	60	38*	66	32*	55
1966	69	63	77	67	62	59
1968	47#	59	43#	65	48	54
1970	75	64	71	68	78#	62
1972	42*	56	52	64	38#	50
1974	45	53	59	65	39	46
1976	48	52	50	63	47	45
1978	56	57	68	64	49	52
1980	56	57	62	60	51	54
1982	54	58	60	61	48	55
1984	50*	60	64	67	39*	54
1986	48*	63	72	71	34*	56
1988	60	66	72	67	52#	64
1990	59*	68	67	69	54*	67
1992	48	47	46	48	49	45
1994	60*	52	53	53	66*	51
1996	58	55	58	54	59	56
1998	73*	65	70	62	75	68
2000	73*	64	64	63	78*	64
2002	64	60	59	58	66	61
2004	64	63	65	62	65	62
Total	57	59	60	63	56	55

Notes: Cells contain the percentage of candidates winning their congressional primaries. The difference of means between men and women is statistically significant at # $p < .10$; * $p < .05$.

candidates in the party's primary, which we expect would decrease the vote share of every candidate. More specifically, Republican women are at a statistically significant disadvantage only in 1960. Among Democrats, the results are striking. In 1986, women are at a significant disadvantage, but in three election cycles—1996, 1994, and 1992—women win primaries significantly more often than do their male counterparts (see Table 2.5 in the Appendix for the regression results on which this analysis is based).

A similar relationship exists between sex and vote share in congressional primaries from 1958 to 2004. Among Republicans, gender does not exert a statistically significant impact on vote share in primary elections, with the exception of 1960. Democratic women were again at a distinct disadvantage only in 1986. With the exception of 2004, in every election since 1990, Democratic women receive more votes than Democratic men in congres-

Figure 2.2 Congressional Districts with Women Candidates, by Party, 1958–2004

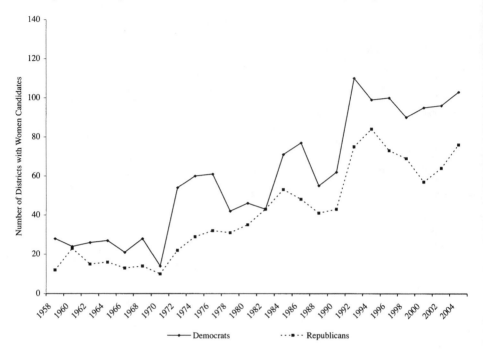

sional primaries (see Table 2.6 in the Appendix for the regression coefficients, standard errors, and goodness of fit).

Across all primaries in the past half century, at the most general level,
the conventional wisdom that scholars have applied to general elections
applies to congressional primaries: when women run, women win and
receive votes at rates equal to their male counterparts, all else equal. Our
analysis reveals, however, that there is variation across parties and over
time and, as we will show, that competition poses more obstacles for
women to overcome.

Gender and Electoral Competition:
The Primary Landscape and Size of the Field

For the majority of incumbents facing primary challenges, the incumbency
advantage, name recognition, and the perquisites of office minimize the
threat of their partisan challengers. Indeed, congressional scholarship that
analyzes members' electoral motivations and strategic behavior focuses on
general elections (e.g., Mayhew 1974). But primary elections can actually
pose the greatest threat to members representing solidly partisan congres-

Table 2.2   Female Republican Candidates' Success, by District

Year	Percentage of Primaries with Winning Female Candidate	Total Female Candidate Victories	Nonincumbent Female Candidate Victories
1958	58	7	4
1960	48	11	4
1962	53	8	5
1964	38	6	2
1966	77	10	7
1968	43	6	3
1970	100	10	6
1972	55	12	11
1974	59	17	15
1976	50	16	12
1978	68	21	18
1980	66	23	19
1982	70	30	20
1984	68	36	26
1986	75	36	26
1988	76	31	19
1990	70	30	22
1992	52	39	26
1994	58	49	36
1996	63	46	31
1998	75	52	33
2000	67	38	24
2002	66	42	24
2004	67	51	29
Total	64	627	422

sional districts. And when incumbents retire or die and their seats are vacated, primaries attract many qualified candidates and generate fierce competition. Our analysis uncovers clear evidence that women face more competition in all cases; it does not matter whether they run as incumbents, challengers, or for open seats. This finding makes the victory rates we present above all the more impressive.

Perhaps the best gauge of a competitive landscape is whether a candidate even faces a competitor in the primary. Among male candidates from 1958 to 2004, more than 37 percent ran unopposed in their primary or advanced to the general election without a real contest. Among female candidates during the same time period, 35 percent avoided an opponent in the primary. While the difference is not large, it does suggest that women are at least slightly less likely than men to get a free pass from fellow partisans to the general election. Perhaps women lack the connections within the political establishment that could ward off primary opponents. Thus, women are somewhat more likely to find themselves devoting energy to fighting candi-

Table 2.3   Female Democratic Candidates' Success, by District

Year	Percentage of Primaries with Winning Female Candidate	Total Female Candidate Victories	Nonincumbent Female Candidate Victories
1958	61	17	6
1960	67	16	8
1962	54	14	8
1964	33	9	4
1966	62	13	5
1968	54	15	11
1970	100	14	10
1972	39	21	15
1974	42	25	16
1976	53	32	22
1978	55	23	13
1980	52	24	16
1982	56	24	16
1984	42	30	20
1986	38	29	19
1988	56	31	21
1990	61	38	24
1992	60	66	47
1994	74	73	42
1996	76	76	55
1998	80	72	40
2000	83	79	43
2002	76	73	35
2004	74	76	47
Total	62	890	543

dates who are leveling attacks at them from different directions at two different stages of the congressional election process.

An additional gauge of primary competition for incumbents and challengers alike is the size of the field. We hypothesized that because women are viewed as more vulnerable, they will be more likely to attract a crowd and, accordingly, face more competition in primaries, and the data support this expectation. In all Republican primaries with a woman, the mean number of Republican candidates is 3.9. In Republican primaries without a woman, the mean number of candidates is only 2.2. This pattern emerges in Democratic primaries as well. Democratic primaries in which a woman competes include, on average, 4.3 candidates. In primaries with only Democratic men, the mean number of candidates is 2.5. The differences in these means achieve conventional levels of statistical significance ($p < .05$).

These results are not driven exclusively by open-seat contests. Like Palmer and Simon (2006), we find that female *incumbents* are more likely than men to generate a crowded field (see also Simon and Palmer 2005). The data presented in Table 2.4 reveal that female incumbents of both parties attract more opposition than do their male counterparts in the other party's primary (differences significant at $p < .05$). Incumbent Republican congresswomen attract more candidates than do men in Republican primaries as well. Differences in views toward women's roles between each party's activists may help explain our findings.

Gender also plays a role in the congressional primary process in that women have become increasingly likely to challenge one another in their own party's primaries. Granted, only 1.4 percent of Democratic primaries and 0.6 percent of Republican primaries include more than one woman candidate.[10] But as Figure 2.3 illustrates, the total number of these races in each election cycle has trended upward over time. Even in 1992, which represents the peak of women challenging women in primaries for both parties, there were only 28 such races. Although we do not want to overstate the implications of these findings—indeed, a primary with more than one woman candidate is a very unusual event—it is important to note that this phenomenon may ultimately stymie some of the potential gains an increasing number of women candidates have on women's overall numeric representation. That is, when women run against women, women defeat women. This may be particularly true for Democrats, who, with the exception of the early 1980s, have always been more likely than Republicans to see multiwoman races.

A similar trend emerges when we turn to the other party's primary; women are significantly more likely to enter primaries to challenge a female incumbent of the other party. In Democratic primaries to challenge a Republican congresswoman, the mean number of women is .25, compared to an average of .15 women running to challenge a Republican congressman. Among Republicans, an average of .20 women run in primaries to challenge a Democratic congresswoman in the general election, compared

Table 2.4 Gender Differences in Incumbents' Primary Competition

	Mean Number of Candidates	
	In Own Primary	In Other Party's Primary
Female Republican incumbents ($n = 200$)	1.7	1.5
Male Republican incumbents ($n = 3,547$)	1.6	1.3
Female Democratic incumbents ($n = 355$)	1.5	1.6
Male Democratic incumbents ($n = 4,845$)	1.6	1.3

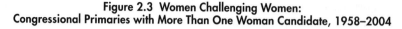

**Figure 2.3 Women Challenging Women:
Congressional Primaries with More Than One Woman Candidate, 1958–2004**

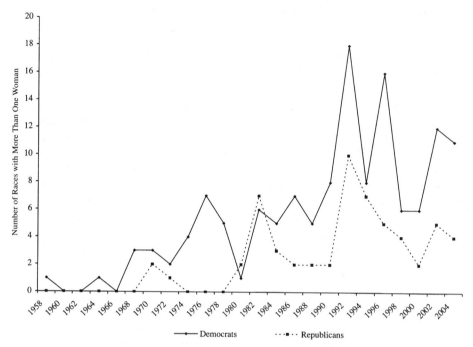

to an average of .09 women who run to challenge a Democratic man. Party leaders, electoral recruiters, and gatekeepers—in addition to women candidates, themselves—may view a woman challenging another woman in the general election as less daunting; the presence of two women may diffuse any gender biases in the course of the general election campaign. The presence of another woman may also nullify any gender advantage a female candidate might have among a subset of voters.

Although our data cannot speak to whether the presence of a female primary candidate attracts other women to the race, or instead, whether women tend to enter races that are also attractive to other women, the fact remains that women are more likely than men to face a crowded primary field, and that crowd is more likely to include a woman.

Discussion and Conclusion

Conventional wisdom derived from the literature on women's electoral success holds that congressional elections yield gender-neutral results. That is, when women run in congressional elections, they win at rates equal to those of their male counterparts. Until now, there has been no systematic, multivariate analysis of primary elections in all types of congressional races over time. Our results show that the gender dynamics of the primary election process complicate the conventional wisdom.

On the one hand, the results are consistent with findings that emerge from studies of general elections. Overall, there appears to be no widespread, aggregate bias against women candidates running in congressional primaries. Granted, the effect of sex varies from election to election and across party. Before the 1980s, women in both parties rarely ran, and when they did, they occasionally fared significantly worse than their male counterparts. Since 1990, however, Democratic women have tended to garner a greater vote share than their male colleagues. Increased party polarization, then, while criticized by Washington pundits and political scientists alike, seems to have helped Democratic women in congressional primaries. When primary voters seek the most partisan—and, therefore, the most liberal— option, they rely on a combination of stereotypes and voting histories that advantage women candidates. Women are viewed as more liberal than men, and Democratic congresswomen are, in fact, more liberal and loyal to their party than their male counterparts. According to *Congressional Quarterly*, Democratic women's party loyalty scores have consistently been higher than men's. Republican women do not enjoy the same advantages with their party's ideological voters, but they generally do not fare worse than their male counterparts. Notably, these results emerge from an unequal playing field, as women face more crowded primaries and a more difficult primary election terrain.

On the other hand, our results indicate that prospects for near-term parity for women in elective office are bleak. Men constitute the vast majority of primary candidates and, unlike the slow but steady increase in the number of women elected to the US House of Representatives in general elections, the number of women entering primaries is actually decreasing, albeit slightly. Further, the gains we have seen in the number of women candidates have been among Democrats. In the 2006 congressional election cycle, for instance, 70 percent of the women who sought their party's nomination were Democrats. If we are to achieve true gender parity and numeric representation for women, then women must emerge from both political parties as candidates in primary elections. Finally, women are more likely to enter primaries in which they would challenge a woman in the general election; there is no net gain for women's numeric representation when women compete against women.

Taken together, our results suggest that primary elections are not gender neutral. And it is likely that these primary election dynamics affect the initial decision to run for office. The candidate-centered system in the

United States, in other words, may hamper women's entrance into public office (Davis 1997; Darcy, Hadley and Kirksey 1993), especially when they need to run in a primary contest. Only the most qualified women may be willing to take on a primary battle, winnowing women from the field before the contest begins. It is, therefore, not surprising that the women who emerge from primaries to compete in general elections are more likely than men to have electoral experience and fund-raising success (Pearson and McGhee 2004). To make it through the primary process, women must be stronger candidates, or at least candidates who are willing to endure greater challenges, and more challengers, than their male counterparts face. Women, in other words, have to be "better" than men in order to fare equally well.

Appendix: Regression Results

Table 2.5 Logistic Regression Results Predicting Candidate Victory, by Party

Year	Coefficient on Candidate Sex	Percentage of Cases Correctly Predicted	Pseudo-R^2	Number of Cases
		Republicans		
1958	.473 (.722)	72.5	.229	255
1960	−3.177 (1.253)*	70.1	.255	294
1962	.072 (.659)	66.0	.146	321
1966	.555 (.919)	70.3	.214	283
1970	−.490 (1.128)	73.4	.331	286
1972	−.366 (.605)	67.7	.197	362
1974	−.078 (.613)	74.5	.310	329
1976	−1.437 (.735)	69.7	.237	366
1978	−.272 (.615)	67.0	.187	339
1980	.150 (.497)	68.2	.178	409
1982	.482 (.427)	67.8	.177	342
1984	−.002 (.420)	68.5	.198	298
1986	.188 (.475)	66.9	.172	248
1988	.110 (.540)	68.3	.189	279
1990	−.243 (.504)	69.4	.237	288
1992	−.203 (.317)	72.3	.208	607
1994	.074 (.300)	73.3	.239	543
1996	.224 (.356)	78.0	.342	500
1998	.518 (.403)	76.2	.331	349
2000	−.305 (.471)	71.9	.267	359
2002	.346 (.375)	77.7	.352	422
2004	.247 (.355)	75.2	.335	383

continues

Table 2.5   continued

Year	Coefficient on Candidate Sex	Percentage of Cases Correctly Predicted	Pseudo-R^2	Number of Cases
		Democrats		
1958	−.106 (.515)	73.0	.250	478
1960	.798 (.568)	78.4	.425	445
1962	−.258 (.649)	77.8	.354	523
1964	−.868 (.682)	80.2	.397	530
1966	−.172 (.820)	79.7	.430	463
1968	−.180 (.571)	80.2	.451	556
1970	1.179 (.773)	75.2	.301	428
1972	−.397 (.394)	77.7	.321	642
1974	−.106 (.360)	78.6	.325	768
1976	.406 (.381)	83.4	.446	736
1978	.558 (.386)	80.7	.413	581
1980	.253 (.421)	81.0	.426	538
1982	.145 (.415)	76.0	.329	499
1984	−.230 (.340)	80.8	.477	604
1986	−1.447 (.483)*	80.3	.509	569
1988	.416 (.372)	77.7	.419	394
1990	.543 (.348)	80.2	.499	348
1992	.513 (.260)*	78.0	.300	650
1994	.832 (.312)*	80.3	.435	517
1996	.760 (.288)*	75.9	.294	469
1998	.379 (.396)	76.1	.386	272
2000	.725 (.378)	75.1	.309	301
2002	.364 (.352)	78.1	.344	356
2004	−.281 (.335)	74.9	.367	362

Notes: Models control for incumbency, total number of candidates in the race, and whether the candidate ever sought that position in a previous election cycle. For Republicans, models for 1964 and 1968 are not estimated because of multicollinearity problems.

Levels of significance: * $p < .05$; ** $p < .01$.

Table 2.6 OLS Regression Results Predicting Candidate Vote Share, by Party

Year	Coefficient on Candidate Sex	Adjusted R^2	Number of Cases
Republicans			
1958	.067 (.073)	.313	255
1960	−.155 (.056)**	.390	294
1962	−.018 (.060)	.361	321
1964	−.088 (.064)	.337	319
1966	.055 (.082)	.408	283
1968	−.130 (.071)	.376	341
1970	−.073 (.081)	.391	286
1972	−.067 (.053)	.285	362
1974	.056 (.049)	.483	329
1976	−.056 (.044)	.382	366
1978	−.008 (.051)	.354	339
1980	−.006 (.043)	.357	409
1982	.045 (.040)	.372	342
1984	.026 (.036)	.371	298
1986	.036 (.040)	.402	248
1988	.057 (.042)	.454	279
1990	.002 (.039)	.441	288
1992	.035 (.022)	.389	607
1994	−.004 (.021)	.456	543
1996	.020 (.027)	.470	500
1998	.040 (.032)	.478	349
2000	−.020 (.036)	.467	359
2002	.013 (.031)	.475	399
2004	.019 (.030)	.462	366
Democrats			
1958	−.029 (.046)	.354	479
1960	.056 (.045)	.501	445
1962	−.068 (.046)	.484	523
1964	−.068 (.041)	.512	530
1966	−.009 (.053)	.471	462
1968	−.005 (.040)	.511	556
1970	.054 (.054)	.478	428
1972	−.035 (.029)	.455	642
1974	−.009 (.024)	.523	768
1976	.008 (.024)	.588	736
1978	.019 (.029)	.558	581
1980	.009 (.030)	.558	538
1982	.008 (.033)	.475	499
1984	−.022 (.024)	.594	604
1986	−.092 (.027)**	.580	569
1988	.041 (.032)	.501	394
1990	.078 (.029)**	.529	348
1992	.093 (.020)**	.480	650
1994	.091 (.021)**	.572	517
1996	.059 (.024)*	.457	469
1998	.072 (.033)*	.499	272
2000	.086 (.034)*	.456	301
2002	.057 (.028)*	.498	346
2004	.051 (.028)	.447	343

Notes: Models control for incumbency, total number of candidates in the race, and whether the candidate ever sought that position in a previous election cycle.

Levels of significance: * $p < .05$; ** $p < .01$.

Notes

We thank Barbara Burrell, Jack Citrin, Richard Fox, John Sides, and Sean Theriault for their comments on previous drafts and help with our data analysis.

1. This is a revised version of Jennifer L. Lawless and Kathryn Pearson, "The Primary Reason for Women's Underrepresentation? Reevaluating the Conventional Wisdom," *Journal of Politics* 70, no. 1 (January 2008): 67–82. Copyright (c) 2008 by the Southern Political Science Association. Used with permission of Cambridge University Press.

2. Party-centered elections characterized the US electoral landscape in the 19th century and gradually faded in the 20th century. In the 19th century, parties printed and handed out ballots, state and local parties controlled nominations, and a norm of rotation made it clear to those nominated that they were subordinated to the party. The party also controlled the key resources necessary for electoral success: strong party organizations ran candidates' campaigns, and voters relied almost exclusively on the party label in general elections. While party cues in vote choice have experienced a significant resurgence in the past decade, primaries today are largely candidate-centered. Hand in hand with other party reforms, direct congressional primaries spread across the country starting in the early 1900s, making the United States unique among democracies for having voters, as opposed to party elites, choose the party standard bearer to compete in the general election.

3. This is true for the vast majority of races we consider. There are, however, some notable exceptions in recent cycles. Dominguez (2005) shows that party congressional campaign committees may get involved in primaries for competitive seats.

4. It is important to recognize that other democracies with relatively patriarchal histories and proportional party list electoral systems tend to see a greater proportion of women in politics because they do not have the winner-take-all and single-member district systems prevalent in the United States (Matland 1998; Norris 1994; Rule 1987). This is not to say, however, that systems of proportional representation with party lists do not have costs of their own. Jane Mansbridge (1999, 652) explains that such systems often facilitate party collusion that leads to noncompetitive races and voter demobilization. Overall, however, she concludes that proportional party list systems are a "flexible" way to promote descriptive representation and women's candidacies.

5. Granted, it is possible that, under certain circumstances, the still existent novelty of women in politics at the national level provides them with more coverage than they might otherwise receive. We thank an anonymous reviewer for raising this point.

6. Even after the creation of the Federal Election Commission (FEC) and the concomitant filing requirements, candidates who do not exceed a minimum threshold of campaign fund-raising ($5,000 in 2006) are not required to file. Collecting data from FEC reports would, therefore, bias our results, as we would miss the weakest candidates.

7. Most of these individuals ran in the earliest cycles, where there were very few women.

8. King and Matland (2003) demonstrate that analyzing the presence of a woman in a primary can be a superior measure of women's electoral success. If two women compete in the same primary, the rate of women's success at the candidate level in that race would be 50 percent, whereas the rate of women's success at the district level would be 100 percent.

9. It is important to note, however, that in this "unique" election cycle, the most significant explanations for women's victories in general elections were hardly unique. Notably, 1992 was a redistricting year, creating a record number of open seat contests in the modern era (Gaddie and Bullock 2000). Most of the new congresswomen won open seats; only 2 of 41 female challengers defeated incumbents, a rate comparable with the general rate of incumbent defeats. In addition, the women who won were "high quality" candidates, i.e., those with experience (Jacobson 2004).

10. Of Republican primaries, 10 percent include one woman (920 races), 0.5 percent include two women (49 races), and 0.1 percent include three women (9 races). On the Democratic side, 13 percent of the races have one woman candidate (1,297 races), 1.1 percent include two women (110 races), 0.2 percent include three women (18 races), and 0.1 percent include more than three women candidates (7 races).

3

Political Parties, Fund-raising, and Sex

Barbara Burrell

FOURTEEN YEARS AND seven elections after the 1992 Year of the Woman in US politics, women's quests for political leadership continued to receive distinctive attention during the 2006 election campaign season. After the seemingly negative contexts of the 2002 and 2004 elections for women candidates with their focus on security and terrorism, media analyses and political activists' commentary suggested that 2006 might be a "mini" year of the woman. The election appeared to provide a positive context for women candidates. But while women have made gains in their numerical presence as members of Congress, they continue to be very much underrepresented at 16 percent given that women are 50 percent of the population. Why?

What primarily accounts for the slow march toward gender parity in numbers among our political leaders is the advantage that incumbents, primarily white males, have had in the electoral process. Increasing women's presence then is dependent upon their taking advantage of opportune situations by running in open seats where incumbency is not an issue, challenging the few vulnerable incumbents in any particular election cycle, and being in strong positions to ride national tides favorable to their party. This chapter tells the story of women's campaigns for the US House of Representatives in 2006 seeking to determine the extent to which taking advantage of opportune situations described their experience in that year's election. I pay particular attention to the role that money and party support played in their quests for seats in the US House. These examinations will help us reflect on the continued distinctiveness of women's quests for political leadership.

The goals of this chapter are fourfold. First, I analyze women's presence as candidates in open seat primaries and as major party nominees in those races. Second, earlier research has shown that women candidates have equaled male candidates as fund-raisers in congressional campaigns. I carry this research forward to the 2006 election as fund-raising has become increasingly central to campaigns for national offices to determine whether parity continues to characterize the financing of men's and women's campaigns for the US House of Representatives. Third, I examine financial support for male and female candidates by party organizations, explore the strategic decisions the parties make, and determine whether those financial decisions disadvantage female candidates. Finally, I reflect on the media focus on 2006 as a mini year of the woman and how the ever-increasing need to raise *lots* of money may negatively impact women, discouraging them from running in the first place.

The Context of the 2006 Election

Context certainly matters in elections. Some elections provide greater opportunity for new or underrepresented groups to make gains than others. The context of the 2006 election had the potential for being a positive year for women as congressional candidates. Media accounts during the campaign season illustrate the positive climate for women candidates. For example, on October 22, the *San Francisco Chronicle* headlined "Big Election Predicted for Female Candidates; Seen as Honest Outsiders, They Could Have Best Showing Since '92."[1] The theme of change ran throughout the political analyses that discussed the prospects for women candidates in that year's elections. Scandals and war weariness were making the public eager for change in national leadership and women continued to be viewed as agents of change at least from the perspective of activists and media personnel. The Center for American Women and Politics at Rutgers University issued a press release in late September in which its director, Debbie Walsh, stated: "When people think the system is broken, it's good news for those who don't look like the congressional candidate from central casting—and that includes women" (CAWP 2006a).

Pundits considered whether it might be another "year of the woman" similar to 1992. Since the number of competitive races was much smaller than in 1992, at most these analysts concluded it would only be a "mini" year of the woman if female candidates were especially successful.[2] Writing in the *New York Times* in March, Robin Toner, for example, noted:

> If the Democrats have their way, the 2006 Congressional elections will be the revenge of the mommy party. Democratic women are running major campaigns in nearly half of the two dozen most competitive House races

where their party hopes to pick up enough Republican seats to gain control of the House. Democratic strategists are betting that the voters' unrest and hunger for change—reflected consistently in public opinion polls—create the perfect conditions for their party's female candidates this year.[3]

This theme was repeated throughout media reports of that year's election campaigns.

In the 2005–2006 election cycle, a total of 211 Democratic and Republican women ran for the US House in the primaries, general election, and in a few special elections. This number was the largest number ever of female candidates for the US House. Women emerged as 137 of the major party nominees in the 2006 general election, second in number to the 2004 election in which 142 women were major party nominees. Table 3.1 shows the electoral situations in which women were candidates in 2005–2006. Of greatest significance is the presence of women in open seat contests as they are where the "action" has been in terms of newcomers being elected to the House (Gaddie and Bullock 2000). It matters very much in which type of races women run.

Women Contesting Open Seats

Crucial for newcomers making electoral gains is their taking advantage of opportune situations. For Congressional candidates in particular, running in open-seat districts—those with no incumbent running for reelection—and especially in open districts favorable to or at least competitive for their party is the key. In 2006, to what extent were women present in such contests? The problem for women in the past has been that they have not seen fit to enter such races to the same extent as men have (Burrell 1994;

Table 3.1   Women Candidates for the US House of Representatives in the 2005–2006 Election Cycle

Type of Candidate	Republicans	Democrats
Incumbent	23	43[a]
Incumbent challenger	12	40
Open-seat nominee	7	12
Incumbent primary challenger	9	13
Opposition-party primary challenger	7	16
Open-seat primary loser	9	12
Special-election candidate	4	4

Note: a. One of these incumbents, Cynthia McKinney of Georgia, was defeated in a primary.

Matland and King 2002; and also Chapter 2 in this volume). Such opportune situations were not plentiful in 2006. Only 27 districts, or 6 percent of
all House seats, were open during the primary season, compared with 91
open seats in 1992.[4] Of these, 8 districts were either safe or likely
Democratic districts based on *Cook Political Report* assessments at the time
of the party primaries, 10 were safe or likely Republican, 5 were toss-ups,
and 2 each leaned in either party's direction.

The presence of women as open-seat candidates should be evaluated
from three vantage points: their overall numbers as candidates; the proportion of districts in which they run, i.e., their presence across races; and their
presence in winnable seats for their party. Many women can run, but if they
only contest a few primaries then voters have little opportunity to cast their
ballot for a woman across the political landscape, diminishing the likelihood of increasing their numbers in the national parliament. Further, if
women disproportionately contest seats where their party has little chance
of being successful, then that is hardly an example of taking advantage of
an opportune situation to increase the numerical presence of an underrepresented group. Sharon Beery, the Democratic nominee in California's 22nd
District was one such sacrificial candidate. She had no opposition in the primary and lost to Republican Kevin McCarthy in the general election, 71
percent to 29 percent. No other Democrat saw fit to seek that party's nomination in such a hopeless district. (Some men were also sacrificial lambs for
their party. It was not a distinctly female practice in 2006.) We need to focus
our attention on the extent to which Democratic and Republican women
were present in primaries in districts considered safe for their party and in
competitive districts, the third vantage point mentioned above. I consider
each of these vantage points in order below to provide an overall assessment of women's strategic presence in open-seat House races in 2006.

Table 3.2 compares the distribution of male and female candidates in
open-seat races in 2006 by party and competitive status of the districts.
Consistent with findings in other contemporary elections as described in
Chapter 2, Democratic women exhibited a greater presence than Republican
women in open-seat races in 2006. More Democratic women ran and more
ran in the most viable races for their party. Twenty-three Democratic women
and 13 Republican women were open-seat primary candidates in 2006 (18
percent of all of the contenders). Women were 23 percent of the Democratic
pool of primary candidates and 13 percent of the Republican pool. In terms
of the proportion of races with a woman candidate, women were candidates
in 16 of 27 Democratic contests (59%) and women were candidates in 10 of
the Republican primaries (37%). Third, regarding party status and the competitiveness of the districts, women were present in six of the seven safe
Democratic seats (86%).Women were candidates in only two (one-third) of
the six safe Republican seats where ultimate victory would be most assured.

Table 3.2   Women's and Men's Presence in Open-Seat Primaries, 2006

Competitiveness[a]	Republicans		Democrats	
	Men	Women	Men	Women
Safe or favored Republican	43 (48%)	4 (31%)	12 (15%)	2 (9%)
Competitive	19 (21%)	7 (54%)	15 (19%)	12 (52%)
Safe or favored Democrat	28 (31%)	2 (15%)	51 (65%)	9 (39%)
Total	90	13	78	23

Note: a. Competitiveness is based on the *CQ Weekly* final election assessment. Competitive seats are seats rated as "leaning" toward one party or the other and "toss-up" races with no clear favorite.

How successful were these women? Women were victorious in 3 of the Republican open-seat primaries (11%) and in 11 of the Democratic open-seat primaries (41%). A Republican woman, Mary Fallin, lieutenant governor of Oklahoma, won her party's primary in one district overwhelmingly favorable to her party. She now represents Oklahoma's Fifth Congressional District in the 110th Congress. The other two Republican women won primaries in more competitive districts. One of the two, Michelle Bachmann in Minnesota's Sixth District, went on to win the general election, while Martha Rainville lost in Vermont's at-large district. Of the 11 Democratic women, 3 won their party's primary in districts highly favorable to their party and were successful in November; 7 of the female Democratic primary winners won in competitive districts, with 2 going on to win in November. Sharon Beery, as cited above, won the Democratic primary with no opposition in a safe Republican district losing overwhelmingly in November.

Table 3.3 provides a number of measures assessing women's success in the 2006 open-seat primaries. When they ran, women were more successful than their male counterparts, winning 37 percent of their races compared to a 24 percent success rate among the male candidates. And they obtained a higher percentage of the vote in contested primaries. Examining women's success from a district perspective (that is, the district is the unit of analysis and not candidates), we see that Democratic women were victorious in 69 percent of the districts in which they ran overall and were successful in 47 percent of the competitive or safe Democratic districts in which they ran. Republican women fared much less well. They were victorious in 30 percent of the races they entered but won in only 17 percent of the competitive or safe Republican districts in which they ran.

Two factors stand out in the story of the women and open-seat primary contests in 2006 that reflect the over-time findings of Jennifer Lawless and

Table 3.3 **Percentage of Winners and Average Percentage of the Vote Obtained in Open-Seat Primaries, by Sex, 2006**

Winners	
Men (%)	24
Women (%)	37
Votes obtained in contested open-seat primaries	
Men (average %)	18.2
Women (average %)	28.7
Uncontested open-seat primaries	
Number of men	11
Number of women	5
Districts with female Democratic candidates	
Number with female candidates	16
Number of female winners	11
Percentage victorious overall	69
Percentage of competitive or safe Democratic districts with a female winner	47
Districts with female Republican candidates	
Number with female candidates	10
Number of female winners	3
Percentage victorious overall	30
Percentage of competitive or safe Republican districts with a female winner	17

Kathryn Pearson in their chapter on women and primary elections. First, over one-quarter of the districts (7 out of 27, or 26%), had no woman candidate in either party, so voters had no opportunity to choose a woman to represent them if they so desired. Second is the party gap; the presence of women in Democratic primaries far surpassed their presence in Republican primaries, and Democratic women were more successful than Republican women in open-seat primaries. The election of 2006 continued the saga of contemporary elections where most of the action by women was on the Democratic Party side of the process. (See Matland and King 2002; Palmer and Simon 2006.) But 2006 was not projected to be a good year for Republicans. Perhaps Republican women made strategic decisions not to run in a year in which the tide was running against their party. They were also less likely to be a presence in Republican-dominated districts, however, suggesting a continuing problem with recruitment and perhaps less ambition than their fellow Democratic female politicos.

Further, the open-seat primary districts were not particularly friendly arenas for the election of women based on the "women friendliness" index Barbara Palmer and Dennis Simon (2006) have developed through a comparison of the geographical and demographic characteristics of districts that have elected women to the US House in recent decades and those districts that have not. Palmer and Simon note that seats that have come open "may not always be receptive to women candidates" (2006, 188). In the

1992–2000 period, they report that the proportion of women-friendly open districts was relatively low, 15.9 percent for the Democrats and 30.3 percent for the Republicans (2006, 188).

By examining four categories of district characteristics: partisanship and ideology, geographic factors, race and ethnicity, and socioeconomic factors, Palmer and Simon created a "women-friendliness index" to measure the types of districts in which women would have the best chance of being elected to the House. Democratic and Republican women have been elected from distinctly different districts and they have been elected from distinctive subsets of districts from that of their male colleagues. "Party-friendliness" and "women-friendliness" are not the same when it comes to electing individuals to the House. Examining the election of women to the House from 1972 through 2000, Palmer and Simon found that with respect to partisanship and ideology, women of both parties represented districts that were more liberal than those of their male counterparts.

> Female Democratic House members tend to win election in districts that are more liberal, more urban, more diverse, more educated, and much wealthier than those won by male Democratic members of the House; they come from much more compact, "tonier," upscale districts than their male counterparts. Female Republican House members tend to win election in districts that are less conservative, more urban, and more diverse than those electing male Republicans; they come from districts that are "less Republican." (2006, 152)

Palmer and Simon report that these results hold true only for white women. The African American women members of Congress, all of whom have been Democrats, have represented districts that were quite similar to those electing African American men.

Among the 27 open seats in 2006, none was particularly friendly for Democratic women candidates based on the Palmer/Simon index. On a scale that runs from 0 to 10 with 10 being the most friendly, 7 was the best score for "friendliness" toward Democratic women among these 27 open seats. Four Democratic women were successful in open seats not having characteristics conducive to their election, and an additional three Democratic women beat Republican incumbents in very "unfriendly" districts. Those three women are facing strong challenges in their campaigns for reelection in 2008. If these women are reelected, along with the other open-seat victors, calculations of the relationship between Palmer and Simon's demographic and political characteristics and women's election to the House may suggest a broader definition of districts friendly toward Democratic women.

Five of the 27 open seats in 2006 had characteristics that were "friendly" for Republican women candidates having a score of at least 8 on the women-friendliness index. However, none of these Republican women-friendly districts had any female candidates seeking their party nomination for the US House seat. In the "most friendly" district for Republican women, the Illinois 6th District, a female state senator who had considered running dropped out and decided to run for state comptroller instead. One of the districts having demographic characteristics that have been shown to be "friendly" for Republican women candidates, Hawaii's 2nd District, was also an overwhelmingly Democratic district hardly conducive to a Republican effort. But given that this predominantly Democratic state has a Republican woman governor and had previously had a Republican woman as one of its two US House members, Republicans might have had a chance to mount an upset campaign had they strategically encouraged a woman to run. But in the end two men but no women sought that party's nomination.

Money and Sex in the 2006 Election

Money is at the center of congressional campaigns and increasingly so. Legally, there is no limit to how much a candidate for the House of Representatives or the Senate can raise and spend. The Supreme Court in the 1976 *Buckley v. Valeo* decision ruled that limits on the amounts that candidates for federal office (or their contributors) might spend to promote their election were a violation of the First Amendment guarantee of freedom of expression. Money equaled speech the court ruled. More than ever, even with some continued campaign finance reform efforts, election campaigns are all about the money. How good candidates are at raising money and how much they can obtain or give themselves are the top two criteria for national party leaders in promoting candidacies. Candidates for the US Senate and House raised more than $1.4 billion in the 2005–2006 election cycle and spent nearly the same amount according to their Federal Election Commission reports, and the national fund-raising committees of the two major parties raised and spent almost as much (nearly $1.1 billion).[5]

When I first tested the conventional wisdom that women were not being elected to national office in major part because of their inability to compete with male candidates in fund-raising, I found that a systematic comparison showed that the amounts of money male and female major party nominees for the US House raised and spent in the elections from 1972 through 1992 tended not to differ. Women had become as good as and sometimes better at raising money to finance their campaigns than their male counterparts. More recent research shows that women candidates have continued to keep pace in accumulating financial resources to run competitive campaigns for Congress (Fiber and Fox 2005; Burrell 2005). We would expect this trend to continue in 2006. Several highlights from that election illustrate women's increasing fund-raising prowess.

- On April 28, US representative Jan Schakowsky (D-IL) held her fifth Ultimate Women's Power Luncheon in a downtown Chicago hotel in which 1,100 women attended and $162,000 was raised.
- In the first reporting period covering fund-raising through 2005 and the first three months of 2006, US senator Hillary Rodham Clinton (D-NY) reported having raised $27,501,536 for her 2006 campaign for reelection to the Senate and possible 2008 run for the White House, twice as much money as the number two senate candidate. She ended the election having raised nearly $40 million.
- US senator Elizabeth Dole was elected by the Republicans in the Senate to head their Senate Campaign Committee. Under her leadership, the committee raised nearly $89 million.
- Republican Katherine Harris contributed $2.6 million of her own fortune to her campaign for US Senate.
- EMILY's List reported contributing over $11 million to Democratic pro-choice women candidates' campaigns.

These anecdotes represent a distinctive face of contemporary gender politics. They illustrate that women have become prodigious fund-raisers in their own right and on their own behalf, that they have organized as women to become formidable players in national politics, and that they have become major actors in their party organizations' efforts to acquire financial resources for their candidates. Now I move from anecdotes to a systematic analysis of the financial aspects of the campaigns of men and women for the US House in 2006 to update our knowledge of the fund-raising aspects of women's campaigns.

Major party nominees facing a major party challenger raised a mean $1,036,931 (up from an average of $876,000 in 2004) and a median amount of $834,844 to fund their campaigns for the US House in 2006. Continuing trends noted in earlier studies (Burrell 1994), women major party nominees facing major party challengers raised more money on average in the 2006 election than their male counterparts did. These women nominees raised a mean $1,239,263 and a median amount of $946,256. Their male counterparts raised a mean of $993,426 and a median amount of $802,757. Figure 3.1 shows the average amount male and female candidates raised by party and candidate status, which allows us to explore whether it was a particular group of women who account for women's advantage or a more general trend. In all but one of the comparisons, the women candidates did better or nearly as well as their male counterparts. Only among Republican open-seat nominees did women, on average, raise less money than men did. At the

Figure 3.1 Average Campaign Receipts for Major Party Nominees, 2006

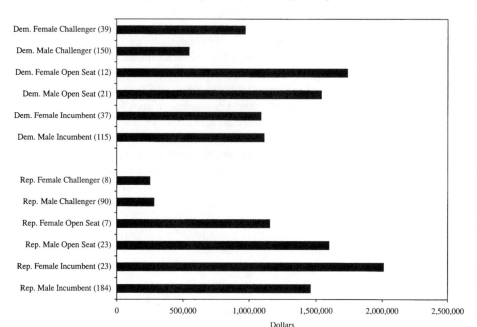

Source: Federal Elections Commission, www.fec.gov.
Note: Contests with a major party opponent only.

same time, female Republican incumbents raised the most money on average. Several of them faced particularly tough challengers (as did many of their male counterparts).

Access to early money is what propels success in opportune situations where often the key is winning one's party primary. Previous research has shown that contrary to accepted wisdom, women candidates in open-seat primaries had achieved parity or had outpaced male candidates in similar situations in raising early money (Burrell 1994). This fund-raising prowess of women continued in 2006. FEC filing reports ending 31 March 2006, listed 28 women and 123 men having filed campaign finance reports as required since they had raised at least $5,000. The 28 women had raised an average of $393,288 and a median $347,737 compared with an average of $268,096 and a median $137,715 for the 123 men. The male and female candidates had raised nearly equivalent amounts of early money from political action committees (PACs); the women candidates had an average of $30,851 and the men candidates had $29,491 in PAC contributions. Here is one more piece of evidence that women who run compete equally with men.

Party Organization Support

Anecdotally one finds little evidence of the national party organizations playing a negative role in the candidacies of women in 2006 opportune open-seat and challenger situations, although one would be hard pressed to find evidence of the National Republican Congressional Committee (NRCC) taking assertive measures to increase the presence and nomination of women in open seats. There was one exception to a lack of assertive measures on the part of the NRCC. Adjutant general of the Vermont National Guard Martha Rainville, who ran in the open seat for Vermont's at-large district, was considered a "prized recruit" for the Republicans. She received money and other fund-raising support from the national party over her primary opponents. As reported in the *Burlington Free Press*, "Five months in advance of the state primary election Vermont Republican leaders have asked the party's national committee to put its financial and organization muscle behind Martha Rainville's bid for Vermont's open U.S. House seat."[6] In his endorsement of Rainville, former Vermont House Speaker Walter Freed stated, "Martha is a stronger candidate of the two. She has far better name recognition, especially around the state. . . . Martha has a better track record and she's shown she has the *ability to raise money*."[7]

When it comes to deciding whether to back a nonincumbent candidate, national political party organizations first ask how much money an individual has already raised and to what extent the candidate can self-finance his or her own campaign. Although campaigns for a seat in the US House or Senate have long been candidate-centered operations, the political parties have reinvented themselves as significant sources of financial assistance and providers of other resources such as consultants and media advisors. In recent campaigns, they have provided millions of dollars in independent and coordinated expenditures in the final weeks of the campaign (see, for example, Dwyre and Kolodny 2006). The decisions they make regarding where they will place campaign ads and send ground forces can make a difference in hotly contested races.

The Democratic Congressional Campaign Committee (DCCC) and the National Republican Congressional Committee (NRCC) raised and spent respectively $69 million and $84 million in the 2006 election. In terms of specific financial support for their individual nominees, I examine coordinated expenditures, independent expenditures for a candidate, and independent expenditures against opponents of their party nominees to determine whether the campaign committees equally distributed financial support to their male and female nominees. The NRCC provided coordinated and independent expenditures for 84 of its 373 2006 nominees (23%) while the DCCC engaged in such financial activity for 171 (or 40%) of its 425 nominees. (Sixty-four of the Democratic nominees got only a token amount of less than $1,000, primarily in coordinated monies.)

On average, the parties' congressional committees were more generous with their female nominees with major party opponents than with their male nominees. The NRCC supplied an average of $410,553 to its women nominees and $195,042 to its male nominees while the DCCC provided an average of $238,715 to its female nominees and $153,140 to its male nominees. Nine Democratic female candidates (9% of female nominees with opponents) and eight Republican female candidates (19% of female nominees with opponents) received $1 million or more. These figures compare with 6 percent of the Democratic male nominees and 7 percent of the Republican male nominees. The Republican figures include three embattled incumbents, Marilyn Musgrave, Thelma Drake, and Heather Wilson. In the Tammy Duckworth–Peter Roskam race in Illinois' Sixth District, one of the most hotly contested open seats, the DCCC spent $3.1 million on Duckworth's behalf and against Roskam, and the NRCC spent over $3.4 million promoting Roskam's campaign and against Duckworth. In the only all-woman open-seat matchup, the Sixth District of Minnesota, the NRCC dropped over $1.3 million in Michele Bachmann's race while the DCCC spent over $1.1 million helping its nominee, Patty Wetterling. Another example of party organizational investment in their women candidates who have proven themselves is the nearly $3 million the DCCC spent on Lois Murphy's ultimately losing effort against Republican representative Jim Gerlach in Pennsylvania's Sixth District. At the other end of the spectrum, however, was Democrat Carol Shea-Porter's surprise victory over incumbent Jeb Bradley in New Hampshire's First District. Shea-Porter raised $353,000 and received only $5,672 in party support money. Bradley raised $1.1 million and the NRCC spent only $21,000 on his behalf.[8]

Winning Votes

Women candidates have shown themselves to be equally capable of obtaining votes as men candidates in previous elections, and this parity is characteristic of the 2006 election also. Figure 3.2 shows the percentage of the vote male and female candidates in each party obtained based on their candidate status of being an incumbent, a challenger, or an open-seat contender in the general election in races with a major party opponent. The Democratic advantage of that election year is reflected in the higher percentages of the vote its candidates obtained across status groups. Female Democratic incumbents led all groups with an average 71.2 percent of the vote while female Republican incumbents slightly lagged behind their male counterparts (57% to 60%). Little difference existed in the vote-getting success of male and female challengers in each party. Democratic challengers, male and female, obtained approximately 10 percent more votes than male

Figure 3.2 Percentage of Votes Obtained, General Election, 2006

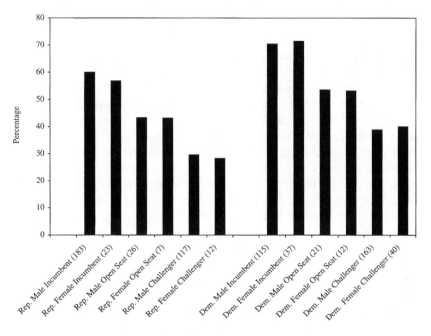

Source: CQ Weekly reports, various dates.

and female Republican challengers (40% to 30%). Parity also characterized the votes of male and female Democratic open-seat candidates and Republican male and female open-seat candidates with the Democratic candidates achieving just over one-half of the votes and Republican candidates receiving about 40 percent of the votes on average. Among the open-seat female candidates, Democratic women won 50 percent of their races and two of the three Republican women were victorious in November.

We still have to determine the relationship between dollars raised and spent and votes obtained for the male and female candidates in 2006. Some previous research has suggested that women have to raise more money and be better campaigners than male candidates to win. (See for example, Palmer and Simon 2006.)

The Winners

In the end, 56 individuals were newly elected to the 110th Congress, 10 women and 46 men. A comparison of the personal characteristics of these men and women shows both continuities with and distinctions from previous first-year classes. Most new members of the House arrive in the chamber between the ages of 35 and 55, so there is a relatively narrow window in each prospective candidate's life when he or she will be "ripe" for a congressional campaign (Gaddie and Bullock 2000, 53). Traditionally women have tended to enter the House of Representatives at an older age than men (Burrell 1994). The conventional wisdom explaining this difference has been that women tend to delay the start of their careers until their children are in school. Thus, as legislators they would be on average older than their male counterparts. Women with young children have also been discouraged from running for office as they and their would-be advisors anticipate receiving criticism on the campaign trail if they tried it (Carroll 1994). However, in 2006, the female victors were actually younger on average than their male counterparts. The average age of the newly elected women was 46.7 years. They ranged in age from 36 to 59. The average age of the male winners was 49.4 years and they ranged in age from 31 to 66. The female winners were also distinctive in being more likely to have law degrees than their male counterparts. Half of the women and 44 percent of the men had law degrees. In the past, female representatives have been less likely to have law degrees (Burrell 1994).

Seven of the 10 women (70%) were experienced office-holders, including two lieutenant governors, two state senators, a state representative, a county commissioner, and a member of the Brooklyn City Council. These seven women won open seats; the three nonofficeholders were incumbent challengers. In 2004, the seven women winning open seats also had office-holding experience, while Melissa Bean, the only challenger to win, did not. Of the newly elected men, 59 percent had elected office experience. The greater elected office experience of the first-term women in the 110th Congress compared with the first-term men is characteristic of the comparative backgrounds of men and women elected to the House since 1992 (Burrell forthcoming). Reflecting recent trends, these women were less likely to be married—70 percent were married compared with 87 percent of the men. Two were single and one was divorced. *CQ Weekly* profiles of new House members list the occupations (in addition to their office-holding experience) of these women as

- Real estate broker, hotel properties manager, state tourism agency official (Mary Fallin).
- Lawyer (Kathy Castor).
- Lawyer, campaign and state legislative aide (Mazie Hirono).
- Local economic development director, day care and youth program coordinator, state legislative aide, state agency aide (Yvette Clark).
- Property management company owner, retail tire company presi-

dent, regional economic and employment analyst (Gabrielle Giffords).

- Pharmaceuticals chemist, teacher, US Environmental Protection Agency chemist (Nancy Boyda).
- Homemaker, US Treasury Department lawyer (Michele Bachmann).
- Community college instructor, social worker (Carol Shea-Porter).
- Lawyer, US Housing and Urban Development Department aide (Kirsten Gillibrand).
- Lawyer, campaign aide, modeling school administrator (Betty Sutton).

Thus, these women newly elected to the US House bring a range of experiences to their service in Congress.

Conclusion

In one sense, this overview of women's and men's campaigns for the US House in 2006 shows a positive face of gender politics, with women competing equally with men as candidates for national office and in some cases even being advantaged. Eight women were newly elected to the US House in 2004, two more were elected in special elections in 2005 and then ten more women were elected in 2006 (although five incumbent women were also defeated). Their fund-raising and vote-winning prowess, women's integration into the top levels of the parties' national campaign organizations, and the election of Nancy Pelosi to the speakership of the US House suggest a lessening of a gendered bias to campaigns for national office. Men and women are running similar campaigns, are equally aggressive candidates, and compete quite equally for votes. But if an election year is touted as a Year of the Woman, then gender is still a factor in the framing of the election season. The biggest lag regarding women's quests for political leadership is observed in their continuing absence as candidates in open-seat contests—the most opportune situations for newcomers to be elected—and especially Republican women's lack of presence in these races. When they run, they win their primaries, they raise lots of money, their party organizations support them, and they get elected to the same extent as their male counterparts.

These results lead to some mixed reflections on the campaign process and women's candidacies. They show that women have become as adept at acting in the political world as men are, that they have adapted to traditional politics, or that they have learned to operate within gendered institutions that are masculine in nature. This aspect of gender politics may have its downside, as it indicates that women elected to public office are not likely to be particular champions of meaningful campaign finance reform and that they will be conflicted over how best to reform the system as they become invested in maintaining the status quo.

Further, it may be the increased pressure to raise enormous amounts of money that is preventing more women from running for office in the first place. And it may be part of the explanation for the lack of growth in the numerical representation of women in state-level office. Why pay such a high price for a position that pays little and is highly contentious? In this context, the lack of campaign finance reform becomes a serious issue for those who would advance the numbers of women in electoral office. Changing the nature of financing our campaigns for public office may be at least a necessary condition but probably not a sufficient condition to increase the number of women running for and winning these positions.

If party organizations do not seem to be obstacles for women candidates and women candidates have proven to be astute fund-raisers, then why should scholars and activists concerned with women gaining political equality be concerned with campaign finance reform? Although women seem to be able to operate quite well in the current system despite any remaining vestiges of gender politics, women continue to lag in taking advantage of windows of opportunity to increase their numerical representation in national office, as we have seen represented by their low numbers in the open-seat contests for the US House of Representatives, especially within the Republican Party. Also, as Beth Reingold points out in Chapter 1, gains in women's presence as lawmakers in state legislatures have leveled off, although there was some slight positive movement in 2006. While women have been shown to be less politically ambitious than men (Lawless and Fox 2005), this factor alone cannot account for *a drop* in women seeking and gaining state-level lawmaking positions in the early elections of the millennium, unless women are becoming even less ambitious. Instead, it may be that the nature of campaigns for these offices has not stimulated women to continue to seek them in ever-increasing numbers, and this may explain why term limits have not advantaged women. The number of candidates running for local office has dropped and elections have been canceled because of a lack of candidates (Marcedo 2005, 66).

We can speculate that one negative factor is the amount of money candidates need to raise and the growing emphasis among political organizational leaders on an individual's fund-raising ability in their recruitment efforts. The emphasis on money may also discourage potential male candidates, but given the underrepresentation of women in political office it has greater significance for them. The amount of money a candidate needs to raise to run a viable campaign has grown with each election season, and among other things, the more money one has, the more one can run ads criticizing opponents, thereby increasing the negativity of campaigns. Women's campaigns have become as negative as men's campaigns (Bystrom and Kaid 2002).

Other factors, such as the increasing polarization of our national legislative process, also contribute to making campaigns for these offices less attractive. Thus, ambitious women may have little incentive to seek public office. They can use their ambition in other ways. It is important to consider whether "clean campaigns" enhance women's entrance into the political fray. Research scholars should examine this other side of the "coin" in studying the reasons why more women are not seeking public office.

In addition, we need to ask why women would want to run for public office in the first place in the contemporary atmosphere of scandal, incivility, and polarization. Potential candidates, both men and women, may ask for what purpose should they run. Currently I am conducting a research project that explores the extent to which men and women potential candidates are taking advantage of windows of opportunity by running in open-seat primaries for the US House (Burrell and Frederick 2007). In this study, 49 percent of the women surveyed about their decisionmaking process regarding seeking election in an open-seat district in 2006 who decided not to run checked that "the ineffectiveness of the U.S. House as policy-making institution" was a "very important" or an "important" factor in their decision not to become a candidate, and 56 percent checked that "the inability of members of the U.S. House to work together" was a "very important" or "important" factor.[9] Institutional problems such as these provide a counterbalancing, sobering perspective and a complexity to women's quests for equal numbers in political leadership positions at the same time that those women who have sought such positions are increasingly successful.

Notes

1. Judy Holland, "Big Election Predicted for Female Candidates; Seen as Honest Outsiders, They Could Have Best Showing Since '92," *San Francisco Chronicle*, 22 October 2006.

2. See, for example, Abby Bar-Lev, "Year of the Woman Begins Tuesday," MDDaily.com, 2 November 2006, www.mndaily.com/artiles/2006.11/02/69686; Allison Stevens, "Tuesday Promises To Be 'Year of the Woman' Part II," 16 July 2006, www.womensenews.org/article.cfm/dyn/aid/2832/.

3. Robin Toner, "Women Wage Key Campaigns for Democrats," *New York Times*, 24 March 2006.

4. Four more seats became open after the primaries. In the 22nd district in Texas, Republican leader Tom Delay resigned his House seat after the primary. The 18th district in Florida and the 18th district in Ohio also became open when Republican members of the House resigned after running into ethical problems. The 17th district in Illinois became open when Representative Lane Evans decided against seeking reelection due to health issues. These races are counted as open in the general election but not in any analyses regarding the financing and vote-getting

in open seat primaries. In addition, the two races in which an incumbent was defeated in a primary are considered open in general election analyses.

5. FEC News Release, 7 March 2007.

6. Sam Hemingway, "State GOP Moves to Back Rainville," *Burlington Free Press*, 6 April 2006.

7. Quoted in the *National Journal*'s Hotline, 20 February 2006 (emphasis added here).

8. This analysis only touches the surface of a systematic investigation into the financial aspects of these candidates' campaigns. In further work, I will conduct multiple regression analyses to more precisely examine factors influencing party financial distribution decisions as well as impacts on candidates' fund-raising efforts.

9. The women who decided not to run were twice as likely as the men who decided not to run to say that the inability of members of the US House to work together was a very important factor in their decision not to become a candidate, 33 percent to 16 percent.

4

Confronting Stereotypes and Double Standards in Campaign Communication

DIANNE BYSTROM

When asked by a reporter if she "planned to run as a woman" during her bid for the Democratic nomination for president in 1988, US representative Pat Schroeder (D-CO) answered, "Do I have a choice?"[1]

In October 1999, Republican Elizabeth Dole announced she was bowing out of the race for her party's nomination for president. "You have to run on something besides the fact that you wear dresses," said Sheila Moloney, executive director of the conservative Eagle Forum, when commenting on the announcement for salon.com.

"I think what we've done is pave the way for the person who will be the first woman president," Dole said at the announcement that she was ending her campaign. "Timing is everything, isn't it?"[2]

Senator Hillary Rodham Clinton (D-NY) entered the race for the Democratic nomination for president in 2007, making it clear that appealing to women voters was central to her campaign. Still, according to Carrie Lukas of the Independent Women's Forum, "I don't think Hillary can count on women coming out for her out of a sense of sisterhood. She'll have to earn women's votes just as other Democratic candidates have really tried to court women."[3]

THE EXPERIENCES OF these three women seeking a major political party's nomination for president in the past 20 years underscore the dilemmas faced by female candidates when they run for public office in the United States. Do they run "as women"? Do they play down their sex? Or, do they try to do both?

This chapter looks at the communication styles and strategies of women political candidates for state and federal office through an analysis of their television advertising and websites. The campaigns of women running for governor and US senator were chosen because they are conducted statewide and thus lead to candidate communication strategies that are directed toward broader audiences, making them more comparable across races than local or congressional district campaigns. In addition, looking at women running for executive (governor) and legislative (Senate) office provides a context to highlight the campaign communication of Clinton as she runs for the 2008 Democratic nomination for the top executive position in the United States—president.

First, I will discuss the stereotypes women candidates face through perceptions by the public and in their media coverage. Next, I will summarize the research on women political candidates' campaign communication through television advertising and websites. Finally, I will show how women political candidates are using communication strategies to define their images and issues—at some times confronting and at other times capitalizing upon stereotypes—through their television advertising and websites.

Public Perceptions of Women Political Candidates

Research shows that voters and the news media have viewed female and male political candidates in stereotypical ways, particularly in terms of their personality characteristics, or image, and in their issue preferences and expertise.

According to a recent poll conducted by Roper-Starch Worldwide and underwritten by Deloitte and Touche on the viability of women candidates for president, one-third of the respondents indicated "there are general characteristics about women that make them less qualified to serve" (Deloitte and Touche 2000, 2). For example, a majority of those polled (51%) indicated that a man would do a better job than a woman leading the nation during a crisis and in making difficult decisions, the top two qualities respondents overall believed were "very important" in a presidential candidate.

Women were favored on the third and fourth most important presidential characteristics—trustworthiness and honesty—as well as the ability to understand people and moral character. Both women and men were considered equal on intelligence and the ability to forge compromise and obtain consensus (Deloitte and Touche 2000).

This poll revealed similar stereotypical assumptions about female and male issue expertise. Respondents said a male president would do a better job than a female president on the top-rated issue of law and order as well as in areas of foreign policy. They said a female president would do a better job on social concerns, such as education, poverty, and homelessness.

Although 44 percent of respondents said that there would be no difference on how well a man or woman president would handle the economy—the number two issue overall—more (31%) thought a man would do a better job than a woman (22%).

A more recent poll by CNN/USA Today/Gallup (Jones 2005) showed similar results when asking respondents whether a female or male president would perform best on issues of national security or domestic policy. The plurality of respondents, overall, said a male president would be best in dealing with issues of national security (42%), whereas a woman president would perform better in the realm of domestic policy (45%).

The 2005 poll showed interesting differences between the perceptions of Democrats, Republicans, and Independents toward female versus male presidential candidates. The poll, taken at a time when Clinton was rumored to be considering a run for the 2008 Democratic presidential nomination, showed that the Democrats polled were more likely to say that a woman president would do the best job in the area of national security (37%) and domestic policy (62%). Comparatively, 31 percent of Democrats said a male president would do the best job on national security and only 13 percent on domestic policy.

Republicans, however, tended to believe a male president would do the best in both national security (57%) and domestic policy (34%). Comparatively, only 8 percent of Republicans said a woman president would do a better job on national security and 30 percent on domestic policy. Independents rated a male president best to handle issues of national security (37%) and a female president best on domestic policy (45%).

The results of this poll (Jones 2005) further suggest that Democrats would be more supportive of a female candidate for president than Republicans would be. In fact, this survey shows that 94 percent of Democrats compared to 76 percent of Republicans would vote for a woman president. When asked if their neighbor would vote for a woman president, 72 percent of Democrats compared to 47 percent of Republicans said yes. The percentage of Democrats and Republicans who would actually vote for a woman for president is thought to be somewhere between what the respondents said about their own support versus what they said about their neighbors' support for a woman candidate for president.

Studies by political scientists (Huddy and Terkildsen 1993a; Kahn 1993; Leeper 1991) also show that voters hold stereotypical views about women political candidates' character traits and issue expertise. Women are perceived to be kind, compassionate, sensitive, understanding, honest, and trustworthy, whereas men are viewed as strong, tough, experienced, and knowledgeable. Women are more likely than men to be associated with such social issues as education, health care, families and children, the elderly, the environment, poverty, and women's issues, whereas men are more likely to be associated with foreign policy, defense, national security, crime, agriculture, and the economy.

However, when voters are asked about actual—rather than hypothetical—women candidates, fewer gender differences emerge. For example, a 2006 survey conducted by Lake Research Partners and American Viewpoint of voters in seven states where five women and two men were running for reelection for governor rated the females higher than the males not only on the attributes of honesty, caring, and cooperativeness, but also on toughness, problemsolving, and decisiveness (Barbara Lee Family Foundation 2007). And, a November 2007 Iowa Poll of likely Democratic caucus participants rated presidential candidate Hillary Clinton the top in a field of eight candidates as the most presidential (27%), fiscally responsible (23%), socially progressive (29%), and most knowledgeable about the world (37%). However, her leading opponent, Senator Barack Obama, was rated most likable (33%) and most principled (25%).

Taken together, these polls show that stereotypes could pose roadblocks to women candidates during election cycles in which voters are most concerned about foreign policy or national security, such as in 2002 and 2004. But these stereotypes may work in the favor of female candidates when domestic or "women's" issues are more salient, such as in 1992, or when voters are seeking change, such as in 2006. The polls also show that actual women candidates—particularly incumbents—can overcome gender stereotypes on both issue and image characteristics. That is, they can be seen as tough and caring and competent on fiscal, social, and global issues.

As Kim Fridkin Kahn noted, female candidates may have held an advantage over male candidates in 1992 because the so-called Year of the Woman election "placed a premium . . . on 'female' issues and 'female' traits" (1994, 191). However, she warns that in most elections, "masculine" issues and traits top the voters' agenda and advises that it may be best for women candidates to "emphasize their leadership ability and to demonstrate their competence in dealing with the traditional 'male' issues" to eradicate voter stereotypes and win campaigns (1992, 512). Clinton seems to be following this advice in her bid for the 2008 Democratic Party nomination for president through political ads that emphasize her leadership, experience, and competence on such issues as the economy, health care, and national security.

Media Coverage of Women Political Candidates

Similar to biases held by voters, female and male political candidates have been treated in stereotypical ways by the media in their news coverage, although recent studies have revealed more balance. Extensive studies by

Kahn examining the newspaper coverage of women candidates running for election in the 1980s found that this medium not only stereotyped female candidates by emphasizing "feminine traits" and "feminine issues," but also accorded them less coverage that often questioned their viability as candidates (1994). However, Kahn also has noted that gender-stereotyped newspaper coverage can sometimes be used to a woman candidate's advantage— for example, by emphasizing her warmth and honesty or expertise on such issues as education or health care—in some electoral environments.

In her 1996 book, *The Political Consequences of Being a Woman: How Stereotypes Influence the Conduct and Consequences of Political Campaigns*, Kahn argues that both women and men candidates can structure their campaign appeals to either capitalize on gendered beliefs or dispel them, depending on the context of the election. Since Kahn's pioneering work, researchers have begun to find more equitable media treatment of female and male candidates running for state and federal office in the mid- to late 1990s and, especially, in the 21st century. For example, Kevin Smith (1997) found that female and male candidates running for governor or the US Senate in 1994 received about the same quantity and quality of coverage, except in open races. And, in his study of 1998 gubernatorial races, James Devitt (1999) found that female and male candidates received about the same amount of coverage, but that women received less issue-related coverage than men did.

Studies of the newspaper coverage of female and male candidates running against each other in gubernatorial and US Senate races in 2000 and 2002 found even more parity, both in terms of the quantity and quality of coverage. In their book, *Gender and Campaign Communication: VideoStyle, WebStyle, and NewsStyle* (2004), Dianne Bystrom, Mary Banwart, Lynda Lee Kaid, and Terry Robertson summarize several studies conducted by members of their research team on the newspaper coverage of female and male candidates running for governor and the US Senate in primary and general election races in 2000. They also present additional findings on the media coverage of female and male candidates running in general election campaigns in 2002.

The authors found that women political candidates running in both primary and general election races for governor and US Senate in 2000 received more coverage than men, and the quality of their coverage—the slant of the story and discussion of their viability, appearance, and personality—was mostly equitable. Still, these women candidates were much more likely to be discussed in terms of their gender, marital status, and children, which can affect their viability with voters.

Similarly, the newspaper coverage of female and male candidates running against each other for the US Senate and governor in 2002 was about even in terms of quantity, with 35 percent of the articles focusing on men and 34 percent on women (Bystrom et al. 2004). However, gender stereo-types were found in the quality of their coverage. For example, in 2002, the media paid significantly more attention to the backgrounds (e.g., the previous occupations and experiences) of female candidates and to the competence of male candidates. Also, male candidates were linked significantly more often with the "masculine" issue of taxes in 2002, whereas female candidates were associated more often with so-called women's issues—such as reproductive choice—and sometimes in a negative manner. Women candidates also continued to receive less equitable coverage than men through news media coverage about their marital status in 2002.

Although recent studies show that female and male candidates running for governor and US Senate are receiving more equitable media coverage, especially in terms of quantity and discussion of their viability, women candidates for president may still receive more stereotyped coverage. For example, studies of Elizabeth Dole's campaign for the Republican nomination for president in 1999 found that she received less equitable coverage in terms of quality and, especially, quantity as compared to her male opponents (Aday and Devitt 2001; Bystrom 2006; Heldman, Carroll, and Olson 2005). Polls consistently showed Dole as a distant runner-up to George W. Bush for the Republican nomination for president; however, she not only received significantly less coverage than Bush, but also less coverage than Steve Forbes and John McCain, who at the time were even further behind in the polls than she was.

In terms of the quality of coverage, again Dole received less issue coverage than Bush, Forbes, or McCain. However, Dole's issue coverage was balanced between such stereotypical "masculine" issues as taxes, foreign policy, and the economy and such stereotypical "feminine" issues as education, drugs, and gun control. Dole also received more personal coverage than her male opponents, including references to her appearance and, especially, personality (Aday and Devitt 2001; Bystrom 2006; Heldman, Carroll, and Olson 2005).

Hillary Clinton's bid for the 2008 Democratic Party nomination for president—which began in January 2007 with the formation of an exploratory committee—provides yet another opportunity for researchers to analyze the gender stereotypes that face women running for the nation's top executive office. Recent surveys (Jones 2005) show that Democrat voters are more supportive of a woman candidate for president than Republican voters. But even if a Democratic woman candidate for president fares better with voters than a Republican woman candidate, she may receive the same biased media coverage.

In fact, according to early studies of the media coverage of the campaign for the Democratic nomination for president, Clinton received more negative news coverage than her closest rivals, Obama and former senator John

Edwards. The Center for Media and Public Affairs at George Mason University found that on-air evaluations of Clinton by television news programs on ABC, CBS, NBC, and FOX were 52 percent negative and 48 percent positive (Rieck 2007). Comparatively, on-air evaluations were 61 percent positive and 39 percent negative of Obama and 67 percent positive and 33 percent negative of Edwards. In this study, Clinton was evaluated more often than all of her Democrat opponents combined. Similarly, a study by the Project for Excellence in Journalism and the Joan Shorenstein Center on the Press, Politics and Public Policy of 48 different outlets in five media sectors—including newspapers, online news, network television, cable television, and radio—found that Clinton's campaign coverage was 38 percent negative and 27 percent positive compared to Obama's 47 percent positive and 16 percent negative coverage (Project for Excellence in Journalism 2007).

Although Clinton's negative media coverage could be attributed to her status as frontrunner for most of 2007 (prior to her loss to Obama in the January 3, 2008, Iowa caucuses), previous studies show that male frontrunners have been subjected to less negative coverage by the media. For example, in 1999, Bush received 57 percent positive trait coverage and 35 percent negative trait coverage as the frontrunner for the Republican nomination for president (Heldman, Carroll, and Olson 2005). Comparatively, Dole received 48 percent positive and 44 percent negative trait coverage, and McCain received 81 percent positive and 2 percent negative trait coverage when they ran for the Republican nomination in 1999.

Women's Campaign Communication

Due to the public's perceptions about female candidates, combined with the added weight of media framing and stereotyping, it remains important for women candidates to define strategically and successfully their own image and issue messages through traditional mass media, such as television, as well as through new communication technologies, such as the Internet. Over time, researchers have found both differences and similarities in the ways in which female and male candidates use television advertising and, more recently, Web technology in their campaigns.

Political Advertising

Studies analyzing the television ads of women and men date back to 1985. Most of the earliest studies found that women candidates were more likely to emphasize social issues, such as education and health care, in their television ads whereas men were more likely to focus on economic issues such as taxes in their political spots (Kahn 1993; Trent and Sabourin 1993). As far as image traits, women were more likely to emphasize compassion and men to stress their strength, although sometimes both sexes emphasized stereotypical "masculine" traits such as competence and leadership (Benze and DeClercq 1985; Johnston and White 1994; Kahn 1993).

As more women ran for political office beginning in the 1990, and especially 1992, campaigns, researchers began to find a more-balanced, and less-gendered, approach in their television advertising styles. For example, in separate studies, Dianne Bystrom (1994) and Leonard Williams (1994) found that women and men running for the US Senate in 1992 balanced "feminine" traits—such as warmth and compassion—with "masculine" images—such as toughness, strength, and activity—in their spots.

In their summary of the results of studies analyzing female and male political commercials in mixed-gender US Senate campaigns from 1990 to 1998, Bystrom and Kaid (2002) found that female and male candidates emphasized similar images in their television commercials. They both emphasized mostly stereotypical "masculine" traits such as strength, aggressiveness, performance, and experience balanced with such stereotypical "feminine" attributes as honesty, sensitivity, and understanding.

As far as issue presentation, Bystrom and Kaid (2002) concluded that the context of the election year was generally more important than the sex of the candidates in choosing what topics to include in their political spots. For example, both women and men focused on education, the environment, and senior citizen issues in 1990; the economy, health care, and taxes in 1992; taxes and crime in 1994; taxes, senior citizen issues, and education in 1996; and taxes, the economy, and senior citizen issues in 1998.

Bystrom and Kaid (2002) further concluded that the presence of a female candidate in a political campaign could change the issue and image discussion of her male opponent. That is, when women run for political office, their male opponents are called into a campaign dialogue that includes attention to issues associated with women and their societal concerns—such as education, health care, and senior citizen issues—as well as presentation of stereotypically "feminine" attributes, such as honesty, trustworthiness, and understanding.

In addition to the content of television ads, it is interesting to look at the effects these appeals have on potential voters. At first, researchers and campaign consultants thought that "masculine" strategies (aggressive, career)—rather than traditional "feminine" (nonaggressive, family) strategies—worked best for women candidates in their political ads (Kaid et al. 1984; Wadsworth et al. 1987). However, it now seems that women are most effective when balancing stereotypical "feminine" and "masculine" traits (Banwart and Carlin 2001; Bystrom 2003).

As far as issues, Shanto Iyengar and his colleagues (1997) found that women are more effective when communicating about stereotypical "feminine" issues such as women's rights, education, and unemployment than such stereotypical "masculine" issues as crime and illegal immigration. Similarly, in their survey of female candidates for state legislatures and the US House of Representatives in 1996 and 1998, Paul S. Herrnson, J. Celeste Lay, and Atiya Kai Stokes (2003) concluded that women are more successful when they run "as women" by emphasizing issues that voters associate favorably with women candidates and targeting female voters. They suggest that female candidates conduct campaigns that employ voters' dispositions toward gender as an asset rather than a liability.

Websites

Similar to television advertising, websites represent a form of communication that is controlled by the politician, rather than interpreted by the media. Thus, researchers (Banwart 2002; Dolan 2005; Niven and Zilber 2001) are beginning to examine websites to see if female and male politicians present themselves differently when they use this form of communication.

In their study of the websites of female and male members of the US House of Representatives in 1998, David Niven and Jeremy Zilber (2001) found that both women and men described their experiences in Washington as "fighting for," "leading," and "being effective." Women listed slightly fewer details about their family than men did, and women dedicated more space than men to their personal qualifications (such as education and work experience) relevant to their position in Congress. Women were more likely than men to mention their record on "women's issues" (women's health research, sexual harassment laws, family leave, child care, and gun control laws); more likely to make "compassion issues"—such as poverty and human rights—a larger part of their website presentation; and more likely to mention their affiliation with a women's group or women's rights group.

Recent studies of the websites of women running for the US Congress show that female and male candidates use a mix of "feminine" versus "masculine" strategies. For example, in her study of female and male candidates running against each other in 2000, Mary Banwart (2002) found that both female and male candidates discussed "feminine" issues much more frequently than "masculine" issues on their websites. Kathleen Dolan (2005) found that women running for Congress in 2000 and 2002 campaigned—on their websites—on a set of topics that were similar to those of their male opponents.

Similar to Niven and Zilber (2001), Banwart (2002) found that women candidates in 2000 were much less likely than men to be shown with their families on their websites. Their studies led Banwart (2002) and Niven and Zilber (2001) to conclude that women portray the personal aspects of their lives—as well as issues and images—differently on their websites than the media do in covering their campaigns. For example, whereas the media often associate female political candidates with fewer and more stereotypical "feminine" issues than male political candidates (Bystrom et al. 2004; Devitt 1999), Niven and Zilber (2001) found that women in the US Congress, through their websites, present themselves with a "much greater diversity of issue commitments that have nothing directly to do with gender" (402). They contend that women politicians can capitalize on "widening Internet use" and "ameliorate media stereotypes" by providing direct, unfiltered messages to their constituents through their websites (403).

Gender, Stereotypes, and Campaign Communication

Although studies have confirmed gender biases and stereotypes by voters and the media in their perceptions of female and male candidates, researchers also have shown how women can use campaign communication to dispel or emphasize such stereotypes, depending on the context of the election year. The following analysis draws mostly upon data collected for a larger project (Bystrom, Banwart, Kaid, and Robertson 2004) to focus on how female and male candidates use image, issue, and strategy appeals to confront or capitalize upon stereotypes held by the public and media and present a more complete picture of their campaigns.

Description of Data Sets

The results reported on communication styles and strategies of women political candidates through their television commercials and websites are based on three sets of data.

1. A quantitative content analysis of 1,389 television advertisements aired by women and men US Senate and gubernatorial candidates running in mixed-gender races from 1990 through 2002. The ads were obtained from the Political Communication Center at the University of Oklahoma. Of the total sample, 686 ads (49%) were from female candidates, and 703 ads (51%) were from male candidates. See Table 4.1 for a complete description of the ad sample by level of office, status and party of candidate, and outcome.

2. A quantitative content analysis of the websites of 48 candidates running in mixed-gender gubernatorial and US Senate races in 2000 and 2002. Of the sample, 54 percent of the websites were from female candidates' campaigns, and 46 percent were from male candidates' campaigns; 48 percent were from gubernatorial campaigns and 52 percent were from US Senate campaigns. A total of 52 percent of the websites represented

Republican candidates, 48 percent represented Democrat candidates, 52 percent were created by candidates in open races, 29 percent were from challenger candidates' campaigns, and 19 percent were from incumbent candidates' campaigns.

3. A qualitative analysis of the political ads and websites of 35 women running for US Senate (22, or 63%) and governor (13, or 37%) in 2004 and 2006. These candidates included 25 Democrats (71%) and 10 Republicans (29%); 17 (48%) were running as incumbents, 9 (26%) as challengers, and 9 (26%) in open-seat races.

In the quantitative analysis of television commercials, ads were coded for demographic and other information about the candidates—including their status as an incumbent, challenger, or open-race contender; their political party; and the outcome of their race—as well as verbal, nonverbal, and production content. This chapter focuses on the analysis of verbal content of the commercials—including the presence or absence of negative attacks, the issues mentioned, the image qualities highlighted, and the structure of the appeals made.

A similar coding instrument was used in the quantitative analysis of candidate websites to record information on their verbal, nonverbal, and production content with additional categories added to analyze interactive content.

In the qualitative analysis, the websites of 35 women running for the US Senate and governor in 2004 and 2006 were accessed to review their content, including examples of political commercials that the candidate had aired on television. Results of this analysis are used to illustrate the findings of the quantitative analyses.

Table 4.1 Political Campaign Advertising Analyzed, 1990–2002

	Total		Female Ads		Male Ads	
Level						
Governor	535	(39%)	282	(53%)	253	(47%)
Senate	854	(61%)	404	(47%)	450	(53%)
Status						
Incumbent	406	(29%)	97	(14%)	309	(44%)
Challenger	393	(28%)	281	(41%)	112	(16%)
Open race	590	(43%)	308	(45%)	282	(40%)
Party						
Democrat	645	(46%)	439	(64%)	206	(29%)
Republican	744	(54%)	247	(36%)	497	(71%)
Outcome						
Won	700	(50%)	292	(43%)	408	(58%)
Lost	689	(50%)	394	(57%)	295	(42%)

In addition, examples of the television commercials and website of Clinton in her campaign for the 2008 Democratic nomination for president are used to compare, contrast, and highlight research findings from lower-level races.

Gendered Communication in Television Political Ads

Although female and male candidates are increasingly similar in the issues they discuss, image traits they emphasize, and appeal strategies they use in their ads, the differences that did emerge (see Table 4.2) are interesting from a gendered perspective. In general, women emphasized mostly "feminine" issues balanced with "masculine and feminine" traits. Both women and men candidates used "feminine" appeals.

For example, the top issue in the ads by women candidates running for office between 1990 and 2002—and one that was discussed significantly more often in females' spots than in the ads for male candidates—was the stereotypically "feminine" concern of education and schools.

Democrat Kathleen Sebelius, in an open-seat race for governor of Kansas in 2002, typified the use of this "feminine" issue in her campaign. Sebelius frequently discussed education in her ads in an attempt, according

Table 4.2 Significant Differences by Gender in Candidate Campaign Advertising (percentage)

	Female Ads ($n = 686$)	Male Ads ($n = 703$)
Issues		
Economy in general	15	9
Education/schools	31	22
Crime/prisons	10	14
Health care	20	13
Senior citizen issues	18	13
Welfare	1	5
Women's issues	9	4
Appeal Strategies		
Incumbency stands for legitimacy	6	11
Use of statistics	17	22
Own accomplishments	31	37
Taking the offensive position	24	18
Attack opponent's record	40	32
Character Traits		
Toughness/strength	36	30
Experience in politics	21	29
Sensitive/understanding	16	20

Note: Percentages indicate frequencies within gender. Gender differences for all significant at levels $p \leq .05$.

to media accounts, to woo moderate Republicans. In one ad, titled "Dedicated," a male voiceover announced: "Kathleen Sebelius. As governor, [she will be] dedicated to our schools, lift teacher pay from 40th in the nation, cut government waste to get more dollars into the classroom, and promote local control so parents and educators decide what's best for their schools." At the conclusion of this ad, Sebelius personally delivers her message that, "As governor, I'll always put our children and schools first."

The ads of female candidates between 1990 and 2002 also discussed other issues—health care, senior citizen issues, and women's issues—considered "feminine" (because they are more commonly associated with women) significantly more often than the ads of their male opponents (see Table 4.2). As with the issue of education, women candidates may be conforming to stereotypical expectations that consider them to be experts on such concerns. However, female candidates also were more likely than male candidates to discuss the economy, which is usually associated more with men than with women and therefore can be considered a "masculine" issue.

In 2004, US Senate candidate Patty Murray (D-WA) demonstrated how "masculine" issues, like the economy, could be interwoven with "feminine" issues, such as education and health care, within the same commercial. In an ad titled "America," Murray is pictured in an orchard behind a cart of red and green apples. She narrates the ad, stating:

> I grew up and raised my family here in Washington State. It's been an honor to serve you in the US Senate. But, today, I'm very concerned about the direction of our country. We need to take care of our own people. Invest in American business. Create American jobs. Improve our own local schools. Lower the cost of heath care right here at home. I'm Patty Murray, and I approved this ad because it's time to change priorities and put America first.

The only issues discussed significantly more often in the ads of male candidates, compared to female candidates, were crime and prisons, a more "masculine" issue, and welfare, a more "feminine" issue. However, some of the male candidates discussing welfare took a hard-line approach, focusing on limiting the number of families receiving such benefits.

The top traits emphasized in the ads by women candidates between 1990 and 2002 were toughness/strength, past performance, leadership, and action-oriented (commonly considered "masculine" attributes) and honesty/integrity (more commonly considered a "feminine" quality). The top traits emphasized in the ads by men candidates were experience in politics, past performance, leadership, aggressive/fighter, action-oriented, and toughness/strength (all "masculine" attributes) and sensitive/understanding (a "feminine" characteristic). Of these traits, women candidates were significantly more likely to emphasize toughness/strength than men candidates, and men candidates were significantly more likely to discuss their experience in politics and emphasize their sensitive side than women. (See Table 4.2.)

The appeal strategies used in female and male candidate ads were closely related to the traits they emphasized and, thus, also are interesting from a gendered perspective. Both female and male candidates were equally as likely to use all of the elements of "feminine style"—which is characterized by an inductive structure, personal tone, addressing the audience as peers, relying on personal experiences, identifying with the experiences of others, and inviting audience participation.

A commercial by Jean Hay Bright, a Democrat who challenged long-time senator Olympia Snowe to represent Maine in the US Senate in 2006, illustrates many of the key elements of feminine style. In a commercial titled "Inside/Outside," Bright narrates:

> Activist politics connects people, empowers people to stand up for what they believe. And that is good. But from my perspective, that empowerment is a means to an end. The bottom line for me is getting our people in positions of power, so we control the agenda, so our side casts the deciding votes, and we take back our America. I'm Jean Hay Bright. Let's all work, march, speak out—and vote—for the America we want to live in.

Male candidates did rely on statistics—a "masculine" strategy—significantly more often than female candidates and were significantly more likely to talk about their incumbency and accomplishments—perhaps not surprising, as incumbents' ads made up 44 percent of the male sample and only 14 percent of the female sample of ads. Female candidates were significantly more likely to take an offensive position and attack the record of their opponent—again, perhaps not surprising, as challenger ads made up 41 percent of the female sample and only 16 percent of the male sample of ads (see Table 4.2).

Does political party affiliation make a difference? When female and male candidates are compared by their political party affiliation, more differences emerged in their television advertising strategies. For example, television ads tended to be more negative in races between female Democrats and male Republicans than in races between female Republicans and male Democrats. Female Democrats were more likely than other candidates to use negative advertising, to attack their opponent's record, to emphasize that they were an aggressive fighter, and to use expert authorities to underscore their strength and competence. Female Democrats also were more likely to discuss education and health care—issues traditionally associated with the Democratic Party—but also taxes, a traditional Republican issue. (See Table 4.3.)

For example, Lucy Baxley, a Democrat challenger running to unseat

Table 4.3 Significant Gender Differences in Campaign Ads by Candidate Party, Status, and Outcome (percentage)

	Democrat		Republican	
	Female (n = 439)	Male (n = 206)	Female (n = 247)	Male (n = 497)
Focus				
Candidate positive	50	69 *	74	59 *
Opponent negative	39	23 *	20	32 *
Comparative/cannot determine	11	8 *	6	9 *
Negative attack present	57	37 *	31	45 *
Emphasis*				
Campaign issues	59	68	—	—
Candidate image	42	33	—	—
Issues				
Taxes	27	19 *	—	—
Economy in general	—	—	16	8 *
Education/schools	39	25 *	—	—
Crime/prisons	—	—	7	14 *
Health care	25	18 *	—	—
Dissatisfaction with government	8	15 *	13	8 *
International issues	1	6 *	—	—
Appeal strategies				
Incumbency stands for legitimacy	5	14 *	—	—
Voice for the state	—	—	31	24 *
Personal tone	—	—	43	32 *
Call for change	—	—	36	28 *
Personal experience	19	28 *	25	18 *
Use of statistics	—	—	9	23 *
Use of expert authorities	24	17 *	12	19 *
Emphasize own accomplishments	30	46 *	—	—
Attack opponent's record	47	30 *	—	—
Makes gender an issue	—	—	6	2 *
Character traits				
Toughness/strength	—	—	40	31 *
Past performance	34	49 *	—	—
Aggressive/fighter	40	30 *	—	—
Leadership	26	45 *	43	34 *
Experience in politics	17	38 *	—	—
Washington outsider	6	13 *	—	—
Knowledgeable/intelligent	11	18 *	18	11 *
Qualified	—	—	26	20 *
Trustworthy	—	—	15	22 *

	Incumbent		Challenger		Open Race	
	Female (n = 97)	Male (n = 309)	Female (n = 281)	Male (n = 112)	Female (n = 308)	Male (n = 282)
Negative attack present	44	30 *	45	67 *	—	—
Emphasis*						
Campaign issues	54	71	60	45	—	—
Candidate image	46	29	40	55	—	—

continues

Table 4.3   continued

	Won		Lost	
	Female (*n* = 292)	Male (*n* = 408)	Female (*n* = 394)	Male (*n* = 295)
Focus*				
Candidate positive	57	70	—	—
Opponent negative	34	24	—	—
Comparative/cannot determine	9	7	—	—
Negative attack present*	49	33	47	55
Issues				
Taxes	32	25 *	—	—
Economy in general	—	—	19	7 *
Education/schools	31	23 *	32	20 *
Crime/prisons	9	16 *	—	—
Health care	24	14 *	—	—
Senior citizen issues	20	11 *	—	—
Environment	—	—	8	4 *
Women's issues	12	3 *	—	—
Appeal strategies				
Incumbency stands for legitimacy	7	15 *	—	—
Personal tone	—	—	36	26 *
Address viewers as peers	24	32 *	34	26 *
Use of endorsements	12	6 *	4	8 *
Use of statistics	19	25 *	—	—
Own accomplishments	37	45 *	—	—
Taking the offensive position	24	17 *	—	—
Attack opponent's record	42	26 *	—	—
Makes gender an issue	—	—	8	2 *
Character traits				
Toughness/strength	—	—	37	28 *
Aggressive/fighter	40	32 *	—	—
Leadership	32	48 *	32	22 *
Experience in politics	26	38 *	—	—
Knowledgeable/intelligent	—	—	16	10 *

Notes: Percentages indicate frequencies within gender.
*Gender differences significant at levels $p \leq .05$. Only significant differences are reported.
— signifies that difference in percentages is not significant.

Governor Bob Riley in the 2006 Alabama gubernatorial race, combined a negative attack with the issue of taxes in her campaign ads. One ad claimed that Riley "didn't pay his taxes for nine straight years . . . but raised your taxes." In an ad titled "Always," Baxley uses clips of Riley from a 2002 election debate to make it appear that Baxley is criticizing himself (instead of a previous opponent) for raising taxes. As clips of Riley and newspaper articles about tax increases play across the screen, a male announcer says: "Bob Riley tried to raise a million dollars in taxes. When voters said no, he raised property taxes without a vote. Now Riley's passed out another billion dollars in no-bid contracts. How is he going to pay for that? Bob Riley. He'll raise your taxes again."

Male Democrats were more likely than other candidates to voice their dissatisfaction with government; address international issues; and emphasize their experience in politics, leadership, accomplishments, and past performance. Female Republicans were more likely than other candidates to discuss the economy, use a personal tone, call for change, act as a voice for the state, and emphasize their toughness/strength and qualifications. Male Republicans were more likely than other candidates to talk about crime/prisons, use statistics, and emphasize their trustworthiness.

Senator Kay Bailey Hutchison, a Republican who has represented Texas since 1993, emphasized her role as a fighter and voice for the state on a number of issues in a 2006 ad. Over photos of Texas scenery and Hutchison riding a horse, talking to senior citizens, and greeting veterans, a male announcer says:

> Texas. 268,000 square miles of mountains, prairies, hills and lakes. And a state this big needs a senator who knows every inch of it. Kay Bailey Hutchison. She's fighting to secure our borders, to make the tax cut permanent. Standing with our veterans and seniors. Working to make sure every child succeeds. Kay Bailey Hutchison. A senator for all Texans.

Political party affiliation—in a sample in which 64 percent of the female ads were aired by Democrats and 71 percent of the male ads were by Republicans—seems to account for some, but not all, of the differences found overall. For example, it could account for women discussing senior citizen and women's issues more often than men overall and men emphasizing welfare. However, political party affiliation, alone, does not seem to account for women's overall emphasis on the economy, education, and health-care issues or characterizations of their strength and toughness.

Does candidate status make a difference? In our sample, 44 percent of male ads were by incumbents, 41 percent of the female ads were by challengers, and 40 percent of the male ads and 45 percent of the female ads were run in open races. When female and male candidates were compared by status, a few differences were found among incumbents and challengers, but not among open-race contenders, who are not bound by status implications—either by the benefits or constraints.

Male challengers ran the most negative ads, dispelling any notion that they would use more restraint against a female opponent. Interestingly, female challengers (45%) and female incumbents (44%) ran about the same amount of negative ads, perhaps showing how they must continue to battle stereotypes to prove themselves even when running as incumbents.

Incumbent male candidates (71%) and female challenger (60%) and incumbent (54%) candidates were most likely to focus their campaigns on issue, as opposed to image, ads; whereas male challengers relied more on image ads (55%) in their campaigns. (See Table 4.3.)

Though not significantly, female and male candidate challengers differ more across character traits than do either incumbent candidates or open-race candidates, with female challengers placing greater emphasis on "masculine" traits than male challengers. Female challengers also discussed issues and used expert authorities more often than male challengers in their ads. Male challengers are most likely to emphasize their honesty/integrity. Female and male open-race candidates are similar across issue agendas and image characteristics, although women are more likely to use a personal tone in emphasizing their aggressiveness and toughness.

Again, candidate status—particularly as a challenger—may explain many, but not all, of the differences seen between men and women in the overall sample. It may explain, for example, women's emphasis overall on the economy, health care, and senior citizen issues (challenger issues), women's issues (incumbent issue), and toughness and strength (open-race trait). Candidate status does not seem to explain women's overall emphasis on education, as both incumbent and challenger women talk about that issue in 31 percent of their ads.

In addition to candidate status, the success of the candidates was compared in the analysis of their television ads. In our sample, 43 percent of the female ads were aired by winners and 57 percent by losers; 58 percent of the male ads were by winners and 42 percent by losers.

Winning female and male candidates used different strategies from losing female and male candidates (see Table 4.3). Specifically, female candidates who ultimately won discussed issues more frequently—taxes, health care, senior citizen issues, and women's issues, in particular—and emphasized being aggressive/a fighter more often than other candidates. Male candidates who won discussed crime and prison issues more frequently and emphasized their leadership, accomplishments, and experience. Women candidates—both winning and losing—talked about education in one-third of their ads and used attacks in almost half of their ads. Losing female candidates were more likely to talk about the economy, use a personal tone, address viewers as peers, and emphasize their toughness and strength. Losing males were the most negative and winning males the least negative of all candidates in their campaigns.

Overall, it is notable that female candidates who won tended to be those who emphasized "masculine" traits and both "feminine" and "masculine" issues (although more "feminine" than "masculine" issues). Winning candidates, both female and male, used substantial issue discussion in their advertising, but this was particularly true of the ads of winning female candidates. Winning male candidates, however, incorporated a mix of "feminine" and "masculine" strategies—such as talking about education as well as taxes, addressing viewers as peers, and touting their own accomplishments—to ensure their success. (See Table 4.3.)

Gendered Communication on Candidate Websites

Websites, like television advertising, represent a form of political communication controlled by the politician, rather than interpreted by the media. Therefore, it is somewhat surprising that male and female candidates are more similar in their issue discussion on their websites than in their political ads. For example, in 2000 and 2002, both female and male candidates discussed "feminine" issues much more frequently than "masculine" issues on their websites. Both female and male candidates were equally as likely to discuss the "feminine" issue of education. On so-called "masculine" issues, male candidates were only slightly more likely to discuss taxes, whereas female candidates were slightly more likely to discuss the economy.

Certainly the World Trade Center and Pentagon attacks on September 11, 2001, and the war in Iraq stimulated increased discussion of international issues and homeland security on both female and male candidate websites in the 2002 and subsequent campaigns. For example, Democrat Jeanne Shaheen, a candidate for US Senate from New Hampshire in 2002, headlined "Enhancing Security" as an issue category on her website, followed by the issue heading of "Ensuring Our Safety After September 11." The text on the site indicated that Shaheen—in her past position as governor of New Hampshire—had acted to secure the state by "stepping up patrols of our harbors and bridges and increasing inspections along our highways."

In the 2006 campaign, the websites of women running for governor and the US Senate continued to focus on issues such as education, the economy, national security, and the war in Iraq. Republican Sarah Palin, running in an open race for governor of Alaska, listed links to 20 different issues on her website, ranging from education, health care, and agriculture to the environment, tourism, and gun rights. Similarly, Amy Klobuchar, a Democrat running in an open race for the US Senate in Minnesota, featured some 15 issues on her website, ranging from promoting homegrown resources, growing our economy, and getting a fair deal for families to changing course in Iraq, supporting our veterans, and keeping our communities safe.

Several 2006 candidates—including gubernatorial candidates Lucy Baxley (D-AL) and Janet Napolitano (D-AZ) and US Senate candidates Dianne Feinstein (D-CA) and Barbara Ann Radofsky (D-TX)—included the issue of "immigration" or "illegal immigration" on their websites. Others— such as Republican Palin and Democrat Baxley—included links to gas prices among their issues. However, Palin titled her link "gasoline" whereas Baxley titled her link "gas price gouging," showing perhaps a partisan presentation of this issue.

Both female and male candidates attempted to establish similar images on their websites, highlighting performance and success, experience, leadership, and qualifications—all stereotypical "masculine" traits. For example, Sebelius and Napolitano noted prominently on their 2006 campaign websites that they had been named among "America's Top Five Governors" in 2005 by *Time* magazine. Also in the 2006 campaign, Sebelius had a home page link titled "leadership," Feinstein and Senator Debbie Stabenow (D-MI) had home page links to "accomplishments," and Hutchison had a home page link to "awards."

Recalling that in their television advertising, female and male candidates emphasized both "feminine" and "masculine" traits, the focus on masculine traits on websites seems significant. This difference in emphasis suggests that candidates recognize that the intimacy of television requires evidence of a more "feminine" style, with traits such as sensitivity, honesty, and cooperation accentuated in their messages. Because websites—as opposed to attack and rebuttal/response ads—do not generate responses, candidates may perceive less need to balance their toughness and aggressiveness, which may be highlighted in an attack ad, with sensitivity and honesty.

Although it may be premature to suggest that websites are a more "masculine" medium, it does seem that websites are still a neutral institution that calls for the emphasis of traits commonly associated with political office—qualifications, experience in politics, leadership, and knowledge on the issues. Surveys by the Pew Research Center for People and the Press (2000) show that those looking for information online—and particularly from candidate websites—may only be seeking clarification, reinforcement, or simply convenience, so it is not surprising that both female and male candidates would choose to focus on the traits commonly associated with political office on their websites.

Candidates, especially men, were also more likely to launch attacks on their websites than in their television ads. In 2002, 56 percent of women's and 86 percent of men's websites contained attacks. Again, the greater use of attacks on candidate websites, as compared to television ads, underscores the difference between these mediums. As websites are most often accessed by people already supporting the candidate, it is "safer" to include attacks. Television ads, on the other hand, have the potential of reaching all voters, who may be turned off by attacks.

Most of the photographs on candidate websites included a combination of the candidate and other people, whether they were located on the candidates' home pages or in their biography sections. Male candidates were slightly more likely (68%) than female candidates (54%) to include pictures of just themselves in their candidate biography section, whereas female candidates were slightly more likely (73%) than male candidates (64%) to include pictures of themselves with other people, perhaps seeking to illustrate that many are supportive of their campaigns. When others were shown in the photos, female candidates were significantly more likely (92%) than male candidates (64%) to have men in their photos and, in many instances, these were men in positions of power and prestige, a strategy undoubtedly designed to lend legitimacy to the female candidate's campaign.

For example, in 2006, US Senate candidates Stabenow and Klobuchar featured photographs of themselves with former president Bill Clinton on their websites, and Senator Hutchison included a photograph of herself with General David Petreaus, commander of multinational forces in Iraq.

Female candidates also were more likely to feature women in their photos (85%) than male candidates (68%), and children and senior citizens played popular roles as well. Although 59 percent of male candidate sites included photos of their families, only 46 percent of female candidate sites included such images. It seems that some female candidates choose not to associate themselves with their families in hopes of not being linked with motherhood and domestic responsibilities, which can diminish their political credibility. For male candidates, however, the presence of "family" can evoke notions of stability and tradition, suggesting that because they have a family to protect, they will govern in ways that will protect the viewer's family as well.

One advantage that websites have over television ads is the potential for interaction with Internet users, allowing the candidates to appear more personal as well as to raise money and recruit volunteers. Female and male candidates seem to be trying to take advantage of the opportunity for interactivity, although in rather limited forms. Female and male candidates in 2002 attempted to include more links from their home pages, as compared to previous election cycles, although male candidates were more likely to offer more links overall than female candidates. Almost all candidates provided a link from their home page to a candidate biography section, issues section, contribution section, and get-involved section. Male candidates were more likely to link to a calendar of events section, which requires more frequent updates and attention than a well-established biography section, contribution section, or even issues section. So male candidates either are more aware of the need to have their websites current and up-to-date or simply have the financial ability to pay someone to do so.

Overall, the websites of candidates running in US Senate and gubernatorial mixed-gender races in 2000 and 2002 were largely similar. Notably, few gender differences emerged. Thus, it appears that the strategies used in political candidate website design are in response to expectations for the medium rather than candidate sex. The ability to present an unmediated message to potential voters makes the campaign website an appealing venue for female candidates in particular, as the qualitative analysis of women candidate websites from the 2004 and 2006 campaigns confirmed.

Discussion and Conclusions

An examination of how female and male candidates present themselves in their political advertising and websites suggests several ways in which communication styles and strategies can be used to either confront, or capitalize upon, gender stereotypes held by the public and media.

Candidates do not have control of how the news media decide to cover their campaigns. In the 1980s and early 1990s, female candidates suffered in this particular genre of campaign information. However, women candidates for US Senate and governor enjoyed more equitable coverage beginning in the late 1990s and, especially, the 21st century election cycles. In fact, in 2000, female US Senate candidates received more total coverage than males. Since 1998, women candidates have also been getting their share of positive coverage, and there are no longer great differences in the viability or electability quotient accorded to female candidates running for governor and US senator.

However, stereotypical news coverage seems to be back in play in Clinton's bid for the 2008 Democratic Party nomination for president. Her coverage not only has been more negative than that of her closest rivals, but also has focused on her dress (including her cleavage), her husband, her likability, and her electability (Media Matters for America 2007; Rieck 2007).

Some areas of news coverage remain troublesome for female candidates at all levels of office. The tendency to emphasize candidate gender, appearance, marital status, and masculine issues in news coverage still haunts female candidates running for state and national office. Candidate gender is still mentioned more frequently for women, reporters still comment more often on a female candidate's dress or appearance, and journalists still refer to a female candidate's marital status more frequently.

Although neither male nor female candidates can directly control news coverage, they can have considerable influence on it. For example, by focusing on a mixture of "masculine" and "feminine" issues, a female candidate can achieve a balance that helps to ensure the media will not leave her out of a discussion of "masculine" issues. Candidates also can use their controlled communication media—television ads and websites—to influence their news coverage. For the past three decades, particularly since the 1988 presidential campaign, the news media have increased their coverage of candidate television advertising. So women candidates can influence their news coverage by producing high-quality ads that will attract media attention. As web campaigning becomes more popular and more developed, it is also likely that the news media will expand their coverage of candidate websites as part of the campaign dialogue.

Television commercials and websites also provide female candidates with tremendous opportunities to present themselves directly to voters, without interpretation by the news media. Political television advertising is still the dominant form of candidate communication for most major-level races in which female candidates must compete with male opponents. And, female candidates are successfully establishing their own competitive styles of political advertising. For example, women candidates have overcome the stereotypical admonition that they must avoid attacks. And, they capitalize on stereotypes by resonating with voters on issues in which they are perceived to have expertise, such as education and health care, yet also confront biases by discussing such "masculine" issues as the economy and taxes and by emphasizing "masculine" and "feminine" traits, such as strength and warmth.

Even as challengers, women candidates have been able to adopt strategies typical of incumbents to give themselves "authority." Female candidates who win also seem to have been successful at achieving a television "videostyle" that is overall positive, emphasizes personal traits of toughness and strength, and capitalizes on the importance of "feminine" issues such as education and health care while also discussing such "masculine" issues as the economy and defense/security.

Television advertising may be particularly important for Republican women candidates, whose numbers are slipping in both state and national office. Republican women can continue to emphasize their toughness and strength, expertise on such perennially important issues as the economy, and calls for change while connecting more with women voters (particularly independents) on such stereotypical "feminine" issues as health care and education.

When it comes to self-presentation in the newest campaign medium, the Internet, research shows fewer differences between male and female candidates. Both men and women candidates' websites are characterized by significant amounts of issue information. And, unlike the balance between "feminine" and "masculine" issues observed in their television commercials, websites for both sexes seem to focus on "feminine" issues. Both female and male candidates also focus on past accomplishments on their sites. Perhaps the "newness" of this medium has not provided sufficient development of different styles for female and male candidates.

The Web may be the best venue for female candidates wanting an equal communication competition with male candidates, especially in situations where resources are limited. A female candidate can do much more for much less on the Web than through television advertising. Female candidates should develop sophisticated websites that provide more specialized messages to specific groups, use innovative types of interactivity, and generate a more personalized presence with voters (e.g., through audiovisual presentations by the candidate and by providing opportunities for citizens to "tune in" for personal chats and question-and-answer sessions with the candidate or campaign representatives). Research on the effects of voter use of websites shows that such techniques have a positive impact on the evaluation of the sponsoring candidate. Candidates with high levels of interaction on their websites are perceived as more sensitive, responsive, and trustworthy. The level of website interactivity also impacts the level of agreement of users with the policy positions of candidates (Sundar, Kalyanaraman, and Brown 2003).

Senator Clinton's campaign for the 2008 Democratic presidential nomination will provide researchers with an unusual opportunity to study how a woman candidate for the nation's top executive office can use Web technology and television advertising to confront stereotypes held about her (and other women candidates) by voters and the media. Clinton's campaign has made tremendous use of Web technology. She announced her candidacy on the Internet, instead of during a live news conference or political event. Clinton's website featured links to "a champion for women" among her issues and "mother and advocate" on her biography, showing how she was reaching out to women in her campaign. Through Web technology, the campaign developed a Women for Hillary network with weekly "Hillgrams" with campaign updates and talking points to share with other colleagues. The campaign also used social networking tools and other Web technology to develop a thousands-strong Women's Leadership Network to promote Clinton's candidacy nationwide, held campaign events, and took part in fund-raising.

Clinton also used television ads in an effort not only to speak out on both "feminine" and "masculine" issues—such as health care, education, senior citizens, energy, and the economy—but also to emphasize her experience (a masculine strategy) and appeal to voters as a voice for change (an attribute of "feminine" style). In her ad titled "Voices," Clinton delivered her message over images of diverse Americans—white, black, and Latino; young and old; at home and at work—with soft music playing in the background. Clinton said:

> In this troubled economy, how can so many millions of people simply not be heard? Well, I hear you. You are asking for health care that covers everyone. Protection from losing your home. You'd like to fill your tank without draining your wallet. And give your kids the future they deserve. If I am your president, I will bring more than my 35 years of experience to the White House. I will bring your voice.

The 2008 campaign will provide additional evidence and insight on how women candidates can manage campaign communication tools in ways that improve their chances of success, despite continuing stereotypes held by voters and the media. Women candidates who present themselves successfully in their television ads and websites may be able to capitalize on these controlled messages to reach viewers and influence media coverage for a synergistic communication effort that compels citizens to vote for them.

Notes

1. Pat Schroeder, *24 Years of Housework and the Place Is Still a Mess: My Life in Politics* (Kansas City, MO: Andrews McNeel, 1998).
2. Jake Tapper, "Another Dole Bites the Dust," Salon.com, 20 October 1999, www.salon.com/news/feature/1999/10/20/dole.
3. David Paul Kuhn, "Hillary Rallies Women's Support," 4 June 2007, www.politico.com/news/stories/0607/4311.

5

Symbolic Mobilization?
The Impact of Candidate Sex

Kathleen Dolan

THE INCREASE IN the number of women who run for and are elected to office in the United States has been accompanied by an expanding literature that examines the impact these women have on our political system.[1] This literature often focuses on questions of representation and the "benefits" that an increasing number of women candidates can bring to the political system, particularly to women citizens. Of course, representation is a complex term, encompassing many different elements of the roles political leaders play in our system. Much has been written about the impact of women on *substantive* representation, resulting in our understanding that having more women in office tends to lead to different policy outcomes and different procedural pathways. There is clear evidence that women and women's issues receive greater representation in law-making bodies as the number of women officeholders increases (Swers 2002; Dodson 1998; Burrell 1994; Kathlene 1995; Thomas 1994; Saint-Germain 1989). Too, scholars find evidence that women elected officials pursue their positions in more open, collegial, and inclusive ways than do men officials, representing a different style of "doing politics" (Norton 2002; Rosenthal 1998; Kathlene 1995).

However, a second aspect of representation, one that is more relevant at the candidacy stage, is that of *symbolic* representation. While the direct benefits of symbolic representation may not be as easily quantified as those of substantive representation, from the perspective of the political community and its citizens, they are no less important. Given the historical exclusion of women from candidacy and elective office, the presence of women candidates can signal a greater openness in the system and more widely dispersed access to political opportunities for all (Burns, Scholzman, and Verba 2001; Reingold 2000; Thomas 1998; Carroll 1994). Women candidates can also

85

serve as role models or symbolic mentors to women in the public, sending the signal that politics is no longer an exclusive man's world and that female participation is an important and valued act (Burrell 1994; Tolleson-Rinehart 1992; Sapiro 1981). Mansbridge (1999) suggests that the increased representation of marginalized identity groups also affirms that members of these groups are capable of governing and can serve to more strongly connect group members to the polity. Finally, women candidates are more likely to campaign on issues of interest to women, which may catch the attention of women voters (Dabelko and Herrnson 1997; Herrnson, Lay, and Stokes 2003; Larson 2001).

The signals of openness, legitimacy, and identity sent by the presence of women candidates can, in turn, stimulate activity and engagement on the part of those members of the public heartened by an increasingly democratic and representative candidate pool. While men may be moved to increase their participation as they see a more open system, it is to women that the benefits of symbolic representation are assumed to accrue. Indeed, according to Lawless (2004a), we can think about symbolic representation as "the attitudinal and behavioral effects that women's presence in positions of political power might confer to women citizens" (p. 81).

Despite the theoretical notion that women candidates could provide tangible political benefits to citizens, particularly women, the empirical evidence of this is still somewhat limited. Most of the work that examines how people respond to the presence of women candidates has focused on a single election or a small number of elections (Burns, Schlozman, and Verba 2001; Sapiro and Conover 1997; Koch 1997) or a limited number of attitudes or behaviors (Atkeson 2003; Hansen 1997). And none of this work has focused on the primary method of citizen involvement in elections, namely voting.

The work presented here examines some of the unanswered questions about whether and how women candidates can mobilize public interest and participation in elections. Specifically, I employ pooled National Election Study data from 1990 to 2004 to examine whether the attitudes and behaviors of those people who lived in states and congressional districts with a woman candidate for US House or Senate are different from those who experience elections with no women candidates.

The Impact of Candidate Sex on the Public

Much of the work on the symbolic impact of women candidates finds some support for the notion that their presence stimulates greater attentiveness to politics, particularly among women. In examining the elections of 1992, Sapiro and Conover (1997) found that women who lived in areas with a woman candidate for governor or US Congress were more attentive to the campaign and more politically active than women who lived in areas with male-only races. That they found no impact on men's attitudes or behaviors supports the expectation that women candidates should affect women and men differently.

Other work also identified 1992 as a year in which women candidates had an impact on the public. Koch (1997) found that women respondents in states with women Senate candidates in 1992 exhibited higher levels of political interest and a greater ability to recall the names of the Senate candidates than those living in states without women candidates. However, he found no impact of women Senate candidates in 1990. Hansen (1997) examined the impact of women candidates for Congress or governor in elections from 1990–1994 on people's political attitudes. She found a consistent impact of women candidates on proselytizing, efficacy, and media use among women in 1992 and no impact in 1990 and 1994.

In the most extensive work on women candidates and their impact on the public, Atkeson (2003) examines gubernatorial and Senate races from the 1990s and finds that women who lived in states with women candidates were more likely to discuss politics and had higher levels of efficacy and knowledge than people who experienced male-only races, although this effect was conditioned by competition. Atkeson found that the impact of women candidates was only present when the woman was engaged in a competitive election. This would suggest that the mere presence of women candidates is not necessarily enough to provide symbolic representation, but that the context of the race must allow them to be known to the public.

Gaps in Our Knowledge

To date, while some research has demonstrated that women candidates can influence the public, particularly women, there is little evidence of a consistent, general effect. Women candidates do appear to affect the attitudes and behaviors of people, but, apparently, only in limited situations, such as in an election year in which gendered issues are particularly salient (such as 1992) or when women candidates are very competitive. At the same time, most of the past research addressing symbolic representation has confined itself to a limited number of offices and/or election years and has not accounted for other important variables such as political party. In an effort to contribute to our understanding of how and when women candidates can provide symbolic representation, this research provides a more comprehensive analysis of the impact of women candidates on public attitudes and behaviors by expanding on current knowledge in several ways. First, I expand the offices and time frame under analysis by examining elections for the US House and Senate from 1990 to 2004. Including all elections since 1990 allows me to capture the time period during which the number of women candidates has steadily increased and provides a chance to see whether any influence of women candidates is more than an idiosyncratic event. Also, including House and Senate races allows for a consideration of whether the level and visibility of the office has any impact on whether women candidates can mobilize public attitudes and behaviors.

Second, I consider the influence of women candidates on a broad range of political attitudes and behaviors by including political efficacy, interest, influencing others, participating in politics, and voting as dependent variables. Examining the potential impact of symbolic representation on voter turnout is a particularly important addition for a couple of reasons. Voting is still the political activity most highly valued by our system and any examination of whether women candidates influence people's participation is incomplete without it. Too, if symbolic representation is demonstrated to have an impact on political attitudes and nonvoting behaviors, then it should be a logical extension of the same argument that the presence of women candidates should excite voter turnout as well. Indeed, an impact on voter turnout would actually be the most tangible sign of an influence. While higher levels of interest and efficacy are certainly positive, an increase in voter turnout would bring a more concrete increase in engagement to the political system. Also, past work on symbolic representation has tended to focus on attitudes and behaviors on which women tend to score lower than men—efficacy, interest, knowledge. The assumption of much of these works is that the presence of women candidates somehow boosts women's attitudes and behaviors to levels equivalent to men (Sapiro and Conover 1997). Yet, because these works employ dependent variables on which there is a "gender deficit," we don't know whether the impact of women candidates is a generalized effect of representation that can excite engagement in any realm or whether it is more of a "compensatory boost" that is limited in its reach. Including voter turnout, an activity on which the gender gap favors women, allows for a test of how the potential mobilizing impact of women candidates operates.

Finally, while the assumption here is that women candidates influence women in the public, it is probably overly simplistic to think that any and all women candidates provide the same signals and benefits to the public. So this research also considers two important contextual variables—political party and the competitiveness of the election. A central aspect of the symbolic representation hypothesis is that women are invigorated by the presence of women candidates because they see someone like themselves on the political stage. Yet, women are no less likely than men to see themselves as partisan, and there is little empirical evidence that women's affinity for women candidates crosses party lines (Dolan 2004, but see Brians

2005). Too, women candidates, like women in the general public, are more likely to be Democrats than Republicans. Among women candidates for Congress in the past two decades, approximately 65 percent have run as Democrats (CAWP 2005). This, coupled with the gender gap in party identification among the general public, could suggest that women would be more likely to be invigorated by the presence of *Democratic* women candidates more so than Republican women. Including party considerations will allow for a test of whether any impact of women candidates is a general phenomenon related to their sex or whether important political variables like partisanship influence how people interact with these women (Dolan 2004).

Another important contextual issue, as Atkeson (2003) suggests, is the competitiveness of the woman candidate. Certainly, for a woman candidate to influence the public, she must be visible enough to enter the political consciousness of the average person. Too, a long-shot or sacrificial-lamb candidacy may actually work to dampen efficacy or excitement: having one of "your own" going down to defeat in a lopsided contest is not necessarily a recipe for engagement. A consideration of the competitiveness of the woman candidate will allow for a test of whether any influence of women candidates is dependent on her viability.

Hypotheses and Methods

If past work suggests that the presence of women candidates can influence women's attitudes and behaviors, we might expect to see this impact in two different ways. First, since the presence of women candidates should provide positive psychological benefits to women, we should expect that women who live in a state or congressional district with a woman candidate for Congress should have higher levels of political efficacy, political interest, and engagement in attempts to influence the votes of others than those who experience male-only races. Too, since women candidates can be an empowering symbol of women's place in the political system, we should expect that women who live in a state or congressional district with a woman congressional candidate would have higher levels of political participation, particularly voting, than those who experience elections with only male candidates.

Given the present-day realities of gender gaps in the partisanship of women candidates and women in the public, this research will also test the expectation that any influence of women candidates on attitudes or behaviors will be strongest when the woman candidate is a Democrat. Finally, the analysis will also test the assumption that women candidates have a stronger impact when they are in more competitive races.

The data employed here are from the National Election Study for all House and Senate elections from 1990–2004. The data are pooled separately for House and Senate races to allow for a test of whether the level of office is relevant to the influence that women candidates can have. NES data are well suited to such an investigation because they comprise the only nationally representative, large-scale data set that evaluates the attitudes and behaviors of citizens who live in election districts that include women candidates. Readers will, of course, note that the NES is not a representative sample of congressional districts and does not include respondents from every state or congressional district. However, since this research examines the attitudes and behaviors of the public in the presence of women candidates, it is the NES respondents who are most important, not the districts themselves. Further, from 1990–2004, there were 999 major-party women candidates for the House and Senate and fully 500 of them ran in states and districts included in the NES sample.[2] For these reasons, I believe that the NES offers the most appropriate source of data to test the questions considered here.

There are five dependent variables employed in the analysis—political efficacy, interest, trying to influence how someone else will vote, general participation such as working for a campaign or donating money, and voting. (See Appendix for all variable constructions.) This will allow for an examination of the impact of women candidates on a variety of attitudes and behaviors. Depending on the dependent variable, I estimate either ordinary least squares or logistic regression equations.

The primary independent variables are those measuring the presence of a woman candidate. Because of the notion that the party of the woman candidate may influence her ability to mobilize the public, I include a variable that accounts for the presence of a woman Democratic candidate and a woman Republican candidate. Also, since past literature finds that the mobilizing influence of women candidates is strongest for women in the public, I interact the presence of a woman candidate of each party with the sex of the respondent. Finally, since women candidates may well be most likely to excite and motivate voters with whom they share a political party, I include a variable that measures party congruence between women candidates and respondents.

The bulk of the variables in the models are those that the literature has long associated with more positive attitudes toward politics and higher levels of participation (Verba, Schlozman, and Brady 1995; Rosenstone and Hansen 1993; Teixeira 1992). These include variables measuring strength of partisanship (from independent to strong partisan), how often respondents follow government and politics, levels of political knowledge and efficacy, and standard measures of sex, age, education, and race.[3] Models estimating House elections include a variable that controls for the impact of a Senate race happening in that state simultaneously. Finally, I include a series of dummy variables to account for the individual election years included in the pooled data set.

All regression models are estimated separately for House and Senate elections for the years under examination to allow me to test whether the level of office has an impact on the influence of women candidates. Further, to test the hypothesis that the competitiveness of the candidate may make a difference, each sample is divided into competitive and noncompetitive races and the models are estimated for each subsample.[4]

Analysis

The symbolic representation literature posits that the public, particularly women members, will be excited and mobilized by the presence of women candidates to higher levels of political attitudes and participation. However, this analysis offers only limited support for this assumption. Tables 5.1–5.4 present the analysis for House and Senate races by level of competitiveness. The variables of greatest interest, measuring whether there was a Democratic or Republican woman candidate for office and the interaction of the presence of a woman candidate and the sex of the respondent, are highlighted at the top of each table. With five dependent variables, there are 80 coefficients that represent the impact of women candidates on symbolic representation. Across elections for the two chambers and the two conditions of competitiveness, there are only 10 instances in which the main variables of interest achieve statistical significance with increased political attitudes or behaviors. This would suggest the presence of a limited effect for women candidates to mobilize the public, but in no way supports an interpretation of a generalized influence.

Taking Table 5.1 first, we see that women candidates in competitive House races can have some impact on the political characteristics of the public. First, we should note that here, as in the other tables, the control variables assumed to be related to higher levels of political attitudes and behaviors perform as expected, such as political knowledge and tendency to follow government leading to higher levels of political attitudes and behaviors. Second, since the models account for party congruence between the woman candidate and respondents, any influence on political characteristics exerted by women candidates is over and above the impact of mobilization based on a shared party identity. Column 2 presents the model estimating political efficacy. Here we see that the presence of a Republican woman candidate actually decreases the efficacy of men and increases the efficacy of women relative to men. This would fit the general assumption that the presence of a woman candidate would make women in the public more like-

Table 5.1 Impact of Women Candidates on Voter Attitudes and Behaviors, 1990–2004: House, Competitive Races

	Voter Turnout	Efficacy	Interest	Influence Other	Participation
Woman Democratic Candidate	**-.014**	**.058**	**-.042**	**.013**	**-.048**
Woman Republican Candidate	**.131**	**-.329***	**-.046**	**.159***	**.353***
Wm Democratic Cand*Woman R[a]	**.281**	**-.098**	**.106**	**.050**	**.236***
Wm Republican Cand*Woman R[a]	**-.195**	**.331***	**.142**	**-.095**	**-.214**
Senate Race in State	.119	.012	-.068	-.006	-.086
Party Congruence	-.005	.093	.026	-.087*	-.187
Strength of Partisanship	.256*	.126*	.140*	.066*	.176*
Follow Government	.509*	.036	.714*	.102*	.325*
Political Knowledge	.224*	.044	.090*	.027*	.038
Efficacy	.126*	—	.016	.006	.051*
Sex	.028	.096	.085	-.046	-.056
Age	.021*	-.003	.004*	-.003*	.003
Education	.309*	.141*	.048*	.010	.072*
Race	.032*	.012*	.009	.003	.002
1990	-1.038*	-.194	-1.012*	-.342*	-.532*
1992	-.095	.128	-.020	-.113*	-.271*
1994	-.500	-.387*	-.880*	-.274*	-.402*
1996	-.061	-.394*	-.709*	-.248*	-.443*
1998	-.562*	-.139	-.972*	-.280*	-.533*
2000	-1.527*	-.500	-.690*	-.298*	-.470
2002	-.449	.938	-.354*	-.156*	-.264
Constant	-4.056*	1.699*	.919*	.117	-.756*
N	1546	1545	1537	1543	1534
Chi Square	330.263				
PRE	77.9				
R^2		.128	.361	.125	.142

Notes: a. Woman Democratic Candidate*Woman Respondent; Woman Republican Candidate*Woman Respondent.
Levels of significance: * $p < .05$.

ly to think that political leaders care about them. But this result also suggests that the presence of a woman candidate may actively suppress the efficacy of men. Too, it is interesting to note that the impact on efficacy is only in the presence of a woman Republican candidate. Democratic women candidates in competitive House races have no significant impact on the public's levels of efficacy. Continuing on to Column 4, we also see that Republican women candidates, but only Republican women candidates, increase the likelihood that respondents will try to influence someone's vote. This increase is experienced by both women and men, counter to the assumption of the symbolic representation hypothesis. Finally (Column 5), with regard to participation beyond voting, the presence of a woman Republican mobilizes both men and women to increase their participation. Additionally, women Democratic candidates mobilize women respondents to higher levels of participation.

Table 5.2 presents the findings for noncompetitive House races, where we see only two significant results. In these races, the presence of Democratic women candidates increases attempts to influence the votes of others and general participation beyond voting among all respondents (Columns 4–5). However, there is no influence exerted by these women candidates on voter turnout, efficacy, or political interest, nor do Republican women candidates have any impact on any of the political attitudes or behaviors. Too, it is interesting to note that the influence Democratic women have on increased influencing and participation is experienced by both women and men, again, something that is counter to the symbolic representation hypothesis. Readers should note that, while women candidates in competitive House races were slightly more likely to mobilize respondents than women candidates in noncompetitive races, competitiveness of the race itself does not seem to be the central variable driving the circumstances under which this influence appears.

Interestingly, women Senate candidates have fewer instances in which they can stimulate the public on political variables. Table 5.3 offers the findings for competitive Senate races. Here we see the only time in which women candidates have an impact is on voter turnout (Column 1). Democratic women Senate candidates in competitive races stimulate voter turnout among women, but not among men. With regard to political efficacy (Column 2), the analysis suggests that Republican women candidates actually drive down the efficacy of women respondents, but have no impact on men. This lowering of feelings of efficacy among women is exactly the opposite of the finding in Table 5.1 that showed competitive Republican women House candidates actually increasing women's efficacy levels. Without a clear theoretical explanation for why Republican women candidates would increase women's efficacy in one set of elections and suppress it in another, we might conclude that these counterintuitive findings are a

Table 5.2 Impact of Women Candidates on Voter Attitudes and Behaviors, 1990–2004: House, Noncompetitive Races

	Voter Turnout	Efficacy	Interest	Influence Other	Participation
Woman Democratic Candidate	**-.050**	**-.095**	**-.012**	**.086***	**.142***
Woman Republican Candidate	**-.081**	**-.038**	**.043**	**.023**	**.010**
Wm Democratic Cand*Woman R[a]	**.186**	**-.118**	**.106**	**-.019**	**-.066**
Wm Republican Cand*Woman R[a]	**-.191**	**.014**	**-.151**	**-.061**	**-.070**
Senate Race in State	.219*	.047	.096*	.030*	.056*
Party Congruence	.157	.007	-.087	-.026	-.036
Strength of Partisanship	.301*	.091*	.148*	.042*	.137*
Follow Government	.405*	.077*	.661*	.124*	.299*
Political Knowledge	.236*	.036*	.083*	.019*	.052*
Efficacy	.084*	—	.026*	.002	.035*
Sex	.151*	.097*	.075*	-.014	-.067*
Age	.028*	-.003*	.004*	-.003*	-.001
Education	.245*	.142*	.043*	.012*	.075*
Race	.005	.004	-.007*	.001	.001
1990	-1.036*	-.326*	-.796*	-.253*	-.473*
1992	-.071	.147*	.050	-.064*	-.211*
1994	-.764*	-.388*	-.660*	-.231*	-.514*
1996	-.033	-.102	-.518*	-.153*	-.293*
1998	-.978*	-.186*	-.904*	-.239*	-.577*
2000	-.273	-.264*	.211	-.111*	-.264*
2002	-.147	.675*	-.380*	-.101*	-.223*
Constant	-4.060*	1.773*	.904*	.045*	-.620*
N	5890	5890	5881	5887	5862
Chi Square	1200.074				
PRE	66.8				
R²		.104	.321	.117	.146

Notes: a. Woman Democratic Candidate*Woman Respondent; Woman Republican Candidate*Woman Respondent.
Levels of significance: * p < .05.

Table 5.3 Impact of Women Candidates on Voter Attitudes and Behaviors, 1990–2004: Senate, Competitive Races

	Voter Turnout	Efficacy	Interest	Influence Other	Participation
Woman Democratic Candidate	**-.564***	**.039**	**.062**	**.002**	**.045**
Woman Republican Candidate	**-.314**	**.065**	**-.192**	**-.032**	**-.331**
Wm Democratic Cand*Woman R[a]	**.333***	**-.093**	**.012**	**.041**	**.121**
Wm Republican Cand*Woman R[a]	**-.858**	**-.963***	**-.061**	**.013**	**.304**
Strength of Partisanship	.240*	.104*	.170*	.051*	.137*
Party Congruence	.124	.003	-.010	-.045	-.178*
Follow Government	.413*	.076*	.688*	.107*	.344*
Political Knowledge	.173*	.031	.109*	.035*	.061*
Efficacy	.169*	—	.015	.012	.051*
Sex	.079	.107	.108	-.036	-.130*
Age	.017*	-.001	.003*	-.003*	.001
Education	.230*	.152*	.026*	.009	.072*
Race	.010	-.001	-.004	.001	-.004
1990	-.944*	-.347*	-.684*	-.303*	-.442*
1992	.993*	.126	-.104	-.114*	-.307*
1994	-.486*	-.359*	-.826*	-.271*	-.563*
1996	-1.761*	-.286*	-.763*	-.178*	-.368*
1998	-.667*	-.219	-1.018*	-.227*	-.632*
2000	-.520	.001	-.062	-.114	-.084
2002	-.425	.764*	-.313*	-.082*	-.169
Constant	-2.930*	1.646*	1.020*	.090	-.714*
N	2408	2438	2434	2437	2425
Chi Square	371.866				
PRE	73.5				
R^2		.108	.336	.106	.148

Notes: a. Woman Democratic Candidate*Woman Respondent; Woman Republican Candidate*Woman Respondent.
Levels of significance: * p < .05.

result of the particular mix of candidates running in the years under consideration. Finally, Table 5.4 demonstrates that there are no circumstances under which women candidates in noncompetitive Senate races influence the political characteristics of the public.

Conclusion

This project began as a test of the assumption that the increased presence of women candidates in the United States has a symbolic importance that is manifested in higher levels of political involvement by the public. This hypothesis is intuitively appealing, since we would expect underrepresented groups to be heartened by the potential for representation by one of their own. In attempting to investigate this relationship, this project expands on past research by evaluating several important considerations at once: different levels of office, differing conditions of competitiveness, different political party conditions, and a longer time frame of elections. The results show, overall, that there is little empirical analysis to support the assumption that symbolic representation is provided by women candidates, or at least there is little support for the idea that their symbolic presence translates into any widespread increase in political attitudes and behaviors.

While the analysis indicates limited influence for women candidates on political variables, there are some general conclusions to make. First, while there are some instances in which the presence of women candidates can influence the political attitudes and behaviors of the public, there is no general or clear pattern to the influence, whether across level of office, political party, or condition of competitiveness. We cannot say that women of a particular party influence the public, or only those women in competitive races, or even women running for one or the other chamber. Additionally, there is no clear pattern to the attitudes and behaviors that are open to influence. Depending on the chamber, party of the candidate, and condition of competitiveness, voter turnout, efficacy, influencing others, and general participation could be influenced by the presence of a woman candidate. But not each of these variables in all, or even most, circumstances. Too, it is interesting to note that women candidates did not excite greater political interest in any circumstance at all.

While the level of office was not a determining factor, the presence of women candidates in House races does appear to have a greater impact on the public than that of women candidates in Senate races. While at first this may seem counterintuitive when we consider the increased visibility of candidates for the Senate; it makes more sense when we recognize that there may be more room to mobilize voters in House races. Senate races, as statewide elections, have more built-in forces that can mobilize the public

Table 5.4 Impact of Women Candidates on Voter Attitudes and Behaviors, 1990–2004: Senate, Noncompetitive Races

	Voter Turnout	Efficacy	Interest	Influence Other	Participation
Woman Democratic Candidate	**-.164**	**.009**	**.004**	**.025**	**-.023**
Woman Republican Candidate	**-.364**	**.140**	**-.027**	**.034**	**-.005**
Wm Democratic Cand*Woman R	**.155**	**.114**	**.047**	**-.005**	**.053**
Wm Republican Cand*Woman R	**.388**	**-.158**	**.126**	**.018**	**.001**
Strength of Partisanship	.365*	.069*	.126*	.035*	.149*
Party Congruence	.058	-.078	-.031	-.024	.025
Follow Government	.425*	.048	.650*	.140*	.314*
Political Knowledge	.243*	.050*	.090*	.017*	.034*
Efficacy	.080*	—	.031	.013	.047*
Sex	.077	.115*	.016	-.022	-.038
Age	.028*	-.003*	.005*	-.003*	-.001
Education	.242*	.144*	.048*	.006	.074*
Race	.011	.010*	-.007*	.002	.005
1990	-1.327*	-.189*	-1.000*	-.234*	-.420*
1992	-.048	.276*	.054	-.088*	-.205*
1994	-.668*	-.329*	-.847*	-.211*	-.423*
1996	-.847	-.619*	-.544	-.078	-.159
1998	-.868*	-.152	-.931*	-.244*	-.476*
2000	-.621	-.396*	.129	-.189*	-.526*
2002	.091	.757*	-.436*	-.132*	-.257*
Constant	-3.911*	1.745*	1.028*	.054	-.604*
N	2655	2702	2691	2702	2688
Chi Square	616.894				
PRE	74.7				
R²		.099	.341	.122	.14

Notes: a. Woman Democratic Candidate*Woman Respondent; Woman Republican Candidate*Woman Respondent.
Levels of significance: * p < .05.

separate from the characteristics of the candidates themselves. In House races, on the other hand, there is less noise and fewer external forces to mobilize political activities. House elections are generally local, low-visibility races. It may be that it is in these circumstances that the impact of women candidates can break through and influence the public's political lives.

Another conclusion to draw is that the competitiveness of the election does not appear to be a central condition for influence, as has been suggested by other work (Atkeson 2003). In this analysis, the difference between competitive and noncompetitive House races was not significant, with women candidates having a limited influence on the public in each condition. However, we should note that noncompetitive Senate races were the only group of races for which there was no mobilization by the women candidates.

The symbolic representation hypothesis suggests that any influence of women candidates will be greatest for women. But these data demonstrate that there are actually more circumstances in which an increase in some attitude or behavior is experienced equally by women and men. It is the case that the presence of women candidates does seem to suppress the efficacy of men experiencing competitive House races. But it is also the case that we see an increase in general participation and influencing behaviors among both men and women. This result is unanticipated by the symbolic representation hypothesis and points us in an area in need of future research.

In the end, the findings here indicate that, over 16 elections for two different offices, the ability of women candidates to mobilize the public to higher levels of political activity is rather limited. In the absence of clear or general patterns, we are left to conclude that the influence of women candidates is, at some level, a function of idiosyncratic circumstances of particular elections—such things as the mix of candidates, their positions, the issues of the day, media coverage, and public awareness. Indeed, this finding is supported by past work that showed that the impact of women candidates depended on the election year and also work that demonstrates that support for women candidates at the ballot box is structured by specific electoral environments (Dolan 2004; Hansen 1997; Koch 1997).

These findings, while compelling, are not definitive, and point us toward avenues for future research. For example, in finding little evidence of a symbolic impact of women members of Congress on the attitudes of their constituents, Lawless (2004a) suggests that we make a mistake in assuming that any influence of symbolic representation is a one-on-one relationship. She suggests that a woman does not have to be directly represented by Hillary Clinton or Mary Landrieu to experience the symbolic benefits of an increase in the number of women in elected office. The same may be true for people observing women candidates. Media attention to women candidates nationally or in other specific races may well demonstrate more openness and diversity to the public, even if they don't have firsthand experience with women candidates. Figuring out a way to measure this more general symbolic representation may help us better identify how the presence of women candidates works. Too, we should strive for more and better data that might allow us to capture the characteristics of women candidates and the contexts of the races in which they do have an impact on the public. Women candidates who stimulate public attitudes and behaviors may take certain positions or highlight certain issues, or run in certain areas of the country or particular election years, or even experience certain kinds of opponents. Without knowing more about these sorts of circumstances, our understanding of the dynamic of when and how women candidates can influence political attitudes and behaviors will remain limited. And since the evidence of a directly symbolic form of representation is weak, we should work to more fully examine the impact that women candidates have on men. Men in this sample increased their involvement in influencing others and general participation in the presence of women candidates. We would do well to understand the context in which the responses of men, as well as women, can be shaped by an increase in women's political candidacies. As women candidates continue to be more fully integrated into our system of government and politics, our research agenda should strive to understand the potential impact of this integration in all its complexity.

Appendix: Variable Construction

Dependent Variables

Voter Turnout—Indicates whether respondent voted in the House and Senate elections in his/her state and congressional district. (0, 1)

Political Efficacy—Indicates agreement or disagreement with the statement "Public officials don't care much what people like me think. (1 = strongly agree, 5 = strongly disagree)

Political Interest—Indicates amount of attention paid to political campaigns. (1 = not much interested, 3 = very much interested)

Influence Others—Indicates whether respondent talked to others and tried to show them why they should vote for or against a particular party or candidate. (0, 1)

Participation—Indicates whether respondent took part in any of six political activities beyond voting. (0–6)

Independent Variables

Woman Democratic Candidate—Indicates the presence of a Democratic woman candidate. (0, 1)

Woman Republican Candidate—Indicates the presence of a Republican woman candidate. (0, 1)

Senate Race in State—Employed in models for House races to indicate whether there was also a Senate race in respondent's state that year. (0, 1)

Party Congruence—Indicates whether respondent and woman candidate are of the same political party. (0, 1)

Strength of Partisanship—Indicates strength of respondent partisanship. (0 = independent, 3 = strong partisan)

Follow Government—Indicates how often respondent follows government and public affairs. (1 = hardly at all, 4 = most of the time)

Political Knowledge—Indicates respondent score on a six-point scale that included identifying political leaders and congressional majorities. (0 = no correct answers, 6 = 6 correct answers)

Political Efficacy—Indicates agreement or disagreement with the statement "Public officials don't care much what people like me think." (1 = strongly agree, 5 = strongly disagree)

Sex—Indicates sex of respondent. (0 = male, 1 = female)

Race—Indicates race of respondent. (0 = nonwhite, 1 = white)

Education—Indicates respondent level of education. (1 = 8 years or less, 7 = advanced degree)

Age—Indicates respondent age in years.

Year Dummies—Indicates the individual election years included in the pooled data set.

Notes

1. Reprinted from Kathleen Dolan, *American Politics Research* 34, no. 6 (2006): 687–704. Used with permission of Sage Publications.

2. The 500 women candidates included in the NES samples from 1990 to 2004 are very representative of the total 999 women candidates on characteristics such as political party and incumbency status, offering further assurances about the appropriateness of the data.

3. The variable measuring efficacy is, of course, not included in the model estimating political efficacy.

4. Competitive races are defined as those races with a 15 point or less margin of victory.

6

Does "Running as a Woman" Mobilize Voters?

ATIYA KAI STOKES-BROWN
AND MELISSA OLIVIA NEAL

WOMEN HAVE MADE significant social gains in US society. Gains in education have been particularly impressive as women are close to achieving parity with men in educational attainment (Spraggins 2000). Women's pursuit of higher education has gone hand in hand with their movement into the labor force. Women have also made significant strides in US politics, as more women move into public office. Albeit small proportionately, the percentage of women in the US Congress and in state legislatures is steadily increasing. The percentage of women in Congress has increased to 16.1 percent (CAWP 2007) while the percentage of women in state legislatures has more than doubled from 1979 to 2007 (from 10% to 23.5%). Recently, political women have also made history serving in visibly powerful positions. Janet Reno became the first woman to serve as US attorney general in 1993. Madeleine Albright, Condoleezza Rice, and Nancy Pelosi have also become women "firsts" serving as secretary of state, national security advisor, and House Democratic whip, respectively. On 5 January 2007, Pelosi again made history becoming the first woman elected Speaker of the House of Representatives.

Despite this progress, there are still significant gender differences in political engagement. While there is little disparity between men and women in terms of voting, women remain less likely to engage in many political activities (e.g., Hansen 1997; Rapoport 1981; Huckfeldt and Sprague 1995; Schlozman et al. 1995). Yet, it is often hypothesized that the gender gap in political engagement closes when female candidates run for office. The presence of female candidates and officeholders is presumed to change the nature of political discourse, thereby encouraging women to feel less alienated from politics and to become more politically active. However, recent work, including the study conducted by Kathleen Dolan in Chapter 5, has given little support to this claim, finding inconsistent evidence of the symbolic effects ascribed to female candidates (also see Lawless 2004a). These studies suggest that the context of the election is an important mediating factor when estimating symbolic representation. In perhaps the most interesting test of this notion, Atkeson (2003), using national cross-sectional data from the 1990s, finds that the presence of competitive female candidates in intergender contests stimulates female political engagement (also see Schlozman et al. 1995).

Notably absent from existing women and politics research is attention to the manner in which candidates' campaigns, specifically candidates' issues, may influence women's attitudes and behaviors. Female candidates are more likely than male candidates to campaign on women's issues (e.g., Larson 2001; Dabelko and Herrnson 1997; see also Chapter 4 in this volume) and gain a strategic advantage at the polls when they do (Herrnson et al. 2003; Plutzer and Zipp 1996). Our study focuses on the importance of candidate gender and campaign issues and their influence on political attitudes and behaviors. Specifically, we argue that female candidates and the issues they stress in their campaigns may jointly influence women's political attitudes and behaviors. Female candidates who play to preexisting gender stereotypes may offer positive psychological benefit to female voters, stimulating female political engagement. We test our hypothesis by drawing on a data set of individual political attitudes and behavior and candidates' campaign issues. We expect the chances that women will discuss politics, proselytize, and engage in nonvoting electoral participation are far greater when female candidates focus on issues of concern to women. However, we expect that female candidates running for office "as women" will have little influence on male political engagement.

Women Running "as Women" and Political Engagement

The integration of women in the public sphere of work and politics has had a profound impact on political participation. Whereas women were once excluded and largely absent from politics and the electorate because of legal barriers (but see Freeman 2000), women are now visibly active as candidates, legislators, and voters. This is clearly evidenced by the increasing number of female candidates and legislators, and current voting patterns. Turnout rates for women in presidential elections now exceed those of men (Beckwith 1986; Leighley and Nagler 1991). In 2004, the rate of voter turnout for women was 60.1 percent, compared with 56.3 percent for men (CAWP 2005). Yet, at the same time, significant gaps between men's and women's participation remain. Women are less likely to engage in a wide range of political activities (e.g., Hansen 1997; Rapoport 1981; Huckfeldt and Sprague 1995; Burns, Schlozman, and Verba 2001; Schlozman et al. 1995; Welch 1977). For example, from 1972 to 2004, women were less likely than men to report any attempts at influencing another's vote (Hansen 1997). This lasting gender difference in political persuasion is important because willingness to engage in public discussion implies an active orientation to politics (Rapoport 1981). Political discussion also enables individuals to make informed reasonable political decisions (Downs 1957; Lupia and McCubbins 1998). If individuals who are interested in politics (more generally or in a particular election) are speaking to others about politics, that discussion presumably will have a meaningful impact as people learn which leaders and policies are in their best interests.

Recent efforts to explain the gender gap in political engagement emphasize cues provided by the political environment. The context and setting of an election influences the individual's decision to participate, as certain cues indicate to the individual that the perceived benefits of participating outweigh the perceived costs (e.g., Bobo and Gilliam 1990). Studies of race and political behavior, particularly the empowerment literature, confirm the salience of contextual effects. Several studies show that the presence of African American and Latino candidates significantly increases political efficacy and interest in elections, which increases African American and Latino political participation (e.g., Bobo and Gilliam 1990; Tate 1991; Barreto, Villerreal, and Woods 2005). The notion that the presence of a minority candidate or elected official provides tangible political benefits to minority citizens is often referred to as symbolic representation. In the case of women, symbolic representation is "the attitudinal and behavioral effects that women's presence in positions of political power might confer to women citizens" (Lawless 2004a, 81). The presence of female candidates signals openness in the public (political) sphere where women were once excluded (Carroll 1994) and affirms the value of female political participation (Burrell 1994). It is also likely that these women are viewed as role models and likely to support issues of concern to women (Burns et al. 2001). Thus, the assumption is that women in the electorate feel represented (symbolic representation) because members of the legislative institution resemble and share certain experiences with these women (descriptive representation) (Pitkin 1967).

A significant body of literature provides theoretical support for the notion that the presence of women in politics encourages women to feel less alienated and to become more active in politics. In her study of female congressional candidates, Burrell (1994) suggests that female officeholders positively influence female political participation. Other studies generally focused on the candidacy stage have found that female candidates also increase female political engagement. Hansen (1997) shows that the pres-

ence of women candidates significantly increased attempts at political persuasion among women in 1992. The presence of female Senate candidates
in 1992 also increased the psychological engagement of women (Koch
1997). However, Dolan's work, the most recent and extensive study of
female House and Senate elections from 1990 to 2004, finds little evidence
of the ability of female candidates to mobilize citizens to higher levels of
political activity and argues that scholars should attempt to

> capture the characteristics of women candidates and the contexts of races
> in which they do have an impact on the public. Women candidates who
> stimulate public attitudes and behaviors *may take certain positions or
> highlight certain issues,* or run in certain areas of the country or particular
> election years, or even experience certain kinds of opponents. Without
> knowing more about these sorts of circumstances, our understanding of the
> dynamic of when and how women candidates can influence political atti-
> tudes and behaviors will remain limited. (p. 99 in this volume, emphasis
> added)

In the absence of a clear pattern of impact caused by the presence of
female candidates, we suggest that greater attention to female candidates
and their campaigns might provide a better understanding of how female
candidates influence political engagement. Just as the presence of female
candidates and the electoral context provided by competitive elections bolster women's political engagement (Atkeson 2003), so too might the issues
stressed by female candidates bolster political attitudes and behavior. When
female candidates run "as women," making women's issues a centerpiece in
their campaigns, they may provide psychological benefits for women who
are then mobilized to higher levels of political activity.

Female candidates are often perceived to be the most competent at handling "compassion" issues such as health care and education, traditional
women- and family-related issues that are of concern to women, and
women's rights issues such as abortion (e.g., Kahn 1996; Huddy and
Terkildsen 1993a; Leeper 1991). Seemingly, these stereotypes can work to a
female candidate's advantage. Women's issues proved highly salient in
1992's Year of the Woman—a year in which candidate gender was highlighted by the media and campaigns. A study of the 1992, 1994, and 1996
congressional elections found that only the electoral environment in 1992
cued voters to employ gender issues in deciding to vote for a female House
candidate (Dolan 2001; also see Plutzer and Zipp 1996).

While the Year of the Woman is a unique case, recent research suggests
that women's issues remain salient despite the relatively "gender-free" electoral environment in post-1992 elections. Female House and state legislative candidates who ran on women's issues and targeted female voters in
1996 and 1998 also gained a significant advantage at the polls, increasing

their probability of winning by 11 percentage points over candidates who did not stress women's issues and target female voters (Herrnson et al. 2003). Individuals have a "baseline gender preference" preferring to vote for a male or female candidate, all things being equal (Sanbonmatsu 2002b). If women are more likely than men to have a baseline preference for female candidates (Sanbonmatsu 2002b) and all voters, regardless of gender, perceive that female candidates better handle certain issues, it is possible that the presence of female candidates who stress those issues may signal to women increased opportunity for women-friendly policymaking (through the election of female candidates). In other words, female candidates who play to the stereotypes the public holds about female candidates may provide a symbolic *and* substantive context that stimulates women's political engagement (Atkeson 2003). Thus, we expect women will be more likely to discuss politics, influence others' votes, and engage in acts of non-voting political participation when female candidates stress women's issues in their campaigns. However, we expect men's political engagement to be unaffected, since gender is a more politically salient cue for women than for men (Sanbonmatsu 2002b; Burns, Schlozman, and Verba 2001). This hypothesis is also supported by prior research findings that show that female candidates have no impact on men's political behaviors (Sapiro and Conover 1997).

Research Methods

We use data from the American National Election Studies (ANES) to test our hypotheses. We focus on Senate and House contests over two election cycles, 2002 and 2004. The data are well suited for this project because ANES examines the political attitudes and behavior of a nationally representative sample of adults. Although the ANES does not include respondents from every state and congressional district, electoral contests from almost every US state are included in the data.[1]

To test whether women running "as women" influence political engagement, we code candidates' issues into several categories. In order to determine the issues on which the candidates focused in their campaigns, we first used LexisNexis to search for newspaper articles about the candidates. We recognize that candidates do not rely solely on the media to get their message out. However, our goal was to capture the issues most likely to be received by voters. While television is the most popular source of news, the decline in newspaper readership has stabilized over the past few years (Pew Research Center 2006). In fact, many Americans—nearly one in three—read newspapers online. We should also note that we relied on articles that did not center on a particular issue, but instead relied on articles that were written for the purpose of comparing the candidates to each other across many issues or discussing a particular candidate's campaign. We also used articles that discussed candidate issues in the context of recent campaign appearances or speeches.[2] We chose an open-ended coding scheme, coding all of the issues mentioned by the candidate.

To paraphrase Karen Beckwith and Kimberly Cowell-Meyers (2007, 554), deciding what constitutes women's issues is probably one of the most problematic tasks in political research. Despite the common perception that women share common interests, women do not share the same experiences. As a result, one's definition of women's issues is defined by context. Given this challenge, most definitions of women's issues tend to be broad (see Beckwith and Cowell-Meyers 2007 for a detailed discussion).[3] Here we define women's issues as issues voters associate favorably with female candidates. This variable (*Women's issues*) includes issues traditionally classified as women's issues—education, health care, social issues, welfare, and children's issues (compassion issues); issues that tap into traditional values; and issues specifically related to women's own physical, social, and economic well-being (women's rights). The candidate's ideological position on these issues or partisan affiliation is of no consequence to this measure or our hypotheses.

Dependent and Key Independent Variables

Our empirical analysis employs three dependent variables: discussing politics, influencing others' votes, and nonvoting electoral participation. Respondents were asked whether they ever talked about politics with family and friends and whether they talked to any people and tried to show them why they should vote for or against one of the parties or candidates. Responses for these questions were coded 1 for "yes" and 0 for "no." The political participation variable measures the number of political acts engaged in by an individual. It is an index of six possible activities: (1) attending a political rally or meeting; (2) displaying a campaign button, sticker, or sign; (3) volunteering for a candidate or party; (4) contributing money to a candidate; (5) contributing money to a political party; and (6) contributing money to groups in support or in opposition to a candidate or party.[4]

In order to measure the effect of female candidates and women's issues on political engagement, first we model political engagement as a function of two key variables: (1) the presence of a female candidate running for office in the respondent's state or district,[5] and (2) the presence of a female candidate who stressed women's issues in her campaign. To better assess the effects of female candidates on women and men, we divide the data among male and female respondents. Given recent findings that candidate gender in and of itself has little influence on female political activity and our theory of women running "as women," we expect the presence of a female candidate running for office in the respondent's state or district to have no impact on women's political engagement and the presence of a female candidate who stressed women's issues in her campaign to have a positive impact on women's political engagement. However, we expect both variables to have no impact on male political behavior.

Our second set of models focuses only on intergender contests—races in which female major-party candidates ran against male candidates. We believe it is necessary to examine these cases more closely as it is often the case that candidates' issues become more significant in female-male races because of voters' stereotypes (e.g., Dolan 1998; McDermott 1997). For the period covered by this analysis, there were 129 intergender contests, and 34 percent (864) of the respondents in the pooled data lived in states or districts featuring intergender House or Senate contests.[6] A majority (55%) of the respondents in the sample of intergender contests are women.

To test whether female candidates who run "as women" in intergender contests positively influence women's political behavior, we distinguish two types of electoral contexts: (1) intergender elections where male and female candidates did not run on women's issues (number of respondents in the sample = 355), and (2) intergender elections where the female candidate ran on women's issues and the male candidate did not (number of respondents in the sample = 455). Ninety-four percent of the respondents fall into these two categories. There were too few respondents to examine the remaining categories: both candidates ran on women's issues ($n = 44$) and only male candidates ran on women's issues ($n = 10$). By separating out our analyses by candidates' issues, we can better track whether the impact of female candidates and campaign issues on the political engagement variables differs when women's issues are introduced into the campaign by female candidates. The main independent variable of interest in these models, *Female*, is a binary variable where 1 indicates a female respondent and 0 a male respondent.

Control Variables

To help rule out alternative explanations for our results, we include several control variables. The first set of control variables included in these models taps general levels of political interest, political trust, and political efficacy, all of which are highly predictive of all forms of political activity (e.g., Rosenstone and Hansen 1993; Campbell et al. 1960).[7] We control for several demographic factors that may explain differences in women's and men's political attitudes and political participation: race, marital status, income, education, and age (Verba and Nie 1972; Welch 1977). Age is measured in the model with two dummy variables (*Age 31–59, Age over 60*), as younger people are more likely to engage in this political activity than are older people (Rosenstone and Hansen 1993). We also control for strength of partisanship (*Partisan intensity*), recognizing that stronger partisans are more likely to be engaged in politics than are weak partisans and independents. We also include *Party congruence* (between respondents and the female candidate) as a proxy to gauge ideological congruence (see Lawless 2004a). It is probable that female candidates are most likely to motivate voters who share their party affiliation. Lastly, we control for the election year (*2004*), expecting higher levels of participation during presidential elections than midterm elections.[8]

Results

The results presented in Table 6.1 show that the engaging effect of women candidates varies across the political behavior variables and gender. While female candidates and female candidates who emphasize women's issues have no impact on nonvoting electoral participation, the combined effect of having female candidates who emphasize women's issues stimulates political discussion among women in the electorate. Yet in the case of proselytizing, candidate gender—in and of itself—has a significant impact on women and men. All respondents who lived in states or districts where female candidates ran for office were more likely to try to influence others' votes than respondents who lived in states or districts where male-only contests occurred. Overall, these findings suggest that when considering various forms of political behavior, female candidates can have an impact on the public. However, the context of the election—in this case, issues—can, in some cases, be an important mediating factor in determining the symbolic effects ascribed to female candidates.

The results presented in Table 6.2 provide additional support for this conclusion. As we can see, the electoral context in intergender contests creates conditions under which the presence of female candidates becomes politically empowering for women in the electorate. Turning to the political discussion model, the first column shows that women are significantly less likely than men to discuss politics with friends and family when neither candidate runs on women's issues. However, when the electoral context changes and female candidates stress women's issues, the gender variable becomes positive and significant, meaning that in this electoral context women are more likely than men to discuss politics.

Taking a closer look at predicted probabilities provides important information about the strength of these variables.[9] The predicted probability of discussing politics for women jumps from a 56 percent chance when none

Table 6.1   **Female Candidates and Women's Issues as a Predictor of Political Behavior**

	Discuss Politics		Influence Others' Votes		Political Participation	
	Female	Male	Female	Male	Female	Male
Female candidate[a]	−.272	.188	.414*	.602**	.029	−.062
	(.248)	(.290)	(.201)	(.203)	(.120)	(.116)
Female candidate stresses women's issues	.555*	−.425	−.231	−.082	.030	.042
	(.266)	(.307)	(.215)	(.226)	(.128)	(.129)
Political interest	1.189***	1.110***	1.045***	1.171***	.435***	.597***
	(.135)	(.153)	(.118)	(.126)	(.067)	(.073)
Trust in government	−.003	−.120	.014	−.037	−.073	.013
	(.148)	(.153)	(.120)	(.119)	(.071)	(.068)
Political efficacy	−.051	−.054	−.030	.055	−.042	−.038
	(.057)	(.062)	(.046)	(.048)	(.027)	(.027)
Partisan intensity	.494***	.236	.298**	.365**	.402***	.341***
	(.147)	(.172)	(.118)	(.128)	(.071)	(.072)
Party congruence	−.317	−.094	−.185	−.245	−.101	.012
	(.279)	(.328)	(.230)	(.247)	(.135)	(.139)
White	.428*	.005	.013	.210	−.102	.089
	(.192)	(.224)	(.164)	(.169)	(.097)	(.098)
Married	.103	−.134	−.190	−.332*	.023	.038
	(.174)	(.199)	(.138)	(.150)	(.080)	(.086)
Income	.137*	.160*	.049	.185**	−.009	.058
	(.081)	(.087)	(.064)	(.066)	(.036)	(.037)
Education	.192***	.279***	.189***	−.063	.121***	.011
	(.062)	(.068)	(.049)	(.051)	(.028)	(.029)
Age 31–59	−.123	−.105	−.159	−.223	.161	.090
	(.239)	(.269)	(.200)	(.211)	(.125)	(.127)
Age 60 and up	−.816***	−.662*	−.388*	−.601*	.366**	.208
	(.260)	(.306)	(.225)	(.240)	(.136)	(.139)
2004	−.275	−.224	.671***	.383**	.256**	−.023
	(.195)	(.205)	(.158)	(.152)	(.092)	(.087)
Constant	−1.970	−.1266	−3.687	−2.975	2.804	2.480
	(.508)	(.590)	(.438)	(.473)	(.261)	(.274)
N	1181	995	1183	996	1183	996
Log-likelihood	−476.483	−374.746	−677.283	−603.877	−951.143	−961.607
Prob > chi square	.000	.000	.000	.000	.000	.000
Pseudo R^2	.169	.152	.134	.119	.091	.073

Notes: Estimates are logistic and ordered probit regression coefficients. Standard errors are in parentheses. All intercepts (not shown) for ordered probit regressions are statistically insignificant.
*Significant at $p < .05$, **significant at $p < .01$, ***significant at $p < .001$, one-tailed test.
a. Female candidate running for Congress in respondent's district or state.

of the candidates campaigns on women's issues to a 74 percent chance when the female candidate stresses women's issues! Clearly female candidates who play to the stereotypes the public holds about female candidates' ability to better handle women's issues encourage political discourse among women.

Table 6.2 Female Candidates "Running as Women" in Female-Male Contests

	Discuss Politics		Influence Others' Votes		Political Participation	
	No Women's Issues[a]	Female— Women's Issues[b]	No Women's Issues	Female— Women's Issues	No Women's Issues	Female— Women's Issues
Female respondent	−.840**	.631*	−.246	−.480*	−.135	.021
	(.345)	(.307)	(.252)	(.249)	(.149)	(.141)
Political interest	.855***	1.469***	1.080***	1.324***	.554***	.573***
	(.254)	(.245)	(.222)	(.206)	(.140)	(.120)
Trust in government	.396	.311	.267	−.029	−.243*	.000
	(.306)	(.247)	(.231)	(.200)	(.144)	(.113)
Political efficacy	.146	.056	.137	.030	−.084	−.014
	(.113)	(.098)	(.087)	(.077)	(.052)	(.043)
Partisan intensity	.509*	.613*	.398*	.391*	.217	.461***
	(.289)	(.267)	(.228)	(.211)	(.137)	(.120)
Party congruence	.135	−.096	−.641*	.149	.012	−.052
	(.363)	(.345)	(.285)	(.269)	(.165)	(.153)
White	.338	.913**	−.066	.565*	−.020	−.281*
	(.367)	(.318)	(.299)	(.270)	(.176)	(.156)
Married	.058	.046	−.588*	−.316	−.025	.031
	(.335)	(.302)	(.266)	(.242)	(.150)	(.139)
Income	.043	.222	.162	.144	−.018	.043
	(.144)	(.143)	(.108)	(.108)	(.062)	(.061)
Education	.442***	.211*	.093	.141*	.137**	.094*
	(.129)	(.110)	(.091)	(.083)	(.053)	(.048)
Age 31–59	−.627	−.066	−.021	−.181	.024	−.047
	(.472)	(.447)	(.360)	(.347)	(.221)	(.199)
Age 60 and up	−1.218**	−1.262**	−.189	−.548	.265	.264
	(.518)	(.491)	(.403)	(.393)	(.242)	(.218)
2004	−.8550**	.620*	.219	.772**	.113	.229
	(.389)	(.321)	(.257)	(.253)	(.151)	(.146)
Constant	−1.945	−3.885	−2.977	−4.052	2.116	2.865
	(.958)	(1.002)	(.792)	(.804)	(.480)	(.449)
N	330	400	330	401	330	401
Log-likelihood	−130.535	−151.698	−198.843	−225.410	−293.671	−333.843
Prob > chi square	.000	.000	.000	.000	.000	.000
Pseudo R^2	.196	.247	.130	.181	.098	.103

Notes: Estimates are logistic and ordered probit regression coefficients. Standard errors are in parentheses. All intercepts (not shown) for ordered probit regressions are statistically insignificant.

*Significant at $p < .05$, **Significant at $p < .01$, ***Significant at $p < .001$, one-tailed test.

a. Intergender contests where male and female candidates did not stress women's issues during the campaign.

b. Intergender contests where female candidates stressed women's issues; male candidates did not stress women's issues.

Contrary to our expectations, men's political engagement is also affected, as the predicted probability of discussing politics among men decreases from a 75 percent chance to a 61 percent chance. The effect of women running "as women" also appears to influence men's attempts to influence others' votes, as male respondents are significantly more likely to proselytize than are women when female candidates in intergender contests run on women's issues. It should also be noted that the presence of women running "as women" slightly depresses both women's and men's willingness to proselytize—the predicted probability of proselytizing is higher for both women (30% chance) and men (35% chance) when neither candidate stresses women's issues as compared to when female candidates stress women's issues (women: 20% chance; men: 29% chance). As for the last dependent variable, the results show that the change in electoral context has no significant impact on nonvoting electoral participation.

Turning to the control variables presented in Tables 6.1 and 6.2, we see that many of them are significant and in the expected direction. In most cases, strong partisans are significantly more likely to be politically engaged than apolitical respondents. Education also appears to have a positive impact—college-educated respondents are more likely to discuss politics, proselytize, and participate in nonelectoral activities than are respondents with little formal education. Interestingly, while there is no racial difference in proselytizing and participation among respondents, white female respondents are more likely to discuss politics than are nonwhite females. Similarly, while there is no racial difference in political discussion, proselytizing, and participation when neither candidate runs on women's issues, white respondents are more likely to discuss politics and attempt to influence others' votes and are less likely to participate when female candidates stress women's issues. Finally, the results show that age is highly predictive across several variables. Respondents age 60 and older regardless of gender are less likely to discuss politics and influence others' votes. Older respondents are also less likely to discuss politics regardless of the issue context.

Conclusion

In this study, we hypothesized that women running "as women" influence political discussion, proselytizing, and nonvoting electoral participation among women. Overall, we find little evidence of the symbolic and substantive effects ascribed to female candidates and their campaigns. Only in the case of discussing politics do we find that the presence of female candidates who run on women's issues positively alters women's political behavior. Contrary to our expectations, these candidates slightly depress attempts to influence the votes of others. Thus, we find limited support for our theoretical argument that female candidates and their issues provide important contextual cues that boost women's political participation.

Interestingly, we find evidence to suggest that female candidates who run "as women," particularly those who run against male opponents, influence male political behavior. Men are somewhat more likely to discuss politics and attempt to influence others' votes when female candidates do not stress women's issues in their campaigns. The fact that female candidates and their issues under various conditions can provide a symbolic *and* substantive context that lowers male political behavior is very intriguing. How might we explain these results? Research suggests that gender is a less salient cue for men and being male is not as strongly correlated with preferring a male candidate as it is for women (Sanbonmatsu 2002b; Burns. Schlozman, and Verba 2001). Yet, it is possible that men are interpreting the same cue that women receive when female candidates run "as women" and are turned off from politics when female candidates seemingly highlight their gender and desire to enact women-friendly policies. Consequently, they then withdraw from politics, perceiving the election as a distortion of politics as usual. While it is not clear from this data that this notion of disillusionment fully explains these findings, our results strongly suggest that the degree to which men are impacted by female candidates warrants additional scholarly attention.

As with most empirical studies, we recognize that there are limitations to this study. First, we acknowledge that examining elections beyond 2002 and 2004 would provide a more rigorous test of our hypotheses. We limited the study to these election years because it was extremely difficult to find information about candidates' issue platforms in elections further back in time. Second, we also recognize that the ANES can be a blunt instrument because of question wording. For example, given the question wording for our proselytizing variable, it is not possible to untangle whether respondents proselytized for or against candidates, parties, or both. We also have no way of knowing *why* respondents attempted political persuasion, or *why* they supported or opposed a particular candidate (or party). Given that individuals who have a baseline gender preference for female candidates (most of whom are women) are more likely to vote for and be represented by a woman, one might assume that the combined effect of candidate gender and issues elicits *positive* behavior from female voters—women attempt to influence others to throw their support to female candidates who stress women's issues. However, it is unlikely that all female candidates provide the same benefits to all women (Dolan 2006). Women are not monolithic in their interests and choices and may choose to speak out against the female candidate.[10]

Despite these limitations, this research has important implications for research on political behavior and gender politics. First, we show that that the impact of candidate gender is at times conditioned by external forces, in this case campaign issues. The presence of female candidates can be a strong and positive cue for both women and men in the electorate (see Table

6.1). However, for two of the three political behavior variables, we see few significant gender differences in political engagement. This is also the case for intergender contests where both candidates do not campaign on issues that are traditionally associated with women. Thus, without a gendered electoral environment, candidate gender in and of itself is an inconsistent cue for women (e.g., Dolan 2001). Second, candidates' issues are influential contextual variables that can play a significant role in understanding the proclivity of political participation. In some cases, female candidates and the issues they stress can help women overcome societal stereotypes of female political indifference and inactivity (e.g., Atkeson and Rapoport 2003). The results clearly show that female candidates and the issues raised in their campaigns can encourage women to discuss politics at higher rates than when female candidates do not stress women's issues. This study highlights the relative importance of female candidates and issues stressed in their campaigns as influential contextual variables that may play a significant role in understanding aspects of both female and male political attitudes and behavior. Future studies of symbolic representation would do well to give greater attention to additional issues that female candidates stress in their campaigns, as doing so will be beneficial to our larger understanding of the influence of candidate gender on political engagement.

Notes

1. States missing from the data include Massachusetts, Mississippi, Nebraska, New Mexico, Oklahoma, and South Carolina.

2. Four of the candidates in our database were not mentioned in any LexisNexis articles. For these candidates, we searched the Internet for web pages. These web pages had an introduction page that listed what issues were important to the candidate. We failed to find any information for two candidates in the data. These candidates ran (and lost) in elections that were overwhelmingly uncompetitive. The issue variables for these candidates were coded as zero.

3. For example, Carroll (1985, 15) defines women's issues as "those issues where policy consequences are likely to have a more immediate and direct impact on significantly larger numbers of women than of men." Thomas (1994, 7), focusing specifically on legislation, defines women's issues as "policies favoring women, children, and families."

4. The scale ranges from 0 to 6 and is internally consistent (Cronbach's alpha = .61).

5. Male-Male contests are coded as 0. Female-Male and Female-Female contests are coded as 1.

6. For 71 respondents (2.8%), a female candidate was running in an intergender contest for both the House and Senate. In this case, we chose to focus on the female House candidate. Doing so in most cases introduced a female candidate for the House of Representatives who was not previously represented in the data set. Of the 71 respondents, 41 were female.

7. The question wording and coding for these variables are as follows: "Some

people don't pay much attention to political campaigns. How about you? Would you say you are very much interested, somewhat interested, or not much interested in the political campaigns so far this year?" Responses range from 0 (not much interested) to 2 (very much interested). "How much of the time do you think you can trust the government in Washington to do what is right?" Responses were coded 0 for "none," 1 for "some of the time," 2 for "most of the time," and 3 for "just about always." Political efficacy measures whether respondents disagree, neither agree nor disagree, or agree with the following statements, "Public officials don't care what people think" and "People like me don't have any say in what government does." Responses range from –2 to 2.

8. We also tested models that controlled for candidate status (*Female incumbent*) and the competitiveness of the election (e.g., Atkeson 2003). These variables are excluded from the models presented here because they were consistently insignificant across all models.

9. The predicted probabilities were calculated using CLARIFY (Tomz, Wittenberg, and King 2003), holding continuous variables constant at their means and nominal variables constant at their modal category. This creates a "hypothetical" respondent and electoral environment. In this case, the "hypothetical" respondent is somewhat interested in political campaigns, trusts government only some of the time, has low political efficacy, has a high school education, is white, is a weak or leaning partisan, earns between $15,000 to $34,999, is married, and is between 31 and 59 years old. As for the electoral environment, the election year is 2004, and the female candidate and respondent do not share the same party affiliation.

10. Clearly, a polarizing female candidate like Hillary Rodham Clinton, for example, is likely to produce this effect.

PART 2
Getting Ahead

7

Policy Leadership
Beyond "Women's" Issues

MICHELE L. SWERS

THE TERRORIST ATTACKS of September 11, 2001, propelled defense policy to the forefront of US politics and made national security expertise a primary criterion for voters when selecting candidates for national office. At the same time, there is a voluminous literature demonstrating that voters hold gender-based stereotypes in which voters trust women candidates less on defense and foreign policy issues but favor female candidates over men on social welfare issues such as education and health (Sanbonmatsu 2002b; Huddy and Terkildsen 1993a; Dolan 2004; Burrell 1994; Alexander and Andersen 1993). This preference for male leadership has grown since the September 11 attacks catapulted national security to the top of the list of voter concerns. Research on presidential candidates demonstrates a dramatic rise in the proportion of voters who identify national security as the most important problem facing the nation. These security-oriented voters are much more likely to favor a male over a female presidential candidate (Kenski and Falk 2004; Falk and Kenski 2006; Lawless 2004b). Thus, the increased saliency of national security as a determinant of voter choice and enhanced media coverage of these issues have primed negative stereotypes about women candidates in a way that could hinder women's advancement to political office.

Despite prevailing assumptions that women are less capable stewards of national security, there are no studies that examine the policy activities of women officeholders on defense issues. Thus, we have no evidence to support or refute the conventional wisdom about women's propensity to engage defense issues. In this study, I analyze the engagement of senators in defense policy in the Democratic-controlled 107th Congress and the Republican-controlled 108th Congress.[1] An examination of senators' involvement in the crafting of the major defense policy initiative considered by Congress, the annual defense authorization bill, finds few gender differences in policy participation. However, the statistical analysis and staff interviews indicate that members act in a partisan and gendered context that skews the policy debate in a way that creates an additional hurdle for women, particularly Democratic women, seeking to establish their reputations on national security.[2] These women engage in compensatory strategies to highlight their defense credentials to constituents and voters.

Making Defense Policy in the Senate: Pitfalls and Opportunities

Senate staffers universally agree that since 9/11 it is both an electoral and a policy imperative for senators to develop a profile on national security. In 2002, the first election since the attacks on the World Trade Center and the Pentagon, terrorism and a potential war in Iraq focused voters' attention on defense policy. Similarly, the competition between President George W. Bush and Senator John Kerry to demonstrate their ability to protect the country in the war on terror and their battles over the proper conduct of the Iraq War dominated the policy debate leading up to the 2004 presidential election, forcing senators, particularly those running for reelection, to continually address security concerns regardless of their planned campaign strategies. The overwhelming importance of security issues and the Iraq war continued in the 2006 election cycle, and the war defines the debate among the 2008 presidential candidates.

The priming of security as the dominant frame for evaluating the competence of officeholders encourages all senators to develop a list of proposals and accomplishments on security. As one staffer put it, a senator's policy agenda is "like a grocery store. If constituents want it you need to have it on the shelf." The higher media profile of senators in comparison to House members means that local and national media will seek the comments of senators on defense issues, allowing them to raise their national profile on these issues—a particularly important goal for presidential hopefuls (Sellers 2002).

Beyond the media and voter expectations, the policymaking process in the Senate encourages widespread participation on defense issues. First, the facts that senators have a greater number of committee assignments than their House counterparts do and most senators have a seat on one of the prestige committees (Appropriations, Armed Services, Finance, or Foreign Relations) means that the vast majority of senators hold a committee seat with jurisdiction over national security issues (Evans 1991; Baker 2001; Smith and Deering 1997). Moreover, most senators serve on at least three committees, allowing them to engage in multiple types of defense questions. Outside of the committees, the protections of minority rights guaranteed in the Senate rules allow senators to force consideration of their defense policy interests through tactics such as offering nongermane amendments to any legislation that comes to the Senate floor and placing holds or threatening a filibuster on legislation until their concerns are addressed (Sinclair 1989, 2005; Binder and Smith 1997; Baker 2001; Evans and Lipinski 2005).

While multiple committee assignments and protection of minority rights expand senators' opportunities to influence defense policy, senators are limited by the established reputations and committee profiles of their same-state counterparts (Schiller 2000). Senators who try to develop policies that overlap with the established expertise of their same-state counterparts will have greater difficulty gaining media attention and by extension voter recognition for their work (Schiller 2000). Additionally, these policy entrepreneurs may earn the ire of the same-state senator.

Clearly, the unique features of the Senate allow senators to tailor their participation on national security to their interests and strengths. This research broadens our understanding of the factors that explain the strategic decisions of senators concerning the substantive content of their defense policy profile.

A Theory of the Impact of Gender on the Defense Policy Activity of Senators

Given the centrality of defense issues to the national agenda and the persistence of voter stereotypes concerning women's lack of expertise in national security, it is important to discern whether there are gender differences in the level and nature of legislators' participation on national security issues. Do these stereotypes about women's defense credentials inhibit or enhance legislators' ability to gain credibility on these issues with colleagues or their voting constituencies? To address these questions, I focus on defense policy activity in the US Senate in the 107th (2001–2002) and 108th Congress (2002–2003).

Taking into account the voter stereotypes that are tied to social norms about the interests and expertise of men and women and the institutional and electoral incentives and constraints faced by senators, I develop a series of hypotheses concerning the role of gender as it influences participation in defense policy. First, I anticipate that despite gender-based stereotypes, there will be no differences in the overall sponsorship of defense-related initiatives by men and women. Instead, the institutional incentives and electoral imperatives that drive senators to be policy generalists will ensure that all senators can point to a mix of defense-related proposals they are pursuing. Thus, the large personal staffs and the breadth of senators' committee assignments that give most senators jurisdiction over some aspect of defense policy combined with the need to reassure voters that they are actively engaged in security issues will lead all senators to develop a profile on defense issues.

However, when one unpacks the substantive content of the defense proposals senators sponsor into "hard" initiatives relating to the training and equipping of the force and "soft" issues relating to benefits for military personnel and veterans, gender differences in participation may emerge. If women bring a perspective to legislating that makes them more likely to consider the needs of families, then female senators may be more active in their sponsorship of the "soft" defense issues that enhance the quality of life for members of the Armed Forces and veterans than are their male partisan colleagues. Alternatively, if negative stereotypes about women's expertise are correct, men should be more active participants than women on the "hard" issues of war, weapons procurement, and transformation of the strategic capabilities of the military.

Furthermore, prevailing negative assumptions about women's lack of expertise on defense issues will make it more difficult for women to establish their national security credentials with constituents and colleagues. To counter these stereotypes, women will engage in compensatory strategies in which they must expend additional resources on position-taking activities that allow them to advertise their defense credentials to constituents and voters. The need to engage in compensatory strategies will be particularly acute for Democratic women who face the double burden of gender stereotypes and association with the party that is perceived as weaker on defense.

The Defense Authorization Bill and the Senate

Although there is a large literature that laments the deference and subordination of Congress to the executive branch on matters of national security, particularly in the initiation and prosecution of wars (for example, Deering 2005; Wheeler 2004), staffers universally agree that the major congressional vehicle for influencing the direction of national security policy is the annual defense authorization bill that is drafted by the Armed Services Committee. While the appropriations bill provides the Pentagon with its funding, the authorization bill allows Congress to create or shape programs and weigh in on policy issues (Deering 2005). For example, the fiscal year (FY) 2006 authorization bill included amendments that limited President Bush's prosecution of the Iraq War and the war on terror by defining torture, limiting the access of detainees to the courts, and designating 2006 as a year of significant transition in the Iraq War with a requirement for quarterly reports on the war's progress and advancement toward drawdown of troops (Donnelly 2005). Through the authorization bill, senators can influence a wide range of defense policies, from missile defense to pay raises and health insurance for the troops.

Given the status of the annual authorization bill as Congress's major policy statement on the conduct of defense policy, I analyzed senators' participation in the FY 2003 and FY 2004 defense authorization floor debates. In the Democratic-controlled 107th Congress, the FY 2003 bill was debated with an eye to the 2002 midterm elections. After Republicans regained control of the Senate in 2003, the FY 2004 authorization bill became a vehicle for both parties to begin positioning themselves for the 2004 presidential election. Senators debated the conduct of the wars and reconstruction efforts in Afghanistan and Iraq. They sought to demonstrate their support for the troops in wartime by proposing increases in military benefits and pay. They argued over weapons systems from missile defense to nuclear weapons research. They sought to protect home-state bases and industries with proposals to alter the mandate of the Base Realignment and Closure Commission and efforts to impose "buy America" provisions on the Pentagon (Towell 2002, 2003; McCutcheon with Cassata 2002; Sorrells 2003).

Measuring Senators' Defense Policy Activity

Clearly, both the FY 2003 and FY 2004 defense authorization bills provided senators with ample opportunities to engage a wide range of national security questions, from weapons procurement and military force structure to taking care of military families and disabled veterans. To assess the influence of gender on the strategic decisions of senators concerning which defense policy debates to engage, I coded the number and policy content of amendments senators filed to these bills, including whether the amendment concerned a hard, soft, homeland security, or constituency-related issue. Hard issues encompass the source of negative stereotypes about the interest of women in defense policy. These amendments concern weapons development, including debates over missile defense and nuclear weapons, as well as questions about the structure and operation of the military, including base closures and waivers of environmental laws for military training facilities. Conversely, soft issues incorporate the more traditional social welfare concerns associated with women's presumed expertise by enhancing various benefits for military personnel in an effort to take care of military families. Soft issues include proposals such as expanding access to TRICARE (the military health insurance program), increasing survivor benefits, and expanding pensions for disabled veterans. The small number of homeland security issues mix domestic and national security concerns by enhancing domestic security in an effort to combat terrorism. Constituency-oriented amendments relate to specific projects benefiting, for example, a military base, defense contractor, or a research organization in the state.

To obtain further evidence of senators' defense policy engagement, I also coded the number and policy content of the amendments senators cosponsored and I examined the factors that determine which members saw their amendments accepted on the Senate floor.

The Impact of Gender on a Senator's National Security Policy Profile

As would reflect the widespread interest in national security policy, Table 7.1 indicates that approximately half of all senators sponsored amendments to the defense authorization bill across the two congresses. In the FY 2003 authorization passed during the 107th Congress, constituency-related projects attracted the most amendments, while hard issues attracted the most amendments to the FY 2004 authorization in the 108th Congress. Across both congresses, more amendments were offered on hard issues than soft issues. However, in the Democratic-controlled 107th Congress, slightly more senators offered soft amendments than hard amendments.

Table 7.2 displays the patterns of amendment sponsorship by gender and party, providing information on the average number of amendments sponsored by each group, the standard deviation, the proportion of the

Table 7.1 Sponsorship of Amendments to the Defense Authorization Bill, 107th and 108th Congresses

Bill Type	Number of Amendments	Number of Members Sponsoring
107th Congress		
Defense	163	57
Subject categories		
Soft	44	28
Hard	54	26
Homeland security	12	9
Constituency	56	35
108th Congress		
Defense	107	42
Subject categories		
Soft	35	19
Hard	49	28
Homeland security	2	2
Constituency	21	14

Note: Amendments are assigned to multiple subcategories if they concerned, for example, both a hard and a homeland security issue.

Table 7.2   Amending the Defense Authorization Bill by Gender and Party, 107th and 108th Congresses

	Mean	Standard Deviation	Median	Percent Sponsor	Minimum	Maximum
		107th Congress				
Democratic men (*n* = 41)	1.7	2.7	1	56	0	13 Cleland (GA)
Democratic women (*n* = 10)	1.7	2.5	.5	50	0	8 Landrieu (LA)
Republican men (*n* = 46)	1.5	2.4	1	56.5	0	14 Warner (VA)
Republican women (*n* = 3)	2.3	1.2	3	100	1	3 Collins (ME), Hutchison (TX)
		108th Congress				
Democratic men (*n* = 40)	.95	1.6	0	42.5	0	8 Nelson (FL)
Democratic women (*n* = 9)	1.4	1.7	1	67	0	5 Landrieu (LA)
Republican men (*n* = 46)	1.1	1.95	0	37	0	8 Inhofe (OK)
Republican women (*n* = 5)	1	1.4	0	40	0	3 Hutchison (TX)

group that sponsored amendments on defense issues, and the minimum and maximum number of amendments sponsored by group members. The small number of Republican women in the Senate, particularly in the 107th Congress, makes it difficult to generalize about the behavior of Republican women. However, interviews with staff overwhelmingly indicate that gender impacts the behavior of senators differently based on whether they are associated with the party that "owns defense issues," the Republicans, versus affiliation with the party that is perceived as weak on defense, the Democrats. Therefore, it is important to investigate how party affiliation influences the behavior of women on security issues.

Upon first inspection, it appears that women are not less active on security issues than are men. In fact, across the two congresses, on average, Democratic and Republican women sponsor equivalent numbers of defense-related amendments in comparison to their male colleagues. This consistent pattern of activity likely reflects the tendency of senators to be policy generalists who as representatives of the interests of an entire state must develop legislative proposals in all policy areas.

To fully understand how gender interacts with the universe of influences on a member's policy decisions, I utilize multivariate regression analysis. Regression analysis allows us to examine the role gender plays in determining the substantive content of senators' security initiatives after taking into account other important motivators of senators' behavior, particularly the senator's party affiliation, ideology,[3] committee responsibilities, and constituent need and interest in defense policy benefits.

To assess constituent interest in defense issues, I utilize data from the census and Department of Defense that measure the importance of defense benefits to the state's economy and the presence of military forces and veterans in the state (for example, see Carsey and Rundquist 1999; Mayer 1991; Carter 1989; Soherr-Hadwiger 1998). These measures include the state's unemployment rate, percentage of active-duty military personnel in the state, the veteran population, Reserve and National Guard pay, total military and civilian contract awards, and the total number of military installations. A measure of whether or not the senator is up for reelection accounts for political imperatives, as senators might increase their activism on defense issues that are salient to voters in an election year.

While all senators are able to offer amendments to the defense authorization bill, a senator's position within the institution also guides his/her decisions on the best use of scarce legislative resources. First-term senators face a greater learning curve and have a more inexperienced staff in comparison to more senior members that will inhibit their ability to develop amendments. The senators who serve on the Armed Services Committee, which has jurisdiction over the defense authorization bill, have the most knowledgeable staffs and the greatest familiarity with the issues addressed by the legislation. Members of other committees that legislate on defense issues, including the Appropriations Subcommittees on Defense and Military Construction, the Foreign Relations Committee, the Governmental Affairs Committee (known as the Homeland Security and Governmental Affairs Committee in the current 110th Congress), the Select Intelligence Committee, and the Veterans' Affairs Committee, may offer amendments that deal with the issues under their committee's jurisdiction. Chairs and ranking members of these defense-related committees and subcommittees are expected to take the lead in advancing national security proposals and they have additional staff to assist them. Finally, members who served in the military possess a base of knowledge and experience that may increase their interest in defense issues beyond their committee position and the needs of their constituency.

Using a negative binomial event count analysis (results not shown), I am able to model, for example, the number of amendments a senator with a given set of characteristics will sponsor in a given period of time.[4] After taking into account the range of influences on senators' policy activity, I find that gender has no impact on a senator's level of engagement in defense issues. Instead, institutional position and the importance of defense benefits to the state drive senators to sponsor amendments to the authorization bill. Members of the Armed Services Committee were the most likely

Table 7.3   Sponsorship of Hard and Soft Defense Issues, 107th and 108th Congresses

	Mean	Standard Deviation	Median	Percent Sponsor	Minimum	Maximum
			107th Congress			
Soft issues						
Democratic men (*n* = 41)	.56	1.2	0	29	0	6 Cleland (GA)
Democratic women (*n* = 10)	.5	.97	0	30	0	3 Landrieu (LA)
Republican men (*n* = 46)	.33	.63	0	26	0	3 McCain (AZ)
Republican women (*n* = 3)	.33	.58	0	33	0	1 Hutchison (TX)
Hard issues						
Democratic men (*n* = 41)	.59	1.3	0	24	0	6 Levin (MI)
Democratic women (*n* = 10)	.6	1.1	0	30	0	3 Landrieu (LA)
Republican men (*n* = 46)	.48	1.2	0	24	0	7 Warner (VA)
Republican women (*n* = 3)	.67	.58	1	67	0	1 Hutchison (TX), Collins (ME)
			108th Congress			
Soft issues						
Democratic men (*n* = 40)	.35	.98	0	17.5	0	5 Nelson (FL)
Democratic women (*n* = 9)	.78	.97	1	56	0	3 Landrieu (LA)
Republican men (*n* = 46)	.26	.8	0	13	0	4 McCain (AZ)
Republican women (*n* = 5)	.4	.89	0	20	0	2 Hutchison (TX)
Hard issues						
Democratic men (*n* = 40)	.48	.78	0	32.5	0	3 Nelson (FL)
Democratic women (*n* = 9)	.44	1	0	22	0	3 Feinstein (CA)
Republican men (*n* = 46)	.52	1.1	0	26	0	5 Inhofe (OK)
Republican women (*n* = 5)	.4	.89	0	20	0	2 Collins (ME)

to offer amendments. Senators from states that received the largest defense-related contracts and those with higher unemployment rates were also more active participants in the amending process. The only feature of a senator's background that impacted participation was military service, a fact that supports the assertion that these senators have special expertise to offer that is valued by colleagues and the media.

It is possible that gender differences will emerge when we look more closely at the substantive content of senators' amendments to the authorization bill. Reflecting voter stereotypes about men's greater expertise in issues of military strategy and weapons development and women's greater expertise on social welfare concerns, Table 7.3 divides senators' policy proposals into the hard and soft defense issues. The results demonstrate that there are few gender differences in the types of amendments that senators offered. Women, like men, offer hard amendments that largely reflect their committee responsibilities and constituent interests. For example, in the 107th Congress, Kay Bailey Hutchison's (R-TX) amendment attempting to alter the criteria utilized in the Base Realignment and Closure process reflects her responsibilities as the ranking member of the Appropriations Subcommittee on Military Construction and the interests of Texas, a state with numerous bases that would be subject to the commission's scrutiny for closure. Similarly, Mary Landrieu's (D-LA) amendment calling for an annual long-range plan for the construction of Navy ships highlights the importance of the shipbuilding industry in her state. The only major gender difference occurs on soft issues. In the 108th Congress, 56 percent of Democratic women sponsored amendments concerning benefits for military personnel and veterans compared to only 18 percent of Democratic men.

While women engage defense policy debates at the same rates as men, it is possible that male senators are more successful in their efforts to get initiatives passed on the floor. However, regression analysis of amendment passage (results not shown), demonstrates that women are just as likely as men to see their amendments passed on the floor. Instead, committee position and constituent interests such as the number of Reserve and Guard members in the state, high unemployment, and the value of defense contracts determined whose amendments were passed.[5]

Finally, I analyzed senators' cosponsorship activity on defense issues. Cosponsorship is a primary method of position-taking for legislators allowing members to advertise positions to constituents on a wide rage of issues regardless of whether the bill comes to a vote on the Senate floor. The level of commitment indicated by cosponsorship varies, with some cosponsors playing pivotal roles in drafting the amendment and building coalitions, while others simply register their support. Still the value of cosponsorship as a signal to voters is universal (Kroger 2003; Wilson and Young 1997). Looking at original cosponsors in Table 7.4, 64 amendments attracted 81 cosponsors in the 107th Congress and 66 members cosponsored 47 amendments in the 108th Congress. Examining bills by policy area, the soft amendments that provide or enhance benefits for military personnel and their families attract the most cosponsors, reflecting the desire of senators to bring benefits to constituents and to support the troops in wartime. Thus, in the 107th Congress, 26 hard amendments attracted a total of 49 cosponsors, while only 19 soft amendments attracted a total of 63 cosponsors.

Table 7.4   Cosponsorship of Amendments to the Defense Authorization Bill, 107th and 108th Congresses

Bill Type	Number of Amendments	Number of Members Sponsoring
107th Congress		
Defense	64	81
Subject categories		
Soft	19	63
Hard	26	49
Homeland security	2	5
Constituency	17	15
108th Congress		
Defense	47	66
Subject categories		
Soft	12	42
Hard	26	42
Homeland security	1	18
Constituency	8	8

While there were no gender differences in sponsorship of amendments, the cosponsorship patterns in Table 7.5 (and in multivariate regression analysis; results not shown) indicate that women are more active cosponsors of defense initiatives than men are.[6] Cosponsorship serves as a primary vehicle for position taking as it allows senators to signal their position on issues to voters. Thus, it is likely that women are engaging in compensatory strategies in which they are utilizing cosponsorship of defense-related initiatives to signal their activism and competence on these issues to voters. Across both congresses, committee position and constituent interest, indicated by higher rates of unemployment during the 107th Congress and total defense contracts in the 108th Congress, are also important predictors of which senators cosponsor amendments to the authorization bill.

Women's higher level of activism in cosponsoring defense bills partially stems from their support for the soft proposals. As shown in Table 7.6, both Republican and Democratic women cosponsor the soft proposals aimed at helping military personnel and their families at higher rates than their male partisan counterparts. These patterns persist when the data is subject to regression analysis; however, gender differences in the cosponsorship of soft amendments appear larger among Democrats than among Republicans.[7] After accounting for the influence of party, ideology, constituent interests, and committee position, I also find that women were more likely to cosponsor hard amendments in the Democratically controlled 107th Congress, but gender had no impact on cosponsorship of hard defense amendments in the 108th Congress.

Overall, women participate in the development of the defense authori-

Table 7.5   **Cosponsorship of Amendments to the Defense Authorization Bill, by Gender and Party, 107th and 108th Congresses**

	Mean	Standard Deviation	Median	Percent Sponsor	Minimum	Maximum
107th Congress						
Democratic men (*n* = 41)	1.5	1.3	1	81	0	5 Cleland (GA), Bingaman (NM)
Democratic women (*n* = 10)	3.1	1.6	3	100	1	5 Landrieu (LA), Carnahan (MO), Mikulski (MD)
Republican men (*n* = 46)	2	1.8	2	76	0	7 Lott (MS)
Republican women (*n* = 3)	4.3	1.2	5	100	3	5 Collins (ME), Snowe (ME)
108th Congress						
Democratic men (*n* = 40)	2.4	2.1	2	80	0	7 Levin (MI), Bingaman (NM), Durbin (IL)
Democratic women (*n* = 9)	3.6	2.6	2	100	1	9 Clinton (NY)
Republican men (*n* = 46)	.74	.95	0	46	0	3 McCain (AZ), Allen (VA), Warner (VA)
Republican women (*n* = 5)	2.4	1.8	3	80	0	4 Snowe (ME), Collins (ME)

zation bill at the same rates as male senators and their participation is motivated by the same factors that influence the decisions of all senators: party affiliation, ideology, committee responsibilities, and constituent interests. However, the higher rates of cosponsorship exhibited by women indicate that female senators are utilizing cosponsorship, a primary tool for position-taking with constituents, to reinforce their defense credentials with voters and combat the perception that women are weak on defense. Additionally, the increased focus of Democratic women on sponsorship and cosponsorship of soft defense policies that provide greater benefits to military personnel and veterans reinforces the association of women and the Democratic Party with greater support for social welfare legislation.

Making Defense Policy in a Partisan and Gendered Context

Interviews with office and campaign staff for Democratic and Republican, male and female senators confirm women's heightened concern with establishing their credibility on defense issues with voters. These interviews also

Table 7.6　Cosponsorship of Hard and Soft Defense Issues, 107th and 108th Congresses

	Mean	Standard Deviation	Median	Percent Sponsor	Minimum	Maximum
107th Congress						
Soft issues						
Democratic men (n = 41)	.9	.86	1	63	0	3 Reid (NV), Johnson (SD)
Democratic women (n = 10)	2.1	.99	2	100	1	4 Landrieu (LA)
Republican men (n = 46)	.7	.81	1	52	0	3 McCain (AZ), Hutchinson (AR)
Republican women (n = 3)	1.7	.58	2	100	1	2 Snowe (ME), Collins (ME)
Hard issues						
Democratic men (n = 41)	.37	.54	0	34	0	2 Bingaman (NM)
Democratic women (n = 10)	.8	.92	.5	50	0	2 Lincoln (AR), Mikulski (MD), Carnahan (MO)
Republican men (n = 46)	1	1	1	61	0	4 Lott (MS)
Republican women (n = 3)	2	0	2	100		2 Snowe (ME), Collins (ME), Hutchison (TX)
108th Congress						
Soft issues						
Democratic men (n = 40)	.85	1.1	0	48	0	4 Kennedy (MA)
Democratic women (n = 9)	1.9	1.8	1	89	0	6 Clinton (NY)
Republican men (n = 46)	.33	.6	0	26	0	2 McCain (AZ), Hagel (NE), Inhofe (OK)
Republican women (n = 5)	1.2	1.3	1	60	0	3 Collins (ME)
Hard issues						
Democratic men (n = 40)	1.1	1.4	1	53	0	5 Levin (MI)
Democratic women (n = 9)	1	1.1	1	56	0	3 Boxer (CA)
Republican men (n = 46)	.3	.55	0	26	0	2 Warner (VA), Sessions (AL)
Republican women (n = 5)	1	.71	1	80	0	2 Snowe (ME)

indicate that defense policy is conducted within a highly partisan and gendered political context.

With regard to partisanship, since Vietnam, national security has constituted one of the core advantages of the Republican Party while Democrats struggle to refute the perception of their party as weak on defense. When one party clearly "owns" an issue, they try to highlight their strength and the opposition party's weakness on the issue, particularly during the electoral season (Petrocik 1996; Sellers 2002). After the terrorist attacks of 9/11 elevated national security to the forefront of voter concerns, Republicans utilized their national security advantage to great effect in the 2002 and 2004 elections. In the months leading up to the 2008 presidential election, polls indicated that President Bush and Republican leadership of the unpopular war in Iraq had reversed the Republican Party's traditional advantage on defense issues. Polls demonstrated that Americans put more faith in Democrats to handle the Iraq War. Moreover, Democrats and Republicans ranked equally in poll questions asking which party voters trust to handle terrorism. Still Democrats remained concerned about demonstrating strength on national security (Benenson and Allen 2007).

My research indicates that extreme issue ownership creates policy skew in which the weaker party is unable to unify around alternatives or check the excesses of the party that owns the issue. In the case of defense, staffers maintained that support for soft benefit issues is easy for Democrats because these represent an extension of the social welfare state programs that Democrats are generally associated with, such as veterans' health and education. These policies give Democrats and all legislators an opportunity to demonstrate they support the troops. However, on the hard security issues of war and strategic choices about weapons development, Democratic defense staff maintain that Democrats are paralyzed by the perception of the party as weak on national security. Thus, Democrats' fear of being labeled as weak on defense and not supporting the troops impacted the vote for the Iraq War Resolution and has hampered their ability to develop a unifying alternative policy on the Iraq War. Democrats have only recently begun to stake out a strong position against the war, and only after public approval ratings of President Bush and the war plummeted. The widespread public opposition to the war is widely seen as the reason Democrats were able to win control of Congress in the 2006 election, and Democrats are struggling to unify their caucus to respond to their perceived electoral mandate.[8]

In addition to the partisan context, senators engaging defense issues work within a gendered context in which stereotypes about women's policy expertise create an additional hurdle for women senators seeking to gain credibility on defense issues. According to staff, the women recognize this vulnerability and devote extra effort to building their reputations on security. Staffers for Republican and Democratic women maintain that establishing their defense credentials with voters and, more broadly, constituents is a primary concern for women senators. According to staff, Republican and Democratic women are very concerned about acquiring seats on defense and foreign policy committees because, as one Democratic staffer noted, "voters don't question a man's ability on defense issues. Senior male senators with no defense experience, no one will say they are not tough. Women need these committees to show they are tough and fit to lead in that area because the women are not likely to have served in the military" (author interview). Similarly, the decision of Hillary Clinton to seek a seat on Armed Services was often brought up as evidence of her desire to show voters she has the capability to become commander-in-chief.

The heightened concern for establishing credibility with voters on defense issues is especially acute for Democratic women who face the double bind of confronting gender stereotypes and being associated with the party that is viewed as weaker on defense. In interviews with campaign managers for Democrats running for reelection in 2004, all managers noted the desirability of securing endorsements from veterans' groups to enhance the candidate's image on national security. But managers for female Democratic candidates expressed more of a sense of urgency and reported working harder to get these endorsements than managers for male Democratic candidates, even those who did not support the Iraq War. Outside the election cycle, staff for Democratic women noted that constituent events related to defense or veterans take on heightened importance for female senators. "All the senators do the Memorial and Veterans Day events but the women are concerned about it to a more extraordinary degree, it is never just another event for them. They also look for legislative opportunities to show their support for the troops" (author interview). These assertions by the staff corroborate the statistical findings concerning women's higher rates of cosponsorship of defense-related amendments and the greater attention of Democratic women to sponsorship and cosponsorship of the soft defense issues that show support for the troops and their families.

Conclusion

Despite long-standing stereotypes that women are less capable stewards of defense policy than men are, the analysis of senators' participation in the development of the annual defense authorization bill provides no evidence that women lag behind men in their focus on national security. Instead, participation reflects the institutional norms and electoral incentives that guide all members' participation on defense issues. Regardless of gender, committee position (particularly a seat on the Armed Services Committee) and the importance of defense benefits to the state were the primary drivers of senators' decisions to sponsor and cosponsor amendments to the bill.

The major gender difference is the greater propensity of women to cosponsor defense-related amendments. The importance of cosponsorship as a vehicle for advertising positions to constituents reflects women's heightened concern with establishing their national security credentials with constituents. Thus cosponsorship serves as an important compensatory strategy for enhancing female senators' reputation for defense policy expertise with voters. Furthermore, the analysis of sponsorship and cosponsorship by issue area indicates that the increased support for social welfare spending that underlies the gender gap in public opinion is reflected in the greater support of Democratic women for initiatives benefiting military families and veterans, and these gender differences remain even after accounting for the traditional association of the Democratic Party with social welfare issues.

The gender differences found in the statistical analysis are magnified by the evidence from the interviews, which demonstrate that national security policy is made in a highly partisan and gendered political environment. Democratic women are particularly disadvantaged by this policy context as they must overcome stereotypes related to gender and their association with the party that is perceived as weaker on defense. Therefore, women engage in compensatory strategies in which they look for opportunities to highlight their defense policy credentials and support for the troops in both their legislative and constituent service activities.

Notes

1. This chapter draws on theory that appears in Michele L. Swers, "Building a Reputation on National Security: The Impact of Stereotypes Related to Gender and Military Experience," *Legislative Studies Quarterly* 32 (2007): 559–596, as well as research from my book manuscript, *Making Policy in the New Senate Club: Women and Representation in the U.S. Senate* (forthcoming).

2. I conducted interviews with 41 Senate staffers associated with 38 senators who served in the 107th and/or 108th Congress, including staffers to 17 Republicans and 21 Democrats. Interview subjects included campaign managers, chiefs of staff, legislative directors, and legislative assistants responsible for defense issues. Some have worked for multiple senators. I have also interviewed one former Democratic senator and one former Republican senator who served in either or both the 107th or 108th congresses. All interviews were anonymous. Direct references to senators are used when the interview subject is not on the personal staff or when permission is granted by the staffer.

3. I utilize Poole and Rosenthal's DW-NOMINATE scores to measure senators' ideology (Poole and Rosenthal 1997). The scores measure preferences across all nonunanimous roll calls. Poole and Rosenthal find that the scores predict more than 80 percent of roll-call voting. While party and ideology are highly correlated, these scores allow me to capture intraparty differences in policy priorities. Additionally, research on defense voting emphasizes the importance of ideology or "hawkishness" as a predictor of member behavior on these issues (e.g., Carter 1989; Lindsay 1990).

4. I use negative binomial analysis to model the total number of defense-related amendments senators sponsor, the number of amendments that are passed on the

Senate floor, and the total number of defense-related amendments senators cosponsor. For the analysis of cosponsorship of hard and soft defense issues, I utilize an ordered logit model. The dependent variable in this model measures whether senators cosponsored 0, 1, or 2 or more, hard or soft defense amendments. I utilize the ordered logit model, rather than the negative binomial, because the distribution of the dependent variable in these cases is bounded with very few senators cosponsoring more than two hard or soft amendments. Negative binomial models were tested and produce substantially the same results. For details on the results of these models, see Swers forthcoming.

5. For more information on these models, see Swers forthcoming.

6. Ibid.

7. Using ordered logit regression analysis, I find that Democratic women across the 107th and 108th congresses are more likely to cosponsor soft defense amendments than are Democratic men. While the coefficient for Republican women is positive across the two congresses, it borders on significance at the .1 level of probability only in the 107th Congress.

8. In a separate analysis (Swers forthcoming), I find that despite polling data indicating that women are less likely to support the deployment of troops, gender had no impact on whether Democratic senators voted against the Iraq war resolution or in favor of amendments to limit the president's authority. Instead, liberal ideology and reelection concerns for those facing the voters in 2002 drove the vote.

8

Committee Assignments:
Discrimination or Choice?

SUSAN J. CARROLL

SCHOLARS OF LEGISLATIVE politics have long recognized the importance of committees to both the work that is done within legislative institutions and the influence that legislators have on legislation (Fenno 1973;
Smith and Deering 1997). Yet, with a few notable exceptions, mostly among
those studying Congress (e.g., Norton 1995, 2002; Swers 2002), scholars of
women and politics have devoted surprisingly little attention to committees
in studying the influence women legislators have on public policy. In particular, the literature focusing on women state legislators has given relatively
little consideration to the possible connections between women's committee
assignments and their legislative priorities and policy-related behavior.

Research on women state legislators has repeatedly demonstrated that
women and men have somewhat different legislative priorities, with women
legislators more likely than their male counterparts to be involved with legislation in the areas of women's rights, the welfare of families and children,
health care, and education (e.g., Dodson and Carroll 1991; Carroll 2001;
Thomas 1994; Saint-Germain 1989). If these differences in priorities and
policy-related behavior among legislators reflect differences in interests
between women and men, one might also expect to find gender differences
in preferences for committees on which legislators might serve.

The preferences of legislators (and any gender differences in those
preferences that may exist) are certainly one factor that comes into play in
determining the committees to which legislators are assigned. However,
final decisions about committee assignments are made by legislative leaders, still predominantly men in most states, who can bring their own attitudes about gender differences to bear on their decisions. Hypothetically,
women and men in the aggregate could end up serving on different commit-

135

tees for any of the following reasons: (1) because women and men prefer different committees, (2) because legislative leaders think women are better (or less) suited to certain committees and assign (or fail to assign) them to these committees despite women's preferences to the contrary, or (3) because of a combination of (1) and (2). Thus, a pattern of women and men legislators serving on different committees could be produced by differences in women's and men's preferences, gender stereotyping by legislative leaders, or both.

This paper provides a thorough and systematic analysis of possible gender differences in state legislative committee assignments to ascertain whether gender differences in committee assignments exist, whether these differences are a reflection of women's preferences or gender stereotyping, and whether gender differences have diminished over time. It also examines the correspondence between committee assignments and legislative priorities to assess the extent to which committee assignments are, in fact, an underexplored link in understanding gender differences in policy-related impact.

Previous Research on Gender Differences in Committee Assignments

Previous research provides some evidence that women and men serving in legislative bodies have received somewhat different committee assignments, although gender differences may have lessened over time. Nevertheless, existing research provides an inconclusive response as to whether observed differences were due to gender stereotyping by those making committee assignments or to actual differences in women's and men's preferences.

Some of the earliest research on committee assignments was conducted by Maurice Duverger. In his work on European legislatures, Duverger found that women were much more likely to be found on committees dealing with topics such as public health, youth, family questions, education, welfare, social policy, and labor; they were much less likely to serve on committees dealing with issues like the budget, finance, and economic policy. Moreover, he concluded that women were less often found on the "important" political committees not because of a lack of interest on their part, but rather because of exclusion by men (Duverger 1955, 95–98).

Much of what we know about the committee assignments of women legislators in the United States is based on the experiences of women in Congress, especially the US House. Former congresswomen Shirley Chisholm and Bella Abzug both wrote about the discrimination they experienced and observed in the House. Noting that her first choice was the Education and Labor Committee, her second choice was the Banking and

Currency Committee, her third choice was the Post Office and Civil Service Committee, and her fourth choice was Government Operations, Shirley Chisholm explained in her autobiography her dismay at learning that she had been appointed to the Agricultural Committee. Chisholm initially thought that perhaps as a "black member from one of the country's most deprived city neighborhoods" (Chisholm 1970, 96) she had been assigned to the committee because it had jurisdiction over food stamp programs and migrant labor, but then she learned that her subcommittee assignments were rural development and forestry. When she protested, she was assigned instead to the Veterans' Affairs Committee. Chisholm viewed this assignment as some improvement, observing, "There are a lot more veterans in my district than there are trees" (Chisholm 1970, 101).

Upon arriving in Congress, Bella Abzug let it be known that she wanted to be appointed to the Armed Services Committee. Instead, she was assigned to Government Operations (Abzug 1972, 22–23). In her autobiography Abzug also reported that of the 12 women serving in the House when she came to Congress, 5 were assigned to the Education and Labor Committee while no woman was assigned to Rules, Judiciary, or Armed Services—three of the most powerful committees (Abzug 1972, 26–27).

According to Irwin Gertzog, the situation for women in Congress vis-à-vis committee assignments has improved over time. Although he found a strong pattern of gender differentiation in committee assignments prior to the mid-1960s, this pattern has not been as apparent in recent congresses. He has argued that women "elected to the House since the mid-1960s have been more successful than their predecessors in securing prestigious assignments, and that they have fared better as a group than the males whose House careers began when theirs did" (Gertzog 1995, 139). Although women continue to be appointed to committees dealing with issues traditionally seen as more compatible with women's interests (e.g., aging, health care, education, and environment), they have also secured assignments to committees that were once all-male domains (Gertzog 1995, 133–136).

Similarly, Sally Friedman, in her analysis of the assignments of congressional newcomers to prestige committees, found change and improvement over time. Although gender differences still exist, white women have fared better in recent decades, particularly in obtaining assignments to committees with mid-level prestige (Friedman 1996). Friedman did not examine African American women separately but rather combined them with African American men, finding that by the 1980s African Americans were receiving committee assignments roughly equal in prestige to those received by white men.

Unlike prior research on assignments to congressional committees, Scott Frisch and Sean Kelly were able to compare actual assignments with the committee requests made by members of Congress. Although the committee assignments requested by women did not differ significantly from those requested by their male colleagues, first-term women members were less likely to be appointed to their preferred committees. Frisch and Kelly also found important differences between the parties, with Republican women less likely than Democratic women to get transfers to their preferred committees following their first term (Frisch and Kelly 2003). Although Frisch and Kelly did not directly investigate the reason why women members were less likely to receive appointments to their preferred committees, they did point to discrimination as a possible explanation, suggesting that, in particular, "the Republican committee selection process had a built in gender bias, that is Republican women were unlikely to have a place at the table [on the Republican Committee-on-Committees, which is responsible for assigning members to committees] from which to advocate the interests of women" (Frisch and Kelly 2003, 18).

Finally, despite the very small numbers of women who have served in the US Senate, Laura Arnold and Barbara King analyzed the assignments women senators received from 1949 to 2001. They found that the breadth of women's committee assignments increased with their numbers, and in the 107th Congress, women were represented on 13 of the 16 standing committees in the Senate (Arnold and King 2002, 311). Nevertheless, women were somewhat underrepresented across all congresses on the Senate's four most prestigious committees (Arnold and King 2002).

Of course, this existing research on gender differences in committee assignments in Congress suffers from two major limitations. The first is that none of the studies, except for Arnold and King's study of the Senate, examines any Congress more recent than the 103rd, which was elected in 1992. The second is that the number of cases is very small, not only for the Senate but also for the House. Even after record numbers of women were elected to the US House in 1992, there still were only 47 women members. And the number of women House members in previous congresses never exceeded 29 (CAWP 2006b).

Fortunately, research on state legislators avoids this problem of a small number of cases. Unfortunately, however, less research exists on gender differences in committee assignments among state legislators, and much of it dates back to the 1970s. Similar to the research on Congress, previous research on the committee assignments of state legislators provides incomplete and somewhat inconsistent answers to the questions of how much gender differentiation in committee assignments exists and why it exists.

Based on her interviews with 50 women legislators selected on the basis of competence and diversity to attend a national conference sponsored by the Center for the American Woman and Politics in 1972,[1] Jeanne Kirkpatrick concluded that there was no discrimination against women in initial committee assignments and in most subsequent assignments. Because she did not systematically compare the committee assignments of women with those of men, she could not draw any conclusions about whether women and men served on different kinds of committees. However, Kirkpatrick did see women's committee assignments as largely a reflection of their preferences. She suggested, "Women assigned to education, public health, child welfare, and other 'women's' subjects are usually there because they have requested the assignment" (Kirkpatrick 1974, 126).

Irene Diamond, in her study of women serving in four New England legislatures in 1971, was more reluctant than Kirkpatrick to rule out discrimination as a possible explanation for gender differentiation in committee assignments. Although women did not appear to be excluded from powerful committees such as judiciary and ways and means, Diamond found that they were concentrated on education committees and on health and welfare committees. Although she admitted that she could not tell from her data whether or not discrimination took place, she described how women who were undecided about their committee preferences were often "channeled" toward certain committees, and she discussed the difficulties women faced when their interests did not coincide with their colleagues' expectations (Diamond 1977, 45–46, 89–91).

More recently, Mark Considine and Iva Deutchman, in their study of legislators in six northeastern states in 1988, found women served disproportionately on "women's and children's committees," which they defined as "committees whose primary charge is legislation where women and children are the beneficiaries such as battered women's shelters, rape reform, infant vaccination and the like" (Considine and Deutchman 1994, 861). They did not, however, examine assignments to other types of committees, and they were not able to determine whether women's overrepresentation on women's and children's committees was a reflection of their preferences or gender stereotyping by those responsible for the appointments.

Kathleen Dolan and Lynne Ford did examine assignments to a wider range of committees in their study of female legislators serving in 15 states in 1972, 1982, and 1992. They found evidence of change over time, with women legislators more likely in 1992 to be serving on committees such as finance, appropriations, commerce, and judiciary than in the two previous decades. However, while Dolan and Ford did not make a direct gender comparison, their data clearly show that even in 1992 smaller proportions of women than men served on these "prestige" committees. Meanwhile, larger proportions of women than men served on education and health and welfare committees (Dolan and Ford 1997, 142, 144, 146).

Similarly, in a study of African American state legislators serving in 1991, David Hedge, James Button, and Mary Spear found that men were much more likely to serve on the "money" committees, such as appropriations and revenue, while women were far more likely to serve on committees dealing with education, families, welfare, and health. Despite these differences, however, women were not less satisfied than men with their committee assignments (Hedge, Button, and Spear 1996, 92).

Viewed as a whole, existing research on women's committee assignments is for the most part outdated, based on samples that are either unrepresentative of the national population of officeholders (e.g., studies of state legislators from a few states) or very small in size (e.g., studies of Congress), and inconclusive. Although most studies point to some gender differentiation in committee assignments, the evidence is less clear as to whether differences in committee assignments are the product of women's own preferences or gender stereotyping by party leaders responsible for appointments. The remainder of this chapter attempts to provide more conclusive evidence regarding questions related to gender differentiation in committee assignments by systematically examining gender differences in committee assignments apparent among nationwide samples of women and men serving in state legislatures in both 1988 and 2001.

Description of the Data Sets

In the summer of 1988 under a grant from the Charles H. Revson Foundation, the Center for American Women and Politics (CAWP) conducted a nationwide survey of women and men serving as state legislators. Four samples of legislators were drawn: (1) the population of women state senators (n = 228); (2) a systematic sample of one-half of women state representatives (n = 474); (3) a systematic sample of male state senators, stratified by state and sampled in proportion to the number of women from each state in our sample of women state senators (n = 228); and (4) a systematic sample of male state representatives, stratified by state and sampled in proportion to the number of women from each state in our sample of women state representatives (n = 474).[2]

A telephone interview of approximately one-half hour in duration was attempted with each of the legislators, resulting in the following response rates: 86 percent for female senators, 87 percent for female representatives, 60 percent for male senators, and 73 percent for male representatives. Respondents did not differ significantly from all the legislators selected for any of the four samples in their party affiliation, the one variable for which we have data for all legislators.

In the summer of 2001 under a grant from the Barbara Lee Foundation, CAWP conducted a similar nationwide survey of women and men serving as state legislators, following the same sampling procedure used in 1988 and replicating many of the questions from the 1988 survey to allow for over-time comparisons. Four samples of legislators were drawn: (1) the population of all women state senators ($n = 396$); (2) a systematic sample of one-half of women state representatives ($n = 718$); (3) a systematic sample of male state senators, stratified by state and sampled in proportion to the number of women from each state in our sample of women state senators ($n = 396$); and (4) a systematic sample of male state representatives, stratified by state and sampled in proportion to the number of women from each state in our sample of women state representatives ($n = 718$).

Response rates for the 2001 survey were 56 percent for female senators, 58 percent for female representatives, 40 percent for male senators, 49 percent for male representatives.[3] As in 1988, respondents and nonrespondents in 2001 did not differ significantly in their party affiliation, the one variable for which data were available for all sampled legislators.

Like the US Senate and US House of Representatives, state senates and state houses are very different political institutions. The lower houses of state legislatures vary considerably in size and influence across the states, while state senates tend to be smaller and show less variation. Because of these differences, state senators and state representatives are analyzed separately throughout this chapter.

Gender Difference in State Legislative Committee Assignments

An Overview

Although previous studies of state legislators have generally found some gender differentiation in committee assignments, most of this research was conducted prior to or near the beginning of the contemporary women's movement. That movement, which is now almost four decades old, has had a profound effect in changing public attitudes toward women, and women have made notable progress in moving into nontraditional fields and careers. Perhaps the impact of changing gender relations has been felt inside, as well as outside, legislative institutions. If so, one might expect to find that gender differentiation in committee assignments, like the widow's succession as a route into Congress for women,[4] is largely a phenomenon of the past. Certainly, one would expect that gender differentiation in committee assignments would have decreased over time.

Table 8.1, presenting the proportions of women and men serving on several major types of committees in 2001 and 1988, indicates that these expectations are only partially met. For most types of committees in 2001, gender differences in committee assignments were not apparent. However, a couple of very notable exceptions exist. Moreover, while gender differences in assignments were less apparent in 2001 than in 1988, for two types of committees they were remarkably persistent.

Table 8.1 Gender Differences in Selected Standing Committee Assignments for State Legislators, 1988 and 2001

| | 2001 | | | | | | 1988 | | | | | |
| | Senate | | | House | | | Senate | | | House | | |
Committees	Women (%)	Men (%)	tau$_b$	Women (%)	Men (%)	tau$_b$	Women (%)	Men (%)	tau$_b$	Women (%)	Men (%)	tau$_b$
Appropriations and Budget	19.9	21.3	-.02	19.0	14.9	.05	20.5	19.7	.01	15.6	16.7	-.01
Ways and Means/Finance	26.9	27.3	-.01	18.2	20.2	-.03	26.2	43.8	-.18***	20.0	23.3	-.04
Judiciary	22.2	23.3	-.01	15.8	18.5	-.04	32.8	24.8	.09	18.8	19.0	.00
Rules	7.4	13.3	-.10*	5.4	7.0	-.03	10.8	13.9	-.05	10.0	8.3	.03
Banking, Business, and Commerce	19.0	18.0	.01	12.2	15.9	-.05	28.7	34.3	-.06	24.9	26.4	-.02
Health and Human Services	35.2	18.0	.19***	26.4	14.6	.14***	40.0	10.9	.32***	31.5	13.2	.22***
Education	30.6	22.7	.09*	25.0	18.2	.08**	30.3	19.7	.12**	22.9	16.1	.09**
Government Affairs	24.1	20.0	.05	15.8	17.2	-.02	38.5	29.9	.09*	24.1	25.3	-.01
Environment	16.7	22.7	-.08	13.6	15.9	-.03	20.0	21.9	-.02	17.1	17.2	.00
Transportation	15.3	18.7	-.05	10.6	11.9	-.02	12.8	18.2	-.08	10.5	15.8	-.08**
Agriculture	13.0	14.7	-.02	7.3	9.3	-.04	9.2	14.6	-.08	10.7	9.5	.02
N	216	150		368	302		195	137		410	348	

Notes: Columns may sum to more than 100 percent because most legislators served on more than one committee.

* Significant at .10 level, ** significant at .05 level, *** significant at .001 level.

With only one exception, women in 2001 were not significantly less likely than men in either house of the legislature to be assigned to what have generally been designated as "prestige" committees (e.g., Duverger 1955; Gertzog 1995).[5] These "prestige" committees include: appropriations and budget; ways and means/finance; judiciary; rules; and banking, business, and commerce. The only notable gender difference among "prestige" committees was for rules committees in state senates to which women were somewhat less likely than men to be assigned (Table 8.1). Women also were not significantly more or less likely than men to be appointed to four other types of committees (government affairs, environment, transportation, and agriculture) prevalent in state legislatures across the country (Table 8.1).[6]

Nevertheless, significant gender differences in committee assignments were apparent in 2001 for two types of committees—education and health and human services (Table 8.1). The differences were particularly large for health and human services committees, with women state senators and state representatives almost twice as likely as their male counterparts to serve on these committees. In both state senates (where about one-third of the women served on health and human services committees and almost one-third served on education committees) and state houses (where a quarter of the women served on each of these types of committees), larger proportions of women were serving on health and human services committees and education committees than on any other type of committee. This was not true for men; male legislators were about equally likely or more likely to serve on several other types of committees as they were to serve on education or health and human services committees.

African American women and Latinas were more likely than male legislators of all races and ethnicities to have assignments to education and health and human services committees. They also were as likely, or slightly more likely, than their white female counterparts to serve on these committees. Among African American women in state houses, 26.5 percent served on an education committee while 30.9 percent served on a committee with jurisdiction over health and human services. Consistent with the finding of Luis Fraga et al. in Chapter 9 that Latina legislators are more likely than Latino legislators to serve on committees dealing with education and health and human services, sizable proportions of Latinas in this study also served on these committees. Among Latinas in state houses, 33.3 percent served on education committees and 40.0 percent served on health and human services committees.[7]

When gender differences in committee assignments are examined over time, they appear less prevalent in the early part of the 21st century than they were in 1988. As Table 8.1 shows, women senators in 1988 were more likely than men to serve on government affairs committees and much less likely than men to serve on ways and means/finance committees. Similarly, women representatives in 1988 were less likely than their male counterparts to serve on transportation committees. By 2001, these gender differences were greatly diminished or had disappeared. Even for health and human services committees and education committees where significant gender differences were clearly evident in both years, gender differences in assignments were somewhat less pronounced in 2001 than in 1988.

Factors Affecting Gender Differences in Committee Assignments

Perhaps factors other than gender help to explain the observed differences between women and men in their appointments to health and human services and to education committees. Maybe Republicans, as the more ideologically conservative party, are more likely to mirror traditional gender roles in their committee assignments than are Democrats. Consistent with the pattern of diminished gender differences over time, perhaps gender differentiation is more apparent among veteran legislators than among newcomers to the legislature.

Perhaps gender differentiation varies by level of professionalism. In less professionalized legislatures, legislators work part-time, have few if any staff, and are not well compensated financially, while lawmakers in the most professionalized legislatures work full-time, have large staffs, and are well paid. More professionalized legislative work environments should be characterized less by traditional cultural roles and more by institutionalized and gender-neutral norms and procedures (see Chapter 10 in this volume). If so, gender differences might be less apparent in "professional" than in "citizen" legislatures.

Similarly, gender differences may vary by political culture, being more apparent in states with more traditional cultures. Daniel Elazar has divided states into moralistic, individualistic, and traditionalistic categories based on their political cultures, with governments in moralistic states more oriented toward serving the public interest and governments in individualistic states more concerned with limiting government intervention except when necessary to keep the marketplace functioning effectively (1984). According to Elazar, governments in more traditionalistic states, located primarily in the South, are more focused on maintaining the social order and preserving traditional roles and relationships. As a result, perhaps women legislators in these states more often than women legislators in other states might be found on committees whose substantive focus is an extension of women's traditional roles in society—for example, education committees and health and human services committees.

Finally, gender differentiation in committee assignments might be more evident in states with lower proportions of women legislators. Women may be concentrated on health and human services committees and education committees when their numbers are small, but as their numbers and proportions increase, women legislators may choose or be permitted by leadership to branch out and distribute themselves across a wider range of committees.

Table 8.2 presents data relevant to these hypotheses, focusing on education and health and human services committees where gender differences in committee assignments were statistically significant for both state senators and state representatives. Gender differences are just as apparent among Democrats as among Republicans. In both parties, women were significantly more likely than men to be appointed to health and services committees, and although the differences are not statistically significant except for Democratic state representatives, women in both parties were slightly more likely than men to serve on education committees.

Consistent with the idea that gender differences in committee assignments may be lessening over time, "newcomer" women who had served in the state senate for four years or less were not significantly more likely than newcomer men in state senates to be appointed to health and human services or education committees (Table 8.2). Similarly, newcomer women who had served in state houses for two years or less were not significantly more likely than newcomer men to serve on health and human services committees although they were slightly more likely than newcomer men to be assigned to education committees.

With the exception of appointments to education committees in state houses, gender differences were much more apparent and statistically significant for veteran legislators who had served more than four years in the senate or two years in the house. Nevertheless, the cohort differences between newcomers and veterans do not occur simply because newcomer women were appointed to health and human services and education committees at lower rates than veteran women. Rather, the differences stem, at least in part, from the fact that veteran men (in three of four cases) less often than newcomer men served on these committees. Unfortunately, I cannot determine from these data whether men among veteran legislators were less likely than women to be appointed to health and human services and education committees in the first place or whether, subsequent to their first term in office, they transferred off these committees at higher rates than women.

Contrary to the expectation that gender differences in committee assignments might be more apparent in "citizen" than in "professional" legislatures, gender differences were very small in states with low levels of professionalization and much larger and statistically significant in states with highly professionalized legislatures (Table 8.2). The more professionalized the legislature, the more likely women state representatives were to

Table 8.2   Gender Differences in Health and Human Services and Education Committee Assignments for State Legislators, 2001

| | Member of Health and Human Services Committee | | | | | | Member of Education Committee | | | | | |
| | Senate | | | House | | | Senate | | | House | | |
Committees	Women (%)	Men (%)	tau_b	Women (%)	Men (%)	tau_b	Women (%)	Men (%)	tau_b	Women (%)	Men (%)	tau_b
Party												
Republican	37.5	18.4	.21**	25.4	16.8	.11+	31.9	22.4	.06	25.6	22.5	.03
Democrat	35.3	15.7	.21***	26.9	11.7	.18***	30.1	24.3	.11	23.8	15.6	.10+
Tenure[a]												
Veteran	37.9	16.0	.24***	26.9	10.0	.21***	31.4	19.1	.14*	25.0	18.7	.08
Newcomer	30.3	20.0	.12	25.0	25.3	.00	28.9	29.1	.00	25.0	18.0	.08+
Professionalization of legislature[b]												
Low	—	—	—	17.2	14.3	.04	—	—	—	17.2	13.3	.05
Moderate	—	—	—	25.3	12.5	.16**	—	—	—	25.8	20.6	.06
High	—	—	—	43.2	19.7	.25**	—	—	—	35.1	21.3	.15+
Political culture[c]												
Traditionalistic	47.7	16.7	.33**	30.0	16.7	.16+	40.9	30.6	.11	40.0	33.3	.07
Individualistic	40.0	25.0	.15+	34.8	12.2	.26***	18.6	11.4	.10	25.0	14.6	.13+
Moralistic	25.7	13.5	.15*	18.9	14.4	.06	33.3	24.3	.10	17.8	13.1	.06
Proportion of women												
Less than 20%	36.8	25.8	.12	32.9	18.0	.17*	31.6	25.8	.06	31.4	31.1	.00
20–24.99%	46.2	18.5	.27**	29.9	19.7	.12	28.8	11.1	.20*	27.6	18.4	.11
25–29.99%	22.7	5.6	.24+	21.6	9.2	.17**	27.3	27.8	-.01	20.1	12.6	.10+
30% or more	27.5	9.3	.22**	23.7	13.5	.13	30.4	20.9	.10	23.7	13.5	.13

Notes: + significant at .10 level, * significant at .05 level, ** significant at .01 level, *** significant at .001 level.

a. For state senators, newcomers are defined as those who have served in the state senate for four years or less; for state representatives, newcomers are defined as those who have served in the state house for two years or less.

b. States were categorized as low, moderate, or high in professionalization of the legislature based on the measure developed by Peverill Squire (2000). Squire's measure is a composite that takes into account compensation, number of days in session, and number of staff. The high and low categories include 12 states each, and the remaining 26 are in the moderate category, consistent with the idea in the literature that most states are neither highly professionalized nor citizen legislatures but rather are in the middle between these two extremes. Because senates are more similar across states in their levels of professionalization while lower houses vary greatly, data are only presented for lower houses.

c. States were categorized as traditionalistic, individualistic, or moralistic based on work by Daniel Elazar (1984). There are 16 states in the traditionalistic category, 17 states in the individualistic category, and 17 states in the moralistic category.

have appointments to health and human services and education committees. Moreover, women state representatives in the legislatures that are most professionalized were more than twice as likely as their male colleagues to be serving on health and human services committees and almost twice as likely to be serving on education committees. The lack of gender differentiation in legislatures with low levels of professionalism may be related to the fact that these legislatures have fewer committees on which to serve. Among state representatives in legislatures with low levels of professionalization, only 49.3 percent ($n = 221$) reported that they served on more than one standing committee, while 91.1 percent ($n = 135$) of state representatives in highly professionalized legislatures served on two or more standing committees. Nevertheless, the degree to which gender differences are apparent in the most professionalized legislatures suggests both that women are more likely to be appointed to health and human services and education committees when more committee choices are available and that greater professionalization does not seem to lead to less gender differentiation.

Contrary to the expectation that gender differences might be more apparent in states with more traditionalistic political cultures, Table 8.2 suggests that gender differences are apparent across states with all three types of political culture (moralistic, individualistic, and traditionalistic), with differences for assignments to health and human services committees that are statistically significant for all but one case. Similarly, the proportion of women serving in a legislative chamber is not related in any consistent way to gender differences in committee assignments. Women in legislatures with proportionately fewer women appear to be slightly more likely than women in legislatures with larger proportions of women to serve on health and human services committees and on education committees, but a similar pattern is evident for men. Gender differentiation in committee assignments exists regardless of the proportion of women in the legislature.

Differences in Preferences or Gender Stereotyping?

Responses to three questions were examined to assess whether gender differentiation in committee assignments is due primarily to differences in the preferences of women and men legislators or to gender stereotyping by legislative leaders who may assign women to committees that are counter to women's own preferences. First, legislators were asked if they were serving on any standing committee to which they initially did not want to be assigned. Second, legislators were asked if there was a standing committee on which they would like to serve but to which they had not been appointed. Finally, legislators were asked to specify which of their assigned committees dealt with legislation that interested them most.

Dissatisfaction with Committee Assignments

As Table 8.3 demonstrates, substantial proportions, about one-third, of legislators were serving on a standing committee to which they initially did not want to be assigned. However, women legislators were not significantly more likely than their male counterparts to be dissatisfied with their committee assignments, and while the data are not shown, this was true for legislators within both parties as well as for legislators in general. Although women representatives who were newcomers were a little more likely than their newcomer male colleagues to be serving on a committee they disliked, women senators who were newcomers were slightly less likely than their male counterparts to express dissatisfaction (Table 8.3).

These findings of similarity between women and men in their level of dissatisfaction with committee assignments in 2001 represent quite a change from 1988 when sizable gender differences were apparent among all senators, newcomers and veterans alike, as well as among newcomers in the state house. Contrary to the pattern for 2001, significant gender differences were evident among state senators in 1988, with 41.0 percent of women but only 26.3 percent of male senators (tau$_b$ = .15, p < .01) dissatisfied with at least one committee assignment. Women state representatives in 1988, like women state representatives in 2001, were not more likely than their male counterparts to be dissatisfied with their committee assignments. Nevertheless, there were gender differences among newcomers to state houses; 37.6 percent of women who had served in the state house for two years or less, compared with 17.5 percent of newcomer men (tau$_b$ = .22, p < .01), were serving on a standing committee to which they initially did not want to be assigned.

Table 8.3 Gender Differences in Dissatisfaction with Committee Assignments for State Legislators, 2001

	Senate			House		
	Women (%)	Men (%)	tau$_b$	Women (%)	Men (%)	tau$_b$
Dissatisfied with a committee assignment						
All legislators	37.9	33.3	.05	35.0	32.6	.03
Newcomers	38.2	43.6	−.06	45.6	38.2	.08
Desires a different committee						
All legislators	49.5	44.4	.05	51.8	50.0	.02
Newcomers	70.1	71.4	−.01	67.6	64.5	.03

Note: None of the differences between women and men were statistically significant.

While overall gender differences in dissatisfaction with committee assignments seem to have dissipated between 1988 and 2001, nevertheless gender differences in dissatisfaction were apparent for legislators who served on some specific types of committees in 2001 (Table 8.4). Among state senators, women who served on several "prestige" committees were more likely than the men on those committees—and significantly more likely in the case of appropriations and budget, ways and means/finance, judiciary, and rules committees—to report that they initially had not wanted to be appointed to these committees. Clearly, a number of women senators who did not request appointments to the so-called prestige committees were assigned to them anyway. Because women in 2001 constituted only 20.1 percent of all state senators and far less than this national average in a number of states, it may well be that leaders in some state senates had chosen to spread the women around to make sure that prestige committees had some female representation.

The pattern is more mixed for state representatives and reversed in some instances, with slightly larger proportions of men than women dissatisfied initially with appointments to several prestige committees (appropriations and budget, judiciary, rules). Women state representatives serving on banking, business, and commerce committees were, however, significantly more likely than men to express dissatisfaction with their appointments to these committees.

In addition to prestige committees, Table 8.4 presents data for the two committees, health and human services and education, on which women were significantly more likely than men to be serving (Table 8.1). As Table 8.4 shows, satisfaction levels on education committees were high; very few

Table 8.4   Gender Differences in Proportions of State Legislators on Various Committees Who Initially Did Not Want to Be Assigned to Those Committees, 2001

	Senate			House		
	Women (%)	Men (%)	tau$_b$	Women (%)	Men (%)	tau$_b$
Appropriations and Budget	9.3	0.0	.21**	5.7	13.3	−.13
Ways and Means/Finance	10.3	2.4	.15*	11.9	6.6	.06
Judiciary	25.0	8.6	.21**	8.6	16.1	−.11
Rules	25.0	5.0	.29*	5.0	14.3	−.16
Banking, Business, and Commerce	17.1	14.8	.03	17.8	6.3	.18*
Health and Human Services	10.5	18.5	−.11	12.4	25.0	−.16*
Education	1.5	5.9	−.12	1.1	1.8	−.03

Note: * significant at .10 level, ** significant at .05 level.

men or women on those committees initially had not wanted to be appointed to an education committee. Dissatisfaction was more evident among legislators on health and human services committees. Gender differences were more apparent here as well, with women less likely than men (and significantly so in state houses) to have been initially dissatisfied with their appointments to health and human services committees.

These findings for education and health and human services committees are evidence that legislative leaders have not engaged in widespread gender stereotyping; they do not appear to have assigned women disproportionately against their preferences to these committees. Although large proportions of women serve on health and human services and education committees, the vast majority of women committee members seem content with their appointments.

Preferences for Other Committees

Findings regarding legislators' preferences to serve on committees other than those on which they serve add further evidence that women legislators have stronger preferences than men for health and human services and education committees. As Table 8.3 demonstrates, about half of all legislators and even higher proportions of newcomers in both chambers expressed a desire to be appointed to a standing committee other than the committees on which they served. Nevertheless, women legislators were not significantly more likely than men to want an appointment to a different standing committee. This was true for newcomers among legislators as well as for legislators overall.[8]

Despite the similarity between women and men in their levels of desire to serve on a committee to which they had not been appointed, clear gender differences were apparent among those legislators who desired an appointment to a different committee. (See Table 8.5.) Among state senators, men were significantly more likely than women to desire appointment to committees focusing on banking, business, and commerce. In contrast, women senators were significantly more likely than male senators to want to be appointed to health and human services committees. While the difference was not statistically significant, women senators also showed a stronger preference than men for appointment to education committees, with one of every five women wanting to serve on an education committee. The three most desired committees among women senators were ways and means/finance, education, and health and human services (with appropriations a close fourth). In contrast, for male senators the three most desired committees were ways and means/finance; appropriations and budget; and banking, business, and commerce. Thus, while men most often desired the

Table 8.5   Gender Differences in Preferences for State Legislators Who Wanted to Be
Assigned to a Committee on Which They Did Not Serve, 2001

	Senate			House		
	Women (%)	Men (%)	tau$_b$	Women (%)	Men (%)	tau$_b$
Appropriations and Budget	13.1	20.6	.10	17.9	24.3	.08
Ways and Means/Finance	22.4	29.4	−.07	18.9	18.4	.01
Judiciary	8.4	10.3	−.03	11.6	6.6	.09$^+$
Rules	2.8	1.5	.04	3.2	2.0	.04
Banking, Business, and Commerce	6.5	17.6	−.17*	8.4	13.2	.08
Health and Human Services	14.0	5.9	.13$^+$	14.2	3.3	.19***
Education	21.5	13.2	.10	23.7	13.8	.12*
N	107	68		190	152	

Note: + significant at .10 level, * significant at .05 level, ** significant at .01 level, *** significant at .001 level.

"money" committees, women's strongest preferences were a mix of "money" committees and the "human interest" committees of education and health and human services.

This pattern of women showing more interest in serving on education and health and human services committees, apparent among senators, also is evident among state representatives (Table 8.5). Men among state representatives who desired assignment to a different committee were more likely than women to want an appointment to an appropriations and budget committee or to a banking, business, and commerce committee although these gender differences were not statistically significant. In contrast, women representatives were somewhat more likely to desire appointments to judiciary committees, and like women in the senate, they were significantly more likely than their male counterparts to want appointments to education committees and health and human services committees. The four most desired committees among male representatives were appropriations and budget; ways and means/finance; education; and banking, business, and commerce. Women state representatives shared with men a high level of interest in appointments to education, ways and means/finance, and appropriations and budget committees. But in contrast to men who preferred banking, business, and commerce committees, the other committee most highly desired by women representatives was health and human services. In contrast, health and human services was one of the least desired committee types among male state representatives.

Interest in the Work of the Committee

Legislators with appointments to multiple committees were asked to identify the one committee that dealt with legislation of greatest interest to them. For the most part, responses to this question provide further evidence of women's preference for health and human services and education committees.

For legislators serving on education committees, women senators were more likely than their male counterparts (65.0% compared to 51.6%) to say that the education committee was the committee whose legislation interested them most; surprisingly, however, these figures were virtually reversed among state representatives where women serving on education committees were less likely than men (51.3% compared to 65.3%) to point to their work on an education committee as most interesting.

For legislators serving on health and human services committees, the pattern was more consistent across the two chambers. Among both state senators (45.1% compared to 24.0%) and state representatives (55.7% compared to 47.2%), women more often than men reported that health and human services was the committee whose legislation interested them most.

Relationship Between Committee Membership and Top Legislative Priority

As one might expect, there is a relationship between membership on various committees and the legislation to which senators and representatives devote their most serious attention. We asked each legislator to describe the one bill that had been her or his personal top priority during the current session. We then coded legislators' descriptions of their top priority bills into 18 broad, content-based categories.

Table 8.6 presents the proportions of legislators serving on education committees, legislators serving on health and human services committees, and legislators in general whose top priority bills fell into four relevant categories (women's issues, the welfare of families and children, health care, and education). First, for those legislators serving on education committees, their strong interest in legislation focusing on education is clearly apparent. Large proportions of women and men in both chambers who served on education committees—and much larger proportions than for legislators overall—reported an education bill as their top legislative priority for the current session. Women legislators on education committees were, however, not more likely than male legislators on these committees to have a top priority bill that focused on education.

The subject matter of health and human services committees is more

Table 8.6 Focus of Top Priority Bills for State Legislators on Education and Health and Human Services Committees, 2001

Priority bill's focus	On Education Committee				On Health and Human Services Committee				All Legislators			
	Senate		House		Senate		House		Senate		House	
	Women (%)	Men (%)	Women (%)	Men (%)	Women (%)	Men (%)	Women (%)	Men (%)	Women (%)	Men (%)	Women (%)	Men (%)
Women's issues	1.5	—	9.0	3.9	9.3	—	15.8	7.1	4.7	2.7	11.0	4.1
Welfare of family and children	12.3	9.1	12.4	9.8	18.7	11.5	15.8	9.5	8.5	5.5	8.4	5.1
Health care	9.2	3.0	9.0	2.0	16.0	19.2	18.9	2.4	11.3	8.9	10.7	6.2
Education	40.0	48.5	33.7	33.3	10.7	11.5	8.4	11.9	17.4	18.5	18.0	15.8

diffuse than that of education committees, a fact seemingly apparent in the findings presented in Table 8.6. Women legislators on health and human services committees in both chambers were more likely than all women legislators to have bills focusing on health care as their top priority legislation. However, they also were more likely than women legislators generally to give top priority to bills dealing with women's issues and with the welfare of families and children—issue areas that, for the most part, would seem to fit under the general rubric of "human services."[9] Women state representatives on health and human services committees were more likely than their male counterparts to have top priority bills in all three issue areas—health care, women's issues, and the welfare of families and children—while women state senators on health and human services gave greater priority than their male counterparts to legislation on women's issues and the welfare of families and children, but not to legislation on health care.

Discussion and Conclusions

Two major patterns and sets of conclusions emerge from the analysis presented in this chapter. The first pattern is one of similarity and convergence in the committee assignments of women and men serving in state legislatures. Fewer gender differences in committee assignments were apparent in 2001 than in 1988, and even for health and human services committees and education committees where gender differences continued to be evident in 2001, differences were less pronounced than in 1988. With the one exception of rules committees in state senates, women in 2001 were just as likely as men to receive appointments to the so-called prestige committees. And contrary to the findings for 1988, women state legislators in 2001 were not more dissatisfied overall with their committee assignments than were their male colleagues. Nor were women legislators in 2001 more likely than their male counterparts to desire an appointment to a committee other than the committees on which they served. Moreover, women and men who were newcomers to state senates and state houses were remarkably similar in their levels of satisfaction with their committee assignments and their desire to be assigned to a committee other than those on which they served.

The analysis in this chapter offers no evidence that legislative leaders in the early 21st century are engaging in gender stereotyping and assigning women to committees that deal with subject matter in which women have traditionally been considered to have special expertise. In fact, to the extent that legislative leaders are assigning women to committees contrary to women's preferences, they seem to be assigning them to prestige committees, perhaps in an attempt to insure that these committees have some female representation.

However, despite all the evidence for similarity and convergence in the committee assignments of women and men, some very critical gender differences are apparent. Women continue to be significantly more likely than men to serve on two types of committees—education committees and health and human services committees. The relative overrepresentation of women on education and health and human services committees constitutes the second major pattern of findings to emerge from the analysis in this chapter.

Women seem largely to serve on these committees by choice. Few women on education committees and notably fewer women than men on health and human services committees reported that they were initially dissatisfied with their appointments. Moreover, proportionately more women than men not serving on education and health and human services committees expressed a desire to be appointed to these committees. Also, sizable proportions of women serving on these committees reported that the work of the committee interested them more than the work of other committees on which they served, and with the exception of state representatives on education committees, women were more likely than men to say this.

The women who served on education committees much more often than women legislators overall gave priority to legislation that focused on education, and women legislators who served on health and human services committees more often than women legislators generally (as well as more often than their male counterparts on health and human services committees) had as their top legislative priority a bill that focused on health care, the welfare of children and families, or women's issues.

In sum, the findings of this analysis show that women legislators are more likely than men to serve on education and health and human services committees. They want to be on these committees. And once on these committees, they work on legislation relevant to the substantive focus of these committees. This cluster of findings suggests that women legislators are, in fact, using their committee appointments as a means to pursue their interests in education and in health care and human services. And the end result is that women legislators give more attention and priority to these issues than their male colleagues do. It is because of the role that committees play in facilitating the expression of these gender-related interests that committee assignments constitute one of the underexplored links in our understanding of gender differences in policy-related impact.

Notes

1. In the 1990s, the Center for the American Woman and Politics changed its name to the Center for American Women and Politics.
2. The men were sampled in this manner to insure that we actually compared

women and men who served in similar political circumstances and not women and men from states with very different political and legislative environments.

3. There are a number of possible reasons for the lower response rates in 2001 than in 1988, including differences in the survey research firms that administered the study, the greater numbers of legislatures in session while we were conducting the survey in 2001, the increased proliferation of voice mail and answering machines making it more difficult to reach respondents, the increase in telemarketing, and the increased rate of turnover in legislatures with fewer legislators consequently aware of the Eagleton Institute of Politics (the parent organization of CAWP and whom respondents were told was conducting the study). However, the major factor leading to lower response rates in 2001 seems to have been the sheer proliferation of surveys of legislators not only by academics, but also by other entities and organizations. Legislators reported that they were asked to participate in several other surveys concurrently with ours.

4. Many of the women who served in Congress prior to the 1970s first gained entry when they were appointed or elected to a seat held by a husband who had died while serving in office.

5. At the state legislative level, of course, the importance and function of these committees vary from state to state.

6. Committee types and titles vary greatly from one state to another, and there were a number of types of committees less commonly found in state legislatures that are not included in Table 8.1. Although results are not presented, there were no significant gender differences in appointments to these less prevalent committee types.

7. Although our main sample included only one-half of all state representatives nationally, we attempted to administer our survey to all women of color who were not included in our initial sample (i.e., the entire population of women of color in state houses) so that we could have sufficient cases for analysis. We were able to complete interviews with 68 (50.0%) of the 136 African American women serving nationally in the lower houses of state legislatures as well as with 15 (40.5%) of the 37 Latina representatives. The statistics reported here are based on the responses of the 68 African American women and 15 Latina representatives who participated in our study. Statistics are not presented for women of color among state senators because of the small number of cases. I also do not compare African American women and Latinas with men in their racial and ethnic groups because of the small number of African American and Latino men in our sample of male state representatives.

8. Although the data are not shown, there were slight partisan differences at the state house level, with Democratic women and men more likely than Republican women and men, respectively, to desire an appointment to a different committee.

9. Issues such as abortion and women's health were included in the women's issues category even though they could also have been classified as health-care issues.

9

Representing Gender *and* Ethnicity: Strategic Intersectionality

LUIS RICARDO FRAGA, VALERIE MARTINEZ-EBERS,
LINDA LOPEZ, AND RICARDO RAMÍREZ

SINCE THE PASSAGE of the Voting Rights Act in 1965, the number of elected officials of color has increased at all levels of government. At present it is estimated that there are over 8,800 African Americans serving in all levels of government, and the number of Latinos is just over 5,000. Since the 1990s, significant increases also have occurred in the number of women of color elected to office. This has especially been the case for Latinos. For example, Table 9.1 (p. 165) displays the gendered patterns of Latino representation in state legislatures in 2004. In that year there were a total of 222 Latino and Latina state legislators serving across the United States. A full 62 of these, 27.9 percent, were Latinas.

In this chapter, we examine whether Latinas elected to state legislatures, relative to their coethnic male counterparts, are more effective advocates for working-class communities of color. Building upon the literature on political incorporation, gender politics, and ethnic politics, we hypothesize that Latina legislators are positioned to be the most effective advocates on behalf of working-class communities of color. We expect this to be the case for three primary reasons:

1. As women, Latina legislators have a propensity to be more focused on the substance of policy of particular interest to working-class communities. Among the issue areas that are of greatest interest to them are education, health care, and jobs. We refer to this as the *substantive policy focus*.
2. As ethnic women, their multiple identities better position them to build cross-group coalitions that are more likely to attain threshold levels of legislative support. We refer to this as the *multiple identity advantage*.

3. As women, they have more opportunities to "soften" their ethnicity by posturing themselves as women, mothers, and community advocates in ways that limit race-based white backlash. We refer to this as the *gender inclusive advantage*.

We argue that the combination of the substantive policy focus, the multiple identity advantage, and the gender inclusive advantage results in *strategic intersectionality*. Latina elected officials are uniquely positioned to leverage the intersectionality of their ethnicity and gender in ways that are of strategic benefit in the legislative process. As such, they are positioned to be the most effective long-term advocates on behalf of working-class communities of color, thus facilitating their political incorporation in US society.

Political Incorporation, Gender, and Ethnicity in Legislatures

Political incorporation can be defined as "the extent to which self-identified group interests are articulated, represented, and met in public policy making" (Fraga and Ramírez 2003, 304). These authors suggest that political incorporation is most comprehensively understood as occurring along three dimensions: electoral influence, representation, and policy benefit.[1] It is important to note that gains can occur along one dimension without necessarily accruing along the other two. They suggest that considerable analytical purchase is gained by understanding the simultaneous clustering of the experiences of historically underrepresented groups along each of these dimensions. Most significantly, in this conceptual framework the end result of the policy process, policy benefit, is placed as a coequal to participation and representation in determining how fully a group is incorporated into American politics.

This linkage of electoral influence, representation, and policy benefit is consistent with Jane Mansbridge's (1999, 2003) arguments regarding the potential benefits to historically underrepresented groups and to the larger political system of effective mechanisms for increasing the voice of distinct interest communities in the larger political process. Political systems that enhance simultaneous gains in electoral influence, representation, and policy benefit are likely to be more robust in the quality of political deliberation, broadening the benefits of social policy to marginalized groups, and even contributing to enhanced legitimacy of the system to members of both majority and minority groups (Mansbridge 1999).

This characterization of political incorporation is useful for understanding some of the most important empirical findings regarding the role of women and racial/ethnic minority elected officials in affecting the US political process. While there is some debate in the literature, there is strong support through consistent empirical findings that the presence of women and racial and ethnic minorities brings distinct perspectives, policy interests, and commitments to the legislative process. However, as noted by Anne Marie Cammisa and Beth Reingold, the vast majority of this research does "not consider how race and gender might interact to distinguish the experiences and activities of black women, white women, black men, and white men" (2004, 206). Our aim is to fill this gap in the literature by focusing precisely on the possible leverage that this interaction or intersection of race/ethnicity and gender may provide Latina state legislators.

Women in Legislatures

Research conducted on legislative women in the 1970s, when many women were first elected to office in sizable numbers, found that they spent more time on constituency service than men, paid more attention to the details of public policy, and were more "problem solvers" than "brokers" (Diamond 1977; Thomas 1994). Lyn Kathlene (1989) found that distinct socialization processes led women to see themselves more as part of communities and also see issues embedded within larger sets of causal relationships, than did men. Susan Carroll (1991) found that women were three times more likely than men to list women-oriented policies among a top concern. Reingold found that women legislators were more likely than their male counterparts to see themselves as representatives of women and to identify women as an important "constituency group" (1992, 509). Sue Thomas's original research on the policy priorities of women legislators in the 1980s found that unlike their male counterparts the "policy priorities" of women were more focused on "women, and children and families" (1994, 79). Interestingly, a number of these authors find variation across states, with some women in some states more likely to articulate interests distinct from those of male legislators. Michele Swers's study of women members in the 103rd and 104th Congress found that among both Democrats and Republicans, women were "more committed to the pursuit of women's interests," especially in the arena of bill sponsorship (2002, 127).

It is the case, however, that a number of studies have found that despite the increased presence of women in state legislatures and despite the growing diversity of strategies that they pursue, there can be major limits to the substantive policy gains that they are able to achieve. Kathlene finds that as women become an increasingly significant percentage of a legislative body, "men [can] become more verbally aggressive and controlling of the [legislative] hearing" to the disadvantage of women (1994, 560). Sally Kenney argues that despite the increases in the numbers of women in major institutions and organizations of power in US society, masculine domination can still be defended, gender can be "reinscribed," and "institutions [can] try to contain progressive change" (1996, 461). Cindy Simon Rosenthal's study of state legislators revealed that there is little "adaptation (and indeed some resistance) on the part of male [legislative committee] chairs when women hold greater institutional power" (2000, 41). However, Alana Jeydel and Andrew Taylor find that women members of the 103rd to 105th House were not any less able to get legislation passed than their male counterparts (2003). Legislative effectiveness, they argue, was the product of "seniority, preferences, and membership in important House institutions" for both groups (2003, 19). Sue Thomas and Susan Welch argue that two factors that lead to women having success in state legislatures are increasing numbers and increasing cohesion such as through the establishment of a women's caucus, allowing them to work together on consensual goals (2001).

Race, Ethnicity, and Gender in Legislatures

Previous research has examined the policy experiences and successes of legislators of color as well as the extent to which the presence of these legislators impacts the substantive representation of minorities. David Hedge, James Button, and Mary Spear found that African American legislators who were male had greater seniority; represented more affluent, predominantly white districts; were outside the Deep South; and reported better race relations in their states generally viewed their "black legislative experience more positively" (1996, 82). Kerry Haynie (2001) finds that African American state legislators are not perceived by their white colleagues as being particularly influential in the legislative process, even when they possess characteristics such as seniority, powerful committee appointments, and policy expertise. He states, "These findings indicate that African American representatives are not viewed by their colleagues as equal participants in the deliberation and debate over matters of public policy" (2001, 104). Chris Owens (2005) and Robert Preuhs (2006) both consider the effects of black legislators in terms of policy influence and reach similar conclusions. Black legislators do influence state policy priorities, measured by the percentage of the state's total budget devoted to a policy area that is important to both black legislators and constituents, as the percent of black legislators increases (Owens 2005). It is also the case that beyond presence, "a highly racialized context and party control condition the nature and degree of policy influence" (Preuhs 2006, 585).

The research conducted on African American women legislators reaches similar conclusions regarding their limited influence in being major players in the legislative process. Mary Hawkesworth finds that "racing-gendering" to the disadvantage of congresswomen of color contributed to the enactment of policies, such as the 1996 "Welfare Reform Act," that were perceived to disserve the interests of working-class communities of color (2003, 548). At the state level, Edith Barrett (1995) looked at the policy priorities of African American women state legislators and found that, when compared to their African American male counterparts and to white female legislators, they had a clear and consistent consensus on policy issues of greatest importance. The issues were "education, health care, economic development, and employment" (1995, 223). Marsha Darling's analysis of African American female state legislators reveals that despite a high degree of unity on the policy issues of greatest importance to African Americans, they report confronting the dual challenges of "white racism" and "paternalism" that can serve as barriers to the attainment of their legislative goals (1998, 162). Kathleen Bratton and Haynie (1999) found that women were as likely to get legislation passed as men, but that African American women legislators were significantly less likely to do so. Wendy Smooth found that there was considerable variation in the policy influence of African American female state legislators (2001). She concludes, nonetheless, that their influence was limited to "specific policy areas in which they have developed some expertise," and "few white legislators consider any African American legislators as influential" (2001, 284).[2] What each of these studies finds is that the intersectionality of race and gender most often serves as a dual disadvantage to African American female state legislators in the process of public policymaking.

Even fewer studies have examined Latina and Latino state legislators. Tatcho Mindiola and Armando Gutierrez (1988) studied legislation introduced by Chicano legislators in the 1981 legislative session in Texas. They found that Chicano legislators were not as successful as their Anglo counterparts in getting legislation enacted. Moreover, most of the legislation introduced by these members did not address issues specific to racial and ethnic groups, and the more the legislation had "major relevance for minorities" or "address[ed] a Chicano concern," the less likely it was to ever be enacted (1988, 357). Arturo Vega (1997) provides a longitudinal analysis of the legislative focus and success of women, African American, and Hispanic legislators in the Texas legislature for the period 1975 to 1995. He finds that female legislators introduced gender-related bills at a rate 2.2 times higher than one would expect given their numbers in the legislature. Interestingly, he also finds that there were no significant differences in the propensity of male and female Hispanic legislators to introduce Hispanic-related legislation; there were also no such differences between African American male and female legislators in introducing African American–related legislation. Lastly, he finds that increases in the number of both women and African American state legislators led to each group having greater success in getting group-related legislation enacted. This, however, was not the case for Hispanics.

Most recently, Bratton considers the patterns of sponsorship and passage of "Latino interest" bills. She finds that in all of the states she considers, except Florida, Latino legislators "sponsor more measures focusing on Latino interests than do their non-Latino colleagues" (2006, 1147). While her model is able to detect the effects of legislator gender, race, and other constituency characteristics, she does not address the potential for the intersection of race/ethnicity and gender to have a distinct influence separate from that of gender or ethnicity alone.

Conceptualizing Strategic Intersectionality

We hypothesize that it is possible for Latina legislators to utilize their intersectionality in ways that are likely to provide them with strategic advantages in the process of public policy making. We in no way mean to minimize the extent to which Latinas can experience the double disadvantage that several authors above noted for African American women. As Aída Hurtado states, women of color, including Latinas, can experience "race, class, and gender subordination . . . simultaneously . . . not only by members of their own group but also by whites of both genders" (1996, 7; see also Crenshaw 1989, 1997). What we are suggesting, however, is that the intersection of gender and ethnicity might position Latina legislators to have a richer set of strategic options relative to Latino male legislators, from which to choose as they negotiate the larger policymaking process and try to serve the multiplicity of constituencies that depend upon them for representation.

As stated above, women representatives tend to bring distinct policy interests to agenda-setting in legislatures. African American female representatives have an even greater focus on issues of interest than do African American men. Do Latina legislators, relative to Latino men, replicate the same intense focus on an identifiable set of issues? If so, what are they? If they do, this issue focus sets parameters that they can use to devise strategies to maximize policy benefit. For example, do the committee choices and leadership positions held by Latina legislators match the policy foci that they identify? In sum, relative to Latino male legislators, do Latina legislators have a clearer and more consistent *substantive policy focus*?

The multiple identities at the heart of intersectionality can serve as a disadvantage by allowing multiple targeting of female legislators of color (as both women and members of ethnic and racial groups) by those who choose to restrict their gains in the policymaking process and the resulting institutional context within which Latina legislators work. However, the key to legislative success in the policymaking process is the building of minimum winning coalitions, often a bare majority on subcommittees, committees, and on the floor. Might not the multiple identities of Latinas, relative to the more narrow range of identities of Latino men, provide Latina legislators with a greater set of potential coalition partners to support legislation that they prefer? It seems possible that Latinas can speak as authentic representatives to their fellow partisans, women, ethnic and racial minorities, mothers, community leaders, and policy experts. Are Latina legislators asked for their advice by a broader set of potential coalition partners than are Latino men? Do Latinas attempt to build more cross-group coalitions among their fellow legislators than do Latino men? We refer to this potential resource grounded in the multiple identities that Latinas have as the *multiple identity advantage*.

Lastly, we hypothesize that the multiple identities noted above not only provide a richer set of options to build cross-group coalitions for Latina legislators relative to Latino men, but also provide them with more choices as to how they position themselves on specific issues. How similarly do Latino and Latina representatives understand their primary constituencies and related representational duties? When confronted with choices where the women's caucus has taken a position on an issue in opposition to the position of the Latino caucus, do Latina and Latino representatives resolve this conflict in the same way? In having a greater set of choices from which to position themselves on an issue, do Latina representatives have a greater capacity to soften the extent to which they are seen as primarily ethnic representatives? If they do, can this lead to a limiting of white backlash by fellow legislators, increasing the chances that a specific legislative proposal will be enacted? We refer to this greater scope of posturing on the part of Latina representatives as the *gender inclusive advantage*.

Taken together, we refer to the three above-described dimensions of the unique position that Latina legislators may occupy, relative to Latino males, as *strategic intersectionality*. We define strategic intersectionality as the distinct, relative to Latino men, set of interests, resources, and strategies available to Latina elected officials to influence legislative policymaking.

The National Latina/o State Legislator Survey

We address the above questions and related hypotheses regarding strategic intersectionality with data from a survey of Latina and Latino state legislators who served in the 2004 legislative year. The survey was entitled the National Latina/o State Legislator Survey (NLSLS) and was cosponsored by the National Association of Latino Elected and Appointed Officials (NALEO). A list of Latinas and Latinos who served in state legislatures was secured from NALEO. This list was further verified with a list of Latino legislators from the National Conference of State Legislators (NCSL). State legislative websites were also reviewed to verify the status of each legislator. Additionally, the office of each legislator was called to verify that the member served during 2004 and that they self-identified as a Latina/o. Offices were also asked with which Latino subgroup the respondent most identified. From June 2004 through January 2005, legislators were called to schedule an appointment to conduct the interview. As many as eight phone calls were made to schedule interviews. All interviews were conducted during this time period. All interviews were conducted with the actual legislator. Legislators were told that their comments would never be attributed to them. Each legislator was given the opportunity to refuse to answer any question she or he wished.

A total of 222 Latina and Latino legislators were identified as having served in 2004: 62 Latinas (27.9% of all Latina and Latino legislators) and 160 Latino men (71.6%). Of these, 35 Latina legislators were interviewed, producing a response rate of 56.5 percent; 88 Latino male legislators were interviewed for a response rate of 55.4 percent. These response rates are well above the norm in published literature on state legislators. At least one legislator was interviewed from 27 of the 32 states in which Latinas and Latinos served. See Table 9.1 for the distribution of Latina and Latino legislators who served and who were interviewed.

The interview consisted of a total of 55 questions in four distinct groupings:

- Involvement in the legislature
- Legislative experiences in 2004
- Legislative environment in the state
- Background demographics

Interview responses were coded and analyzed using the computer program SPSS.

Findings

Substantive Policy Focus

Dissimilar to one of the most consistent conclusions in much research on women and politics, we find that there are not meaningful differences in the policy priorities of Latina and Latino legislators. As revealed in Table 9.2, both groups identify education as the most important issue of concern to them; 54.8 percent of Latina legislators rated education as their top priority as compared to 52.4 percent of Latino legislators. The issue area that received the second highest percentage of first-place rankings was health

Table 9.1 Latina/o State Legislators, NLSLS Responses, 2004

	Latinas	Latinas Interviewed	Latinos	Latinos Interviewed	Totals	Interview Totals
Arizona	4	3	11	5	15	8
California	12	6	15	4	27	10
Colorado	2	1	5	4	7	5
Connecticut	4	1	2	0	6	1
Delaware	0	0	1	0	1	0
Florida	1	1	16	9	17	10
Georgia	0	0	3	2	3	2
Hawaii	1	0	0	0	1	0
Idaho	0	0	1	0	1	0
Illinois	5	3	6	3	11	6
Indiana	0	0	1	1	1	1
Kansas	0	0	2	1	2	1
Maryland	1	1	3	1	4	2
Massachusetts	1	0	3	1	4	1
Michigan	0	0	1	1	1	1
Minnesota	0	0	1	1	1	1
Nebraska	0	0	1	1	1	1
Nevada	1	0	1	1	2	1
New Hampshire	0	0	1	1	1	1
New Jersey	2	0	3	1	5	1
New Mexico	13	10	31	24	44	34
New York	2	1	12	7	14	8
North Carolina	0	0	2	0	2	0
Oregon	0	0	2	2	2	2
Pennsylvania	0	0	1	1	1	1
Rhode Island	1	1	2	0	3	1
South Carolina	1	1	0	0	1	1
Tennessee	1	1	0	0	1	1
Texas	8	4	30	16	38	20
Washington	2	1	1	0	3	1
Wisconsin	0	0	1	0	1	0
Wyoming	0	0	1	1	1	1
Total	62	35	160	88	222	123

care; 19.4 percent of Latinas rated it first, as did 19.5 percent of Latino men. The only statistically significant difference between Latinas and Latino men was on the priority of the budget. No Latina legislators listed the state budget as their number one policy priority, yet 7.3 percent of Latino men did.

In the fashion similar to Barrett (1995), we grouped the top three issues together to see if an overall pattern of top priorities and resulting substantive policy focus might exist to a noticeably greater extent for Latina legislators as compared to Latino men. (See Table 9.2, columns 3 and 4.) There is a statistically significant difference in only one issue area. Economic development and jobs comprise 16.7 percent of responses from Latino legislators, whereas this category only received 2.9 percent of responses from

Table 9.2   Most Important and Top Three Policy Issues Among Latina/o Legislators (percentage)

	Most Important Issue		Top Three Issues	
Policy Issue	Latinas	Latinos	Latinas	Latinos
Education	54.8	52.4	34.5	31.3
Health care	19.4	19.5	25.0	21.7
Economic development/jobs	3.2	4.9	2.9	16.7*
Taxes	3.2	3.7	1.1	5.0
Environment	9.7	2.4	8.3	3.7
Family/children assistance	3.2	3.7	8.3	3.3
Budget	0.0	7.3*	1.1	3.7
Crime/criminal justice	3.2	2.9	4.7	5.0
Housing	0.0	0.0	2.3	1.6
Other issues	3.2	3.2	5.9	7.5
Total	99.9	100.0	94.1	99.5
N	31	82	84	239

Notes: Question posed to legislators: Numerous public policy issues are of great concern to you as a legislator. Please rank the three issues that are of greatest concern to you. Which issue is: most important, second most important, third most important?
    * $p \leq .05$, two-tailed test of gender differences.

Latina legislators. This difference, however, is overshadowed by the similarity among Latina and Latino legislators. Education was mentioned most often by Latina legislators; these responses comprised 34.5 percent of the responses to the top three issues of concern. Education comprised 31.3 percent of the top three responses from Latino men. Both Latinas and Latinos also had health care as their second largest grouping among the top three responses. Health care comprised 25.0 percent of the responses of Latinas and 21.7 percent of the responses of Latino legislators. These data reveal that a greater substantive policy focus does not characterize the policy priorities of Latina legislators as compared to those of Latino men. There are more similarities in their priorities than there are differences.

We also examined differences in policy priorities as measured by committee membership. (See Table 9.3.) Committee membership has often been a primary way in which legislators position themselves to better address their policy priorities. The only difference between Latina and Latino legislators that attains statistical significance appears in the propensity to serve on the education committee. Almost one-quarter, 24.2 percent, of all Latinas served on education committees, whereas only 11.2 percent of Latinos did. Although other differences appear, such as on the propensity to serve on health and human services committees (see Chapter 8 in this volume) and on committees dealing with natural resources, these differences do not

Table 9.3   Eight Most Frequently Cited Committee Assignments, by Gender (percentage)

Committee Assignments	Latinas	Latinos	Latinas and Latinos
Appropriations	15.1	17.9	17.2
Education	24.2*	11.2	14.7
Finance	9.0	12.2	11.4
Health and Human Services	36.3	22.4	26.2
Insurance	15.1	8.9	10.6
Judiciary	15.1	10.1	11.4
Natural Resources	3.0	11.2	10.6
Transportation	15.1	12.3	13.1
N	33	89	122

Notes: Question posed to legislators: On which committees do you serve?
* $p \leq .05$, two-tailed test of gender differences.

attain statistical significance. Unlike previous research, there was no major difference in the likelihood of Latinas to serve on appropriations and finance committees. Although 17.9 percent of Latino male legislators served on appropriations committees, a very similar 15.1 percent of Latina legislators also served on such committees; 12.2 percent of Latinos served on finance committees, and yet 9.0 percent of Latinas also served on them. It is possible that a greater substantive policy focus exists for Latina legislators in influencing legislation affecting women, families, and children given their greater presence on education committees. In 2004, however, this greater focus did not come at the expense of limited participation on appropriations and finance committees, traditionally considered among the most powerful committees in any state legislature.[3]

A final way in which we examined potential differences in the substantive policy focus between Latina and Latino legislators was through a detailed specification of the ranking of representational duties. Each legislator was asked to rank possible duties that included elements of constituency service, governmental oversight, conflict resolution, and interest advocacy on a scale from 1 = not important to 5 = extremely important. Mean responses and the full listing of 13 representational duties are displayed in Table 9.4. Our analysis of their ranking of these duties distinguishes between those representatives from districts with majority Latino populations and those from districts with non-Latino majorities. Although some differences appear, what is most clear is that there is no discernible difference in the ranking of representational duties between Latina and Latino legislators. No differences by gender reach levels of statistical significance. Surprisingly, this is even the case for the representation of women's interests and the representation of Latino interests. All representatives list

Table 9.4 Interest Representation: Mean Scores of Legislators' Ranking of Representational Duties, by Gender and Latino Majority Districts

	Latinas		Latinos	
	Latino Majority	Non-Latino Majority	Latino Majority	Non-Latino Majority
Helping people in the district who have personal problems with the government	4.61	4.81	4.89	4.77
Making sure that the district gets its fair share of government funds and projects	4.72	4.44	4.80	4.36
Keeping track of the way government agencies are carrying out laws passed by the legislature	4.33	4.13	4.28	4.00
Keeping in touch with the people about what the government is doing	4.44	4.69	4.67	4.57
Smoothing out conflicts and effecting compromise with other representatives	3.83	4.00	3.98	3.82
Working on legislation that benefits one's district	4.61	4.56	4.65	4.56
Working on legislation that benefits the broader interests of the state	4.72	4.50	4.48	4.44
Working on legislation that benefits women's interests	4.28	4.31	4.35	4.00
Working on legislation that benefits Latina/o interests	4.61	4.40	4.50	4.21
Working on legislation that benefits African American interests	4.28	4.33	4.30	3.82
Working on legislation that benefits Asian American interests	4.27	4.27	3.93	3.69
Working on legislation that benefits children's interests	4.83	4.69	4.78	4.62
Working on legislation that benefits immigrants' interests	4.67	4.12	4.39	3.92
N	18	16	46	39

Notes: Question posed to legislators: Here is a list of things people often think of as duties of a representative. Please evaluate the importance of each item to you where 1 is not important at all and 5 is extremely important.

"smoothing out conflicts and effecting compromise with other representatives" as lowest on their ranking of representational duties. These data suggest that in terms of representational duties, there is much more unity than distinctiveness across gender lines between Latina and Latino legislators. This is even the case controlling for whether or not Latinos comprise a majority of the district's population. As measured by ranking of representational duties, no greater substantive policy focus appears for Latina legislators as compared to Latino men.

Multiple Identity Advantage

We use two distinct measures to determine if Latina state legislators utilize a multiple identity advantage to better position themselves to influence public policy making. Table 9.5 displays how often Latina as compared to Latino legislators report being asked for advice from groupings of their colleagues ranging from coethnics to party leaders. It also displays the reported frequency with which Latina and Latino legislators form coalitions with groups of fellow legislators. Relative to Latino legislators, Latina legislators

Table 9.5   Coalition Partners: Mean Propensity to Ask for Advice and Propensity to Form Coalitions, by Group

	Asked for Advice on Legislation		Frequency of Coalition Partners	
	Latinas	Latinos	Latinas	Latinos
Latinos	2.77	2.79	2.86	3.17
Latinas	2.60	2.52	2.72	3.04
African American males	2.48*	2.13	2.38	2.69
African American females	2.25	2.26	2.09	2.58*
Asian American males	2.00	1.68	2.40*	2.00
Asian American females	2.58*	1.61	2.50	1.76
Caucasian males	2.21	2.36	2.21	2.46
Caucasian females	2.41	2.35	2.27	2.38
Democratic Party leaders	2.55	2.63	2.56	2.85
Republican Party leaders	1.82	1.87	1.84	2.01
Legislative leaders (e.g., Speaker)	2.52	2.37	2.65	2.62
Governor	1.59	1.77	1.79	2.07*
Lieutenant governor	1.47	1.52	1.42	1.75*

Notes: Question posed to legislators about asked for advice: How many times in the last session did the following legislators ask for your advice? Never = 1, Some of the time = 2, Most of the time = 3, Always = 4. Question posed to legislators about frequency of coalition: Please indicate the frequency with which you have formed coalitions with the following legislators or leaders. Never = 1, Some of the time = 2, Most of the time = 3, Always = 4.

 * $p \leq .05$, two-tailed test of gender differences.

are asked for advice from African American male legislators and Asian American female legislators at higher rates that are statistically significant. It is possible that Latinas are therefore better positioned to form coalitions with these groups than are Latino men. Latino legislators, by contrast do not report being asked for advice at higher rates than Latinas from any of the subgroups specified. We expected to find that fellow Latinas would be more likely to ask advice from each other. Bonds of solidarity based upon ethnicity and gender seem plausible given the raced and gendered hierarchies that predominate in state legislatures. We also expected that Latina legislators would report being asked for advice more frequently from fellow Caucasian and African American female legislators. We did not find any such differences that attained statistical significance.

Frequency of building coalition partners did reveal some interesting differences between Latinas and Latinos. Latina legislators reported building coalitions more frequently with Asian American males than did Latinos. These higher rates also attained levels of statistical significance. Latino male legislators reported building coalitions more frequently with African American females, the governor, and the lieutenant governor. These differences attained levels of statistical significance.

What these data reveal is that a multiple identity advantage of Latina legislators exists. In half of the six instances where differences between Latinas and Latinos attained statistical significance, these differences worked to the advantage of Latinas. However, this advantage did not fall into a consistent pattern based upon either Latino ethnicity or gender identity.

Gender Inclusive Advantage

Finally, we examine whether Latina legislators position themselves on controversial issues in ways that are distinct from those of Latino legislators to build upon what we earlier termed a gender inclusive advantage. If Latina legislators do position themselves in distinct ways, are these positions ones that limit the extent to which they can be pegged as being ethnic representatives and build upon their gender identity? We specify the patterns of issue posturing through three hypothetical scenarios where legislators are given very clear signals as to the preferences of their district constituency, the Latino caucus, and the women's caucus.[4] In each scenario, the interests of one group are in direct opposition to the position of another. Given the significance of district constituency interests in the first two scenarios, we report the results by whether or not Latinos are a majority of the population in a legislator's district.

Table 9.6 reveals that there is no difference between Latina and Latino legislators when forced to choose between constituency interests and those of the Latino caucus. To similar degrees, both Latina and Latino legislators

Table 9.6   Conflict Resolution: Mean Scores for How Legislators Would Vote When Group Interests Are Incompatible, by Gender and Latino Majority Districts

	Latinas		Latinos	
	Latino Majority	Non-Latino Majority	Latino Majority	Non-Latino Majority
Constituency opposes/ Latino caucus supports	−.33	−.16	−.02	−.42
Constituency opposes/ women's caucus supports	−.66	.33*	−.38	−.58
Latino caucus supports/ women's caucus opposes	.33*	.40*	.76	.64
N	17	16	44	37

Notes: Questions posed to legislators: (1) Suppose that you were considering how to vote on a bill that your constituency *strongly opposed* but that the Latino Caucus had introduced and *strongly supported.* Is it more likely that you would . . . ; (2) Suppose that you were considering how to vote on a bill that your *constituency strongly opposed* but that the Women's Caucus had introduced and *strongly supported.* Is it more likely that you would . . . ; (3) Suppose that you were considering how to vote on a bill that the Latino Caucus *strongly supported* and that the Women's Caucus *strongly opposed.* Is it more likely that you would. . . . Responses were coded as 1 = vote in favor of the bill; −1 = vote against the bill; 0 = abstain from voting.
  * $p \le .05$, two-tailed test of gender differences.

reported they were more likely to vote with their constituency *against* the preferences of the Latino caucus. Further examination of Table 9.6 indicates that Latina representatives, by contrast, are more likely to vote in favor of a bill that is supported by the women's caucus and opposed by their constituents, than are Latino legislators. This occurs, however, only in cases where the Latinas represent non-Latino majority districts. This difference is statistically significant. There is, however, no statistically significant difference between Latinas and Latinos in this scenario when they both represent majority Latino districts. In majority Latino districts, constituency preferences dominate. Lastly, a statistically significant difference between Latino and Latina legislators was also found when the scenario required legislators to decide between supporting the preferences of the Latino caucus or the women's caucus. Latina legislators, although still tending to vote in favor of the bill supported by the Latino caucus and opposed by the women's caucus, reported rates of such voting that were noticeably lower than those of Latino legislators. This was the case when Latina legislators represented either Latino majority districts or non-Latino majority districts. Latina legislators were more supportive of the position of the women's caucus than were Latino legislators.

The findings in Table 9.6 indicate that Latina legislators, in two distinct scenarios, are more likely to support the position of the women's caucus than Latino men. In these two scenarios, one restricted to those Latinas representing non-Latino majority districts and the other in cases of representing both Latino majority and non-Latino majority districts, Latina legislators indicate a propensity to identify with gender more strongly than constituency or ethnicity. In these cases, Latina legislators build upon their multiple identities to support the women's caucus. Stated differently, Latina legislators are both committed constituency advocates and committed gender partisans. Latina legislators can pursue a gender inclusive advantage in choosing to position themselves in conflictual situations such that they are authentic representatives, focusing however on their gender authenticity and not as much on their ethnic authenticity.

Strategic Intersectionality and Latina State Legislators

Building upon the literature on gender, race, and ethnicity in legislative politics, we developed a model of strategic intersectionality to outline how it is that Latina state legislators may bring unique perspectives, strategies, and opportunities to the legislative process that are distinct from those of Latino men legislators. We specified the three primary components of strategic intersectionality: substantive policy focus, multiple identity advantage, and gender inclusive advantage. We then tested our model with responses from a national survey of Latina and Latino legislators who served in the 2004 legislative year.

We find little evidence for the presence of a substantive policy focus among Latina state legislators, contrary to much previous research on the way in which gender-based identity contributes to a commitment by women legislators, including African American female legislators, to a specific set of policy priorities distinct from their male counterparts. Our data demonstrate that both Latina and Latino state legislators focus on the same types of issues, with education and health care being at the top of the list for both groups. We did find a modest difference in the types of committees on which Latinas and Latinos serve. Latina legislators have a greater propensity to serve on education committees relative to Latino men. This finding is consistent with previous research. However, we also found that the propensity to serve on these committees did not come at the cost of lower rates of membership on appropriations and finance committees. Additionally, we find no significant difference in the rankings Latina and Latino legislators give an extensive set of representational duties and related interests. There is more unity than distinctiveness on substantive policy focus across gender lines.

We did find evidence consistent with our model that Latina legislators report being asked for advice and developing legislative coalition partners in ways that are consistent with a multiple identity advantage. Latina legislators indicate that some distinct subsets of fellow legislators may be especially useful to them as they pursue their work in the policymaking process. Interestingly, these subsets of legislators who seem especially prone to work with Latina legislators do not fall neatly along either Latino ethnic or gender lines. All potential coalition partners for Latinas, however, do come from historically underrepresented groups. Clearly, Latina legislators, as distinct from Latino men, are sought out by and develop relationships with coethnics at higher rates than Latino legislators, but not with Latino coethnics.

Finally, we found that Latina legislators, relative to their Latino male counterparts, do position themselves distinctly, pursuing a gender inclusive advantage, when forced to confront a set of hypothetical incompatibility scenarios. Although both Latinas and Latinos report a tendency to vote against legislation that is supported by the Latino caucus and yet opposed by their constituents, the pattern is much more distinct when confronted with scenarios where the women's caucus supports legislation that is opposed by their constituents and where the women's caucus opposes a piece of legislation supported by the Latino caucus. Latina legislators who represent non-Latino majority districts are more likely to support the women's caucus even when it is not consistent with the preferences of their constituents, unlike Latino men legislators who represent such districts. All Latina legislators, regardless of whether they represent Latino majority or non-Latino majority districts, support the position of the women's caucus in opposition to the Latino caucus noticeably more than do Latino men.

What our model of the strategic intersectionality of Latina legislators reveals is a complex, multilayered pattern of advocacy, representation, and potential policy influence. The legislative lives of Latina state representatives and senators are both similar and different from those of their male counterparts. This finding is consistent with Thomas (1994, 158) regarding women generally and Barrett (1995, 2001) and Smooth (2001) regarding African American female state legislators. There is no singular experience of any female legislator.

Our subsequent analysis of the similarities and differences of Latina and Latino state legislators will systematically examine state context to see if the general patterns in the model of strategic intersectionality noted in this chapter can be specified more precisely. Do state-based variations in legislatures by partisanship;[5] number of women representatives; number of Latina/o, African American, and Asian American representatives; position of Latina and Latino representatives within the majority or minority party; and party affiliation of statewide elected officials set important parameters that affect the use of strategic intersectionality? Moreover, our analysis must be informed by the patterns of success that Latina and Latino legislators have in getting their policy priorities enacted into law. Fortunately, these analyses are well under way.

We are confident that our model of strategic intersectionality holds promise to better understand the ways in which the simultaneous growth in gender and ethnic-racial empowerment affects American politics. All indications are that such empowerment will only grow in the future. The course of progress that such empowerment will chart may well depend on how effective strategic intersectionality is in effecting change in many traditional patterns of US politics and policymaking.

Notes

This research would not have been possible without a magnificent team of undergraduate research assistants at Stanford University including Maria Lizet Ocampo, Teresa Mosqueda, Evan Otero, Kiyomi Burchill, Darya Landa, and Jessica Flores. We also thank the Office of the Vice Provost for Undergraduate Education (VPUE) and the Political Science Program for Undergraduate Research at Stanford. Luis R. Fraga would also like to thank the Immigrant Incorporation Cluster at the Radcliffe Institute for Advanced Study, Harvard University, for providing a wonderful environment in which to work during the 2003–2004 academic year. An earlier version of this chapter was prepared for delivery at the annual meeting of the American Political Science Association, Washington, DC, August 31–September 4, 2005.

1. Preuhs (2006) makes a distinction between *simple incorporation* and *institutional incorporation*. The model of political incorporation that we utilize goes beyond a dichotomous categorization and instead allows for a multidimensional continuum of political incorporation.

2. Smooth expands upon this analysis in Chapter 10 of this volume.

3. We also examined differences in committee chairmanships. We found no major differences in the propensities of Latinas and Latinos to serve as committee chairs. We also found no significant differences in the types of committees on which they served as chairs.

4. We well recognize that not all states have a Latino caucus or a women's caucus. In those states where respondents indicated that no such caucus existed, we asked them to consider the scenario under conditions where a clear majority of either Latino or women legislators have preferences consistent with the scenario. In cases where there are so few Latina and Latino legislators that no such grouping of preferences is possible, we did not pose this scenario to the respondent.

5. Very few of our respondents were Republican, and they largely were in Florida.

10

Gender, Race, and the Exercise of Power and Influence

WENDY G. SMOOTH

THE INCREASING NUMBER of African American women elected to state legislatures coupled with the transferring of power back to the states necessitates an increased focus on the legislative experiences of African American women state legislators. Based on in-depth interviews of African American women in three state legislatures—Georgia, Maryland, and Mississippi—this chapter chronicles the experiences of African American women as they attempt to translate their policy preferences into legislative realities. Specifically, I consider whether African American women have garnered institutional power in these states and whether or not their colleagues view them as influential actors in the legislature.

One of the most monumental successes of the civil rights movement was the passage of the 1965 Voting Rights Act, which provided opportunities for African Americans to increase their participation in electoral politics. This landmark legislation created the structures necessary for African Americans to elect the representatives of their choice for the first time since the Reconstruction Era. African Americans traded in their protest-style social movement strategies for electoral politics and the promise of inclusion and full participation through the democratic process (Tate 1993).

As African Americans elected members of their racial group to public office following the passage of the Voting Rights Act, the diversity of state legislatures in particular increased significantly. Southern states especially realized an increase in black representatives (Bositis 1999). An increase in the numbers of women soon followed. Between 1971 and 1996, the numbers of women elected to state legislatures grew steadily. However, by the mid-1990s, the overall rate of growth for women elected to state legislatures actually began to stagnate, a trend that remains today (Sanbonmatsu 2006a;

see Chapter 1 in this volume). Despite the plateau in the numbers of women overall elected to state legislatures, the numbers of African American women and other women of color continue to increase. Today's state legislatures are more representative of society and are more diverse than ever in the nation's history.

At the same time that state legislatures are becoming more gender and racially diverse, their importance as sites of policymaking is also increasing. State governments are assuming a more prominent position in domestic policymaking as the national government continuously scales back its responsibilities in the domestic policy arena (King-Meadows and Schaller 2006). State legislators deliberate on a wide range of domestic policies such as welfare policy, the environment, health insurance coverage, and reproductive rights. State legislatures are faced with more demanding legislative sessions and the issues they are deliberating are likewise growing ever more complex (A. Rosenthal 1998).

For all these reasons, it is important to understand how state legislatures are responding to their increased diversity. In this chapter, I focus on the experiences of African American women state legislators, a group that stands at the nexus of race and gender and is among the most understudied groups in politics. In particular, I explore the extent to which African American women are considered influential members of the legislature by their colleagues. Being considered as influential is an important step in successfully representing constituents and the policies that are key to their political, economic, and social interests.

Legislative scholars, while differing in their approaches, conclude that certain institutional attributes contribute more to a legislator's influence than do others. For example, those who are influential in legislatures have commonly been identified according to the positions they hold within the institution (Hamm, Harmel, and Thompson 1983; Meyer 1980), their legislative activity (Matthews 1960; Frantzich 1979), and their reputations among their peers (Francis 1962; Best 1971; Haynie 2001, 2002). In interviews with state legislators in three states, I find that legislators identified several factors contributing to a legislator's influence, including character traits, legislative activity, and holding institutional positions of power in the legislature. And, in this regard, the legislators' definitions affirm the existing literature on legislative influence.

However, in examining their evaluations of their colleagues in the legislature, it is evident that other attributes also are important in determining influence in the legislature. In this chapter, I focus on not only legislators' definitions of influence, but also the attributes of those they perceive as influential in their state legislatures. According to my findings, in addition to holding institutional positions of power, being legislatively active, and being senior members in the institution, there are additional factors that impact whether or not legislators are regarded as influential among their peers.

I argue that legislators' gender and race also play significant roles in determining whether they are regarded as influential members of their legislature. Data collected from interviews with members of the Georgia, Maryland, and Mississippi legislatures suggest that gender and race act as mediating factors negatively impacting legislators' evaluations of one another's influence. For African American women, influence appears at first glance beyond their reach because they lack the leadership positions that their colleagues link to influence. Yet, upon closer examination, the data show that African American women's lack of influence is linked to their denied access to the informal circles of power within the legislature.

Further, my findings indicate that the legislative context plays an important role in whether or not African American women wield any influence at all among their peers. Among other contextual factors, the level of legislative professionalization impacts the prospects of African American women being regarded as influential among their peers in the legislature. State legislatures vary along a continuum from professional to citizen legislatures. More professional legislatures meet annually with some, such as the California legislature, meeting year round, while more citizen legislatures in comparison meet for shorter periods with some even meeting biannually. Legislators in more professional bodies are usually full-time legislators and are paid salaries reflective of their full-time status. More professional legislatures attract careerist politicians as compared to citizen legislatures whose members are part-time and usually have other occupations. More professional legislatures also have the benefit of larger staffs of assistants than do citizen legislatures. In more citizen legislatures, strong personal relationships and ties are often more significant than political partisanship (Ellickson and Whistler 2000). With longer sessions and more staff dedicated to legislators, more professional bodies have greater capacities for lawmaking and as a result they tend to enact more legislation (Reingold 2000). Of the three legislatures in this study, the Maryland legislature approximates the characteristics of the more professional legislature, while Georgia and Mississippi approximate more citizen legislative bodies.

These findings echo those of Kerry Haynie (2002), who finds that African American legislators were not considered effective by their peers, even when holding formal positions of power. For African American women in this study, their limited access to the informal circles of power—which contributes to their inability to garner influence among their peers—illustrates the extent to which state legislatures remain not only gendered but also racialized institutions that adhere to the gender and racial norms and preferences that African American women defy by their very existence.

Existing Literature and Hypotheses

As the numbers of African Americans and women have increased in state legislatures, researchers have begun evaluating their activities as legislators. However, most of these studies have focused on the experiences of *either* African Americans, most of whom are men, *or* women, most of whom are white, with few studying those at the intersections of race and gender— women of color. Despite considering African Americans and women as mutually exclusive groups, they reach similar conclusions. Those studying African American legislators find that their committee assignments (Friedman 1996; Orey 2000), the types of legislation they introduce (Barrett 1995; Bratton and Haynie 1999; Haynie 2001; Owens 2005; Miller 1990), and their success in navigating legislation through the process (Bratton and Haynie 1999; Hamm, Harmel, and Thompson 1983; Menifield and Shaffer 2000; Orey and Smooth 2006) all impact the extent to which they make a difference as legislators. Women likewise are increasingly more successful in accessing leadership positions and successfully getting their legislation passed (Saint-Germain 1989; Carroll, Dodson, and Mandel 1991; Thomas and Welch 1991; Kathlene 1994; Bratton and Haynie 1999; Orey and Smooth 2006).

Taken together, scholars note that both African Americans and women do make a difference in state policymaking. Yet, few studies have focused on how the legislative institution has responded to these new entrants. The ability of these representatives to make a difference for their constituents is connected to their abilities to establish themselves as effective, influential legislators. Questions regarding influence among members of legislative bodies have long been a central point of inquiry in the study of legislative institutions. These studies have indicated that legislators who hold leadership positions are typically more influential in the institution (Best 1971; Hamm, Harmel, and Thompson 1983; Meyer 1980). Likewise, those legislators who have an established track record of getting legislation passed have also been denoted as the most influential (Frantzich 1979; Matthews 1960). These studies laid important groundwork for understanding how influence operates in legislative institutions, but the findings of these studies are based on legislatures that were largely homogeneous institutions. As Gary Moncrief, Joel Thompson, and Karl Kurtz (1996) conclude, the state legislature of today is quite different from its early days and its increased diversity has significantly changed the operations of the institution.

Revisiting questions regarding legislative influence in light of the increased diversity of these institutions has contributed new understandings about influence and has produced new knowledge concerning the experiences of women and people of color once they are elected to the legislature. For example, Haynie (2001, 2002) finds that race plays a significant role in determining legislative influence. Lobbyists and fellow legislators consistently ranked African American legislators as less effective than their white peers regardless of their membership on prestigious committees, seniority, profession outside of the legislature, or leadership position, which are all attributes traditionally associated with effectiveness in the legislature. In addition, Diane Blair and Jeanie Stanley's (1991) study of perceptions of power among state legislators shows that gender makes a difference in determining legislative influence. Women legislators thought the old boys' club atmosphere of the legislature limited the ease with which they functioned among their colleagues and impeded their abilities to be viewed as equals among their male colleagues.

While these studies have added to our understandings of influence in light of increased diversity in the legislature, we have no knowledge of how the intersection of race and gender impacts perceptions of influence. In that these studies focused on influence across the institution, we also have little knowledge as to whether these legislators exert influence in specific policy arenas, particularly those in which they have placed the bulk of their legislative energies. Previous studies of legislative influence conclude that there are different types of influence legislators can wield in the institution (Best 1971; Francis 1962). Legislators can either be influential in a specific policy area or they can wield influence across the institution. Wayne Francis (1962) concludes that area influence precedes general influence. To the contrary, James Best (1971) finds that those influential in specific policy areas were much less likely to be perceived also as generally influential. Instead, those who were generally influential were much more likely to be regarded as influential in specific policy areas. Hence, Best (1971) concludes that legislators' influence goes in one direction from impacting the policy agenda across issue areas to impacting policy in specific areas. His conclusions support the argument that general influence is a more favorable commodity because it can be transferred to specific policy areas, but influence in a specific policy area does not necessarily translate into influence across issue areas.

Having influence in a specific policy area is the equivalent of providing technical competence, while being generally influential across policy areas is more likely to result in genuine institutional power. The literature suggests that women legislators are less likely to garner the type of power that would make them revered throughout the institution. A woman legislator interviewed by Blair and Stanley (1991) begins to point to the differences between being generally influential and having influence in specific policy areas. In terms of her own legislative effectiveness, she asserts, "It's a philosophy of issue versus process; being effective in the process as opposed to being effective on an issue. Now I consider myself effective on the issues, on my issues, but I don't consider myself totally effective in the process."

The authors assert that women legislators had not yet become influential to the extent that they were capable of influencing the process of legislating (Blair and Stanley 1991). I expect that the same will be true for African American women in this study. Given the findings of previous studies, African American women are more likely to be regarded as capable of providing technical expertise in policy areas in which they have had some prior experience. I expect that their technical competence will not translate into their being regarded as influential across policy areas, which is also more likely to translate into genuine institutional power.

Data and Methodology

The data and findings presented in this chapter are drawn from a larger project in which I seek to determine the impact of gender and race on legislative influence. I pursued this analysis conducting a national survey of African American women state legislators and case studies of three state legislatures—Georgia, Maryland, and Mississippi—during the 2000 legislative session. The analysis discussed in this chapter draws upon the case studies of these states. These states were selected because, of all the states, these states had the largest numbers of African American women serving as legislators. In all three legislatures the Democratic Party held control of both the upper and lower chambers during the 2000 legislative session. The party in control exercises considerable power in selecting the chairs of committees and assigning members to the committees. The members of the leadership are members of the party in control of the legislature. All of the African American women in these legislatures were Democrats, which suggests that they would have access to leadership positions and important committee assignments.

The case studies uncover subtleties concerning the effects of gender and race that could not be easily understood or revealed using survey methodology. In the case studies, I approached African American women's influence from the perspective of their colleagues. While the focus of my analysis is African American women's influence, the data are inclusive of all the members' perceived influence.

During the 2000 legislative session, I conducted 94 semistructured interviews with members of the three state legislatures, including interviews with most of the African American women serving.[1] In order to understand legislators' thinking about power and influence, I interviewed a cross-section of legislators in both the upper and lower chambers of the legislature. I interviewed legislators with years of service in the legislature as well as members in their first term, both Democrats and Republicans, and both African American and white men and women. This provided the broadest understanding of influence across seniority rankings, party lines, race, and gender.

A portion of the semistructured interviews followed the format of Wayne Francis's (1962) and James Best's (1971) studies of legislative influence in which they asked respondents to identify the most influential legislators in the institution. Further following their approach, I also instructed legislators to identify the most influential legislators in particular policy areas. Legislators were asked to identify those who were influential in the policy areas in which African American women consider themselves experts—education, health care and health-care reform, economic development and employment, children's issues, and women's issues.[2] Legislators were not asked to focus on specific pieces of legislation, but instead were directed to consider their most influential colleagues in these policy areas, more broadly defined. This process prompted legislators to look beyond the success or failure of one piece of legislation and encouraged them instead to consider a range of legislative initiatives that encompassed more than actual introduction and passage of legislation. Most important, this approach not only allows us to explore whether African American women are influential or not, but it also provides information regarding African American women's influence in areas that they have defined as significant to their legislative agendas.

Findings: General Influence

Just as Best (1971) concluded decades ago, general influence continues to be concentrated in the hands of only a few members of the legislature. It is also the case that those considered generally influential are also perceived as influential in specific policy areas, but not vice versa. Those legislators who were perceived as influential in specific policy areas were less likely to be considered generally influential, which also mirrors Best's conclusions.

The few legislators regarded as generally influential, with influence across policy areas, held formal leadership positions for the most part. A Maryland legislator offered a summation of general influence that is applicable to all three state legislatures:

> Of the 141 members in House of Delegates less than 10 percent are truly influential. Those 10 percent consist primarily of leadership, standing committee chairs, the Speaker, the majority leader, the Speaker pro-tem, and some committee chairs. Those are the only ones who have the real influence over the macro agenda.

Whether legislators agreed or disagreed with the policy positions of certain members, they nevertheless acknowledged their influence in the institution. One legislator found that the leadership's desires were fulfilled no matter what. He contended, "If leadership decides that something is going to be done, one way or another it happens. That's the way it normally works." What makes this highly problematic is that this concentration of power and influence is not reflective of the legislatures' diversity. Though some African American men had gained entry into these circles of influence, the absence of African American women from these power circles was keenly noticeable.

Table 10.1 shows the distribution of leadership positions in the three state legislatures during the 2000 legislative session. In each of these legislatures, white men held the majority of the party leadership positions while African American women held very few (if any) party leadership positions. For example, only one African American woman held a party leadership position in the Maryland House of Delegates, while there were none holding party leadership positions in the Maryland State Senate. In addition to holding few party leadership positions, the few positions African American women held were in the lower tier of the leadership structure. In the Georgia House of Representatives, for example, an African American woman was the secretary of the majority caucus, and in the Georgia Senate the one party position held by an African American woman was that of assistant to the administrative floor leader. The positions held by African American women in the party structure of these legislatures are not traditionally regarded as highly influential positions.

The Upper Tier of Influence: Formal Institutional Leaders

Holding formal leadership positions is the key to being regarded as generally influential in all three legislatures, though the positions conferring influence differed in each state legislature. In Maryland, all the members considered the Speaker of the House, president of the Senate, and the majority leaders to be influential across policy areas. Maryland legislators did not regard other party leaders as generally influential. According to one Maryland legislator,

> Influence is not being a subcommittee chair or it's not being a whip, a deputy whip, or a deputy, deputy whip, which we do a lot of down here. The reason I say that is not influence is because frequently, in getting an assignment like that, legislators make a commitment that—at least on important calls—they will go along with the Speaker and the president.

During his sixth term in office, Maryland Speaker of the House Casper Taylor expanded the party leadership structure to include more members in the organized leadership and added subcommittees to the committee structure, which created even more coveted positions in the leadership hierarchy.

Table 10.1   Distribution of Leadership Positions in the State House and Senate

	Percentage of Leadership Positions in the House	Percentage of Members in the House	Percentage of Leadership Positions in the Senate	Percentage of Members in the Senate
Georgia				
African American women	7	7	8	9
	(1)	(12)	(1)	(5)
African American men	7	12	8	9
	(1)	(21)	(1)	(5)
White women	7	13	—	7
	(1)	(24)	(0)	(4)
White men	79	68	85	75
	(11)	(123)	(11)	(42)
Total	100	100	100	100
	(14)	(180)	(13)	(52)
Maryland[a]				
African American women	4	7	—	6
	(1)	(10)	(0)	(3)
African American men	7	13	18	13
	(2)	(19)	(2)	(6)
White women	44	26	27	13
	(12)	(36)	(3)	(6)
White men	44	52	55	66
	(12)	(74)	(6)	(80)
Total	100	100	100	100
	(27)	(141)[a]	(11)	(47)
Mississippi				
African American women	—	7	—	4
	(0)	(8)	(0)	(2)
African American men	50	21	—	13
	(1)	(26)	(0)	(7)
White women	—	7	50	8
	(0)	(8)	(1)	(4)
White men	50	66	50	75
	(1)	(80)	(1)	(39)
Total	100	100	100	100
	(2)	(122)	(1)	(52)

Notes: Numbers do not total 100 percent due to rounding.

a. In Maryland, two legislators in the House are identified by race as "other" and are not included in this table.

Members perceived that Taylor's reason for including more members in the leadership structure was to decrease the likelihood that they would go against his leadership. According to Delegate Mike Busch, chairman of the Economic Matters Committee in the House, "More people are invested in the system, and as a result they respond."[3] Though Speaker Taylor expanded the leadership structure to include more members, it appears that very little institutional prestige or influence is afforded to the members in these expanded leadership positions. While Maryland's leadership structure offered the appearance of a more expanded distribution of power, legislators regarded this quite differently. Maryland legislators contended that the extensive leadership structure served to only solidify the influence of the Speaker. As one legislator concluded, "When they [the leadership] want something, they normally get what they want because they have created all these layers of leadership, so they can get the votes." As discussed previously, African American women held positions at this lower level of legislative leadership in Maryland.

In Georgia, legislators included all the party leadership as influential across the institution. In fact, most legislators were content to divulge *only* the names of those in the party leadership position as the most influential. "I guess we are just disciplined to follow the leadership," one legislator in Georgia remarked after realizing that she only considered those in top leadership as influential in the statehouse. Mississippi's lack of a strong party system or party competition allowed legislators to be more varied in terms of the members having general influence. Likewise, with a more limited leadership structure—only two official party leadership positions in each chamber, Mississippi legislators included a broader group of influentials beyond the formal leaders. While Mississippi legislators were consistent in their feelings about the influence of the Speaker and the lieutenant governor, there was more variation in the other members they also considered to be influential.

The Second Tier of General Influence: Committee Chairs

Those legislators in the top party leadership positions were without question considered to be the most influential across policy areas. Legislators were also likely to consider committee chairs as generally influential; however, the power of the committee chairs varied from one institution to the next. For example, in Maryland, the small number of committees extended more power to all committee chairs, and as a result most legislators considered *all* committee chairs generally influential. In fact, committee chairs in Maryland were afforded more institutional prestige than members holding low-level party leadership positions. However, in Georgia and Mississippi, influence worked quite differently. With many more committees and committee chairs, not all committee chairs were considered influential.

In all three legislatures, legislators considered the chairs of committees such as Appropriations and Budget and Taxation, essentially those dealing with allocating funds or the state's budget, as influential across issue areas. Those chairing the so-called money committees carried extraordinary amounts of general influence, and as one Mississippi legislator concluded, "If you're the Appropriations Chairman you control how much bond indebtedness the state incurs and for what projects. So, the money makes you the most powerful. Who controls the gold makes the rule. That's the golden rule down here."

As is the case with party leadership positions, white men held the majority of committee leadership positions while few, if any, African American women did. (See Table 10.2.) In Maryland, for example, there were no African American women serving as committee chairs. In Georgia and Mississippi, African American women served as committee chairs;

Table 10.2   Distribution of Committee Chairs in the State House and Senate

	Percentage of House Committee Chairs	Percentage of Members in the House	Percentage of Senate Committee Chairs	Percentage of Members in the Senate
Georgia				
African American women	3	7	9	9
	(1)	(12)	(2)	(5)
African American men	12	12	9	9
	(4)	(21)	(2)	(5)
White women	6	13	4	7
	(2)	(24)	(1)	(4)
White men	76	68	78	75
	(26)	(123)	(18)	(42)
Total	100	100	100	100
	(33)	(180)	(23)	(52)
Maryland[a]				
African American women	—	7	—	6
	(0)	(10)	(0)	(3)
African American men	17	13	33	13
	(1)	(19)	(2)	(6)
White women	17	26	17	13
	(1)	(36)	(1)	(6)
White men	67	52	50	66
	(4)	(74)	(3)	(80)
Total	100	100	100	100
	(6)	(141)[a]	(6)	(47)
Mississippi				
African American women	3	7	6	4
	(1)	(8)	(2)	(2)
African American men	17	21	15	13
	(6)	(26)	(5)	(7)
White women	8	7	3	8
	(3)	(8)	(1)	(4)
White men	72	66	76	75
	(26)	(80)	(26)	(39)
Total	100	100	100	100
	(36)	(122)	(34)	(52)

Notes: Numbers do not total 100 percent due to rounding.

a. In Maryland, two legislators in the House are identified by race as "other" and are not included in this table.

however, they did not chair committees typically regarded as the most powerful. In Mississippi, it is of note that for the first time in the state's history, an African American woman chaired one of the Senate's major committees—the Senate Education Committee, which was also a first for an African American legislator in the Mississippi Senate.

In the case of Georgia and Mississippi, influence was further complicated by the nature of committee chair selection. Legislators were able to become institutions unto themselves as a result of the committee chair selection process, which limited the distribution of influence among legislators. In Georgia, once a legislator is appointed to chair a committee, it is customary that he or she serves as the chair of that committee as long as he or she is continuously elected to the legislature (Fleischmann and Pierannunzi 1997, 147). This allows legislators to cultivate one area of expertise on the issues their committee typically addresses. It also has the effect of closing the field of legislators who can garner influence in these areas.

Committee chairs in Mississippi are appointed to serve only one four-year term as chair of a particular committee and are not appointed for consecutive terms, though they often chair the same committees in multiple nonconsecutive terms. For example, three senators appointed to chair major committees in the Senate during the 2000 session had chaired those same committees in prior legislative sessions.[4] Further, the same legislators rotate through the major committee assignments, allowing them to gather legislative expertise on a number of issues because they have chaired multiple major committees dealing with various policy areas. These two factors surrounding committee chair appointments greatly impact which members are considered generally influential and maintain a small, select group as those with the greatest influence in the institution.

The Secret Powerhouse: The Informal Leadership Team

In the Georgia and Mississippi legislatures, a select group of members are considered influential based upon their membership in informal leadership groups. These informal leadership groups consist of a small number of legislators who hold the confidence of the top legislative leaders. In addition to the official leadership of the Georgia and Mississippi legislatures, these informal groups serve as the final decisionmakers, providing members of these groups immense power. These informal leadership groups emerged as key organizing features of the Mississippi and Georgia legislatures but not an organizing feature of the Maryland legislature.

In Georgia, this group was referred to as the "Green Door," alluding to the fact that it had the power to determine what legislation continued on the path to becoming law. Similarly, in Mississippi, the group holding this same function was referred to as the "Go Team." These informal groups were mostly comprised of committee chairs; however, not every committee chair was included, only a select group of committee chairs. In Mississippi for example, legislators identified members of the Go Team as the chairs of the money committees and several of the most senior legislators. These Go Team members also were supporters and backers of the lieutenant governor's and House Speaker's election bids. Legislators were not afforded membership in these groups by virtue of their leadership positions alone, and not every legislative leader and committee chair was included in these groups.

The Green Door and the Go Team were not official groups in these legislatures in that they were not acknowledged in any of the official documents of the institution, but they were nevertheless a key factor in the legislative process. What was most interesting about these groups was the extent to which they operated as not only elite, but also clandestine groups. In Georgia, the group was described as "an elite and secretive cadre of about a dozen leading Democrats who do the real work of finalizing state budgets and setting the agenda."[5] Their anonymity precluded them from being held accountable by other legislators or even constituents. In 1999, in response to the Georgia House passing an open records and open meetings bill that applied only to local governments, Representative James Mills launched a campaign retaliating against these informal groups by proposing that the Green Door's meetings be open to all members wanting to attend.[6]

Much like the infamous "Board of Education" operating in Congress prior to the reforms of the 1970s, the Green Door and the Go Team were also institutional entities that garnered power through informal norms governing the institution as opposed to the institution's official rules. According to the *Atlanta Journal-Constitution*, the Green Door Committee is "probably one of the most powerful collections of politicians in the state" and "decides what millions go into the state budget and what millions get cut."[7] In effect, these informal groups have the powerful job of managing the flow of legislation in these legislatures. Legislators are included in these groups by invitation only, and those who are not members speculate as to who actually constitutes the group's membership. While it was speculative as to which legislators held membership in these circles, it was unquestionable that they were an influential group that held the fate of much legislation, and legislators were quite cognizant of their influence. As one Mississippi legislator described, "the way the process works, if you are one of the big boys—on the Go Team is what we call it—you are going to have influence on just about anything. Basically, four legislators run this place because they have a lot of say."

When asked how these legislators acquired that type of influence, the legislator explained that they not only supported the lieutenant governor's campaign, but they fit a "psychological and political profile" appealing to the legislature's formal leaders. This group varied by party affiliation, but shared more important characteristics according to this legislator. Their status as "white southern gentlemen" aided them in securing such influence in the institution. These groups no doubt limited the distribution of influence among legislators.

In Maryland, the leadership team under Senate president Mike Miller was a much larger, less select group than in either chamber of the other two states. Miller was known as a consensus builder and included a large legislative leadership team on many decisions. He was also known to bring in rank-and-file members as a way of solidifying consensus (A. Rosenthal 1998, 273). Likewise in the Maryland House, the leadership team was larger than those in the other two states, which again avoided the cloud of secrecy associated with the leadership teams in Georgia and Mississippi.

General Influence and African American Women Legislators: A Question of Access

Though some African American women served in select leadership roles and chaired a few committees, they still had not secured membership among the elite group of legislators who engaged in the final legislative decisionmaking. When asked about their relationship with those in the top leadership positions, African American women in Georgia and Mississippi crafted their remarks in terms of their exclusion from the leaderships' inner circles. While nearly all of the African American women interviewed considered themselves to have a good relationship with those in the top leadership posts of their respective chambers, all acknowledged that despite good working relationships, they were not a part of these innermost groups where many significant decisions were made. As one African American woman legislator remarked, "I am included on some things, but I know that I'm not included on a lot. I'm not involved in the power meetings, not on every level. Though I chair a committee, I am not a member of the team that makes the final decisions on budget items."

Even in moving into the formal leadership, African American women described that there were times in which they were excluded from some circles of decisionmaking. As one African American woman detailed, there were often leadership meetings that were just a formality and it was evident that the meeting in which she was participating was not being held to make real decisions.

> I'm one of the individuals that the Speaker meets with weekly on the basis of my committee leadership. But, sometimes I really think that some meet-

ings are held before the meeting. Some meetings are held the night before or the week before. We can tell that the meeting has already occurred because some decisions have already been made. So, it does make a difference when you're on that committee, you at least have an opportunity to voice your opinion about certain things, even if the decision seems final.

As a result of these institutional norms perpetuated by the top leaders in Georgia and Mississippi, power in these legislatures was concentrated in the hands of only a few, which were near exclusively white men. The legislators interviewed did not mention an African American woman as a member of one of the highly selective circles surrounding the top legislative leaders in Georgia or in Mississippi, nor did African American women consider themselves among this group. It is very difficult to definitively conclude that their exclusion was a direct result of gender and race bias; however, it is unquestionable that their influence was compromised as a result of not gaining this level of access to power.

Issue-Specific Influence

During the interviews, legislators were also asked to identify their peers whom they consider influential in specific policy areas—education, health care and health-care reform, economic development and employment, women's issues, and children's issues—all of which correspond with African American women's areas of expertise. As expected, African American women had some influence in the policy areas in which they have developed expertise. However, the advantage associated with being a formal leader in these policy areas in question cannot be minimized. African American women who chaired committees dealing with the policy area were far more likely to be considered influential than those who did not.

The distribution of issue-specific influence was different in each state and reflected the legislatures' institutional values and norms. A number of different factors impact legislators' influence and they vary not only according to the legislature, but also according to the policy area under consideration. A factor that is valued in one legislature and as a result affords a legislator influence is not highly regarded in another. Holding a position as the committee chair with jurisdiction over the issue afforded considerable influence in all three states' legislatures.

Aside from being a committee chair, having knowledge and expertise of an issue and holding membership in an institutionalized group that addressed the issue area were additional factors contributing to legislators' influence in specific policy areas. The impact of these two factors varied from state to state. In Maryland, knowledge and expertise were highly valued, and in Georgia and Maryland having a women's caucus and/or a black caucus provided important sources of institutional influence. African American women were much more likely to be regarded as influential on specific policies by other African Americans, which suggests that race was also an institutional norm that played a significant role in determining legislative influence.

The Power and Influence of the Chair

The fact that most legislators considered only committee chairs influential did not bode well for African American women given the small numbers holding committee chairs. Because African American women were legislatively active in these policy areas, it was expected that they would be mentioned as influential by virtue of their work and attention to these policy issues. In Georgia and Mississippi, however, influence by and large only came as a result of holding an institutional position of power. Making note of her own tendency to denote only committee chairs as having any influence on the policy areas in question, one legislator remarked,

> You notice that I stay with the chairmen. The chairmen are so powerful that a lot of times if any other person is doing something on the issue they have to come through a chairman. Unless the person has a burning issue that they push, it is very, very hard to know that they are working on the issue.

The majority of legislators considered only the committee chairs whose committee had jurisdiction in that policy area as influential. This was most consistently the case on policy issues in which the committee handling the topic was easily identified, such as education, health care and health-care reform, and children's issues.[8] Influence on policy issues that fell under the jurisdiction of multiple committees, such as women's issues and economic development and employment, was more widely distributed among legislators and included rank-and-file members.

Because committee chairs in Mississippi had a history of serving as chairs of several major committees over their legislative careers, often legislators chairing other committees retained influence in a policy area over which they once had jurisdiction. This had the effect of confining influence to a very small group of legislators.

Legislators shared different opinions about the influence committee chairs held. Some legislators respected and had confidence in the committee chairs, acknowledging the chairs as the most qualified members to lead the committee. For these legislators, committee chairs were influential by virtue of their qualifications. Others understood the influence of the committee chairs as simply a function of holding the institutional position, and the chair may or may not have knowledge and competence in the policy area. A Maryland legislator differentiated between chairs having influence because of the formal position and chairs having influence because they know the issue and their committee members respect them and are willing to follow their leadership. According to this legislator, "it's one thing to be a chairman of a committee and use that to try and swing votes. It's another thing to be a chairman of a major committee and also have the respect of the members so that they will take what you say seriously and they will look to you as an expert in the field or any other." Despite whatever doubts legislators may have had regarding the chairs of various committees, they nevertheless understood these members as influential in accordance with the norms of the legislature.

The Power of Prior Knowledge and Expertise

Previous studies suggest that as legislators become experts on specific policy issues, their influence in these areas also increases (Francis 1962; Best 1971; Keefe and Ogul 1989; Weissert 1991). Knowledge and expertise did not always yield influence in these three states. The extent to which knowledge and expertise were prized depended upon the values or norms of the legislative institution. Knowledge and prior expertise were much more valuable in Maryland than in the other two states, and as a result, influence in specific policy areas was more widely distributed among rank-and-file members in Maryland. Because state legislatures are handling more and more complex issues, legislators are finding it increasingly more important to seek fellow members with strong knowledge bases in particular issue areas. Education and health care were two issue areas in which several African American women legislators in Maryland had prior expertise, and their colleagues frequently looked to these members to weigh the merits of proposed legislation in these areas. One African American woman's experience with the leadership exemplified Maryland's inclusiveness and emphasis on knowledge and expertise:

> There was an education issue on the floor, and I was not on the education committee at that time, but I asked questions on that bill and was able to stop that bill on the floor. The Speaker told the chairman of the committee handling education, "Don't bring any other education issues before the floor unless you talk to Delegate X." I was not in the leadership, but here was someone saying, "She has some knowledge. If she can stop what we're trying to do in the leadership, then we need to communicate with her."

Though rank-and-file members were acknowledged as having prior expertise and exerting some influence based on their knowledge of particular issues, even in Maryland, the stigma of not being an official member of the leadership was still a factor impeding their influence. A Maryland legislator described the dilemma of being very knowledgeable on an issue, yet not being a member of the leadership. She described the experience of one African American woman, who was in such a situation:

> Delegate X is very knowledgeable, but I don't see her as influential. She's very knowledgeable, but she is not in a leadership role, so she cannot always get her agenda accepted. You know they say that, "A little bit of knowledge is a dangerous thing, a lot of knowledge can get you a long way." So, whatever committee X is on, they always look to her because she has worked for health on the national level.

While acknowledged for her in-depth expertise of health issues and her work on the national level, this delegate's influence was mitigated because she did not hold a formal leadership position, and her agenda was stifled as a result.

Prior expertise and experience were not preferenced as highly as other factors in the other states. As an African American woman in Mississippi's legislature explained:

> The issues do not matter. What matters is that you are a part of the leadership. The leadership makes the decisions. While there are many legislators who have spent their entire lives working on an issue, like education, they come to the legislature and that expertise is seldom taken under consideration. We have members who were teachers, principals, school superintendents—and many of them are African American, African American women, and because they are not in the leadership [in the House] they are not influential. The issue doesn't matter—leadership is the key!

Privileging knowledge and expertise has a positive impact on African American women's influence. While selection as a committee chair is not within a legislator's control, cultivating expertise and in-depth knowledge of a subject matter are indeed factors that legislators can control. Therefore, when knowledge and prior expertise were valued in the legislature and widely accepted as an institutional norm, African American women stood to benefit as demonstrated in Maryland's case. Preferences for knowledge and expertise are associated with more professional legislatures. While Maryland is not considered among the most professionalized legislatures in the country, it more closely approximates the characteristics of a professional legislature than do the citizen legislatures of Georgia and Mississippi (Squire 1992).

Beyond Simply Gaining Access

The existing literature on state legislatures suggests that the key to gaining power and influence rests with gaining access to key legislative positions, including top leadership posts and committee chairs. However, much of the evidence here suggests that the road to influence for African American women legislators is much more complex. African American women who have leadership positions describe that they are not members of the top leaders' inner circles, precluding them from participating at all levels of decisionmaking. This certainly impacts the extent to which they hold general influence. Likewise, the values of the institution also determine whether they are considered influential, even on the issues of importance to them. Merely gaining access to positions typically associated with influence may not be the key to accessing influence for African American women.

One example from the Mississippi legislature suggests that those in power are willing to use even the most Machiavellian tactics to retain their long-standing power in the institution. During the 2000 legislative session, the legislative leadership broke the traditional committee leadership norms at the same time an African American woman was appointed as chair of the prestigious Education Committee in the Senate. This changed the long-standing norm of having white men control the most powerful committees, but in the midst of this historic moment, legislative leaders still managed to preserve white male control over the legislative policy area and protect the customary structure of power in Mississippi. The African American woman's power as the chair of the Education Committee was curtailed by a maneuver on the part of the Appropriations chair, who broke with the traditional norm of appointing standing committee chairs as chairs of the subcommittee in Appropriations dealing with the same policy area. Under the old system, committee chairs held control over both the policy agenda and appropriating funds. However, with the Appropriations chair's change, this African American woman was forced to co-chair the Appropriation's Subcommittee on Education with her vice-chair of the Education Committee. Several legislators interviewed indicated that the leadership orchestrated the change in normal legislative procedures as a result of their resistance to placing that much power in her hands alone. According to one Mississippi legislator, the leadership sufficiently curtailed her influence under this new system.

> For the first time, I think it is basically because of Senator X, the Appropriations Committee chairman decided he was going to go with a system of co-chairs of the subcommittees. Now, a white male shares co-chairmanship of the Subcommittee on Education in the Appropriations Committee with X. Her power has been diluted because she can't make a move without her co-chairman.

This legislator and others who mentioned the new system instituted by the chair of the Appropriations Committee concerning subcommittee chairs indicated that this new system was deliberately executed to weaken the

African American woman's power. Several suggested that members of the leadership team were fearful of an African American woman controlling such a major area of public policy. Another Mississippi legislator went further in analyzing the influence of the Education chair in light of the change in the Appropriation Committee's subcommittee structure:

> When you talk about influence, there are some people that head the policy committee as well as the subcommittee on that particular area of appropriations—that is what makes them influential. . . . If you head the policy committee and the money committee, then you could just about get what you want through the legislature. If you head the policy committee and you need the money to implement what your policy is, then you don't have real influence over the issue.

Increasing the number of African American women committee chairs is an important means of garnering institutional positions that confer power and influence. However, this example suggests that selection as a committee chair may not result in the same institutional powers that are afforded to others holding the same position. In this case, the unwritten rules or norms were changed to maintain the existing power structure. It cannot be definitively concluded that the Appropriations chair instituted this rule as a means of specifically countering the power of the first African American woman to chair a major committee in the Senate, but it has had the effect of weakening this major committee chair's power.

Conclusion: Complexities of Race and Gender Norms

This study reiterates the complexity of influence in legislative institutions. Though scholars have always pointed out this reality, few have attributed this complexity to these institutions' inability to adapt to their increased diversity. This research contributes to our understandings of how legislative institutions are responding to difference. While much of the traditional knowledge about the nature of legislative influence remains constant, this study and others are showing that gender and race problematize even the most stable categories such as party leader or committee chair. The effects of gender and race on legislative influence are substantial. Gender and race mediate avenues that would otherwise lead to influence for African American women. These findings indicate that an African American woman party leader or committee chair conveys a different meaning in the minds of her colleagues. Unfortunately, when African American women move into such positions that traditionally convey power, it may not result in actually holding the power conveyed by the position. For these women, acquiring influence is more rich and complex than simply gaining access to positions of power previously denied them.

In examining African American women's influence, it is clear that they have not yet become the power brokers in the big leagues able to influence the legislative process across policy areas. However, as expected, influence in specific policy areas is slightly more open and they are indeed more likely to provide the equivalent of technical competence in the policy areas in which they have cultivated their expertise. Further, African American women are more likely to find themselves afforded some influence in legislatures like the Maryland General Assembly where knowledge and prior expertise in a policy area are preferenced. Such norms are far less exclusive and subjective. African American women and others seeking to influence their colleagues can acquire knowledge on a particular policy area more easily than they can appeal to and appease their colleagues' various notions of "quality character traits." More research on professional legislatures is needed to understand the extent to which these legislatures are more inclusive of women and people of color.

In this chapter, I have argued that state legislatures privilege attributes predominantly held by white male legislators. These preferences have become a part of the institution's norms and are instrumental in determining institutional power. The preservation of these institutional norms is critical to maintaining the current power structure and in the end determining policy outcomes.

At the time this study was conducted, the Democratic Party controlled all three of these state legislatures and African American women enjoyed some benefits from belonging to the party in control. Recently, the Republican Party has gained control over a number of state legislatures across the South, including both the Mississippi and Georgia state legislatures. As a result, African American women may find themselves experiencing even greater marginalization with ever more limited access to even symbolic power.

African American women legislators are resilient in the face of these circumstances. Though the legislative institution has not responded favorably to their difference, they remain active legislators. In my larger study of African American women's influence, I find that they are delivering for their constituents by finding creative means of ensuring their viability in the legislative process. They are successfully using their affiliations with both the women's caucus and the black caucus to leverage their influence. For the most part, African American women have positioned themselves as a bridge on issues that both caucuses consider important. Therefore, these legislators are able to play important roles on the policy issues that impact the communities they serve in the face of the legislative institution's resistance.

Notes

1. I conducted the largest number of interviews in Maryland ($n = 37$), followed by Mississippi ($n = 29$) and Georgia ($n = 28$).

2. These policy areas were derived from Barrett's (1995) findings and the national survey conducted in conjunction with this study.

3. T. Waldron and D. Dresser, "Handful of Lawmakers Pulls General Assembly's Strings: Leaders Drive Outcome for Most Legislation," *The Baltimore Sun*, 16 January 2000.

4. These include Jack Gordon who chaired the Appropriations Committee from 1988 to1992, Bill Minor who chaired the Finance Committee from 1992 to 1996, and Robert "Bunky" Huggins who chaired the Public Health and Welfare Committee from 1988 to 1992. Jack Elliott, "North Mississippi Senators Capture Lion's Share of Senate Leadership," *The Clarion Ledger* (Jackson), 13 January 2000.

5. Doug Nurse, "Legislative Notebook: Mills Rebuffed in Push for Open Session," *The Atlanta Journal Constitution*, 18 February 1999.

6. Ibid.

7. Kay Powell, "Frank Pinkston, Ex-Legislator," *The Atlanta Journal Constitution*, 28 March 2000.

8. This applies only to Georgia, the only state of the three with a committee designated to handle only children's issues.

11

Climbing Higher: Opportunities and Obstacles Within the Party System

CINDY SIMON ROSENTHAL

The more things change, the more they stay the same.[1]

WOMEN TODAY SERVE IN the US Congress in greater numbers than ever before, and Speaker Nancy Pelosi's (D-CA) rise to power marks a historic moment for women in leadership. In spite of this apparent progress, hints of resistance and the problem of invisibility persist both in the political science literature and the institution. Women in congressional leadership are exceptional, in three senses of the word—being a rare occurrence, deviating from the norm, and being held to higher standards and expectations.

In this chapter, I attempt to redress the relative absence of gender analysis in congressional leadership studies by first recounting the current status of women leaders in Congress and in the literature. Then, I show how gender analysis can provide new research insights by testing hypotheses about congressional leadership elections and analyzing leadership contests as socially constructed media events. Finally, I close with an argument for the incorporation of gender into the study of congressional leadership.

Utilizing an original data set of House leadership elections between 1975 and 2007, I analyze the gendered patterns of those elections. I find that women members of Congress more so than men are associated with contested leadership races in the last decade. As the number of lower-level leadership posts expanded in the 1990s, so too did the frequency of leadership contests involving women, both those challenged by men and those opposed by other women. Women's rise to congressional leadership confronts the obstacles of numbers, districts, informal processes, and outright resistance.

In recent leadership races, the media coverage suggests important differences in gendered discourse. The media pay much greater attention to, but impose contradictory interpretations of, Representative Pelosi's leadership style, which could be due to perceived incongruities of her femininity with the unspoken masculinity of congressional leadership. I argue for more gendered analyses of congressional leadership and suggest that current theoretical assumptions be challenged as distinctly gendered.

The Status of Women in Congressional Leadership

The 110th Congress enjoys a considerable presence of women in the ranks of the US House and Senate leadership. Seven of the 16 women in the US Senate hold positions of leadership or committee chairships in the 110th Congress. Speaker Pelosi is the first woman ever to lead her party in either chamber of the Congress and now serves as the first-ever female Speaker of the House. Table 11.1 reports the women of the 110th Congress by leadership positions in both parties and chambers.

Both parties have found ways to incorporate female members into some arena of leadership in spite of their lack of seniority. While leadership comes in different forms, this analysis generally focuses on those positions of elected, not appointed, leaders.[2] Table 11.2 illustrates the number and percentage of women in each party conference and as a percentage of different leadership roles. On average, women have less seniority, a factor also related in part to the fewer number of women serving as committee chairs or ranking members. Specifically, in the Senate, only one woman ranks in the top one-third of seniority, and similarly, only four women senators hold positions as chairs or ranking minority members of committees. Among House Republicans, only four women rank in the top third of party seniority, and only one of those has achieved the status of a ranking minority member on a committee. Among House Democrats, the picture is somewhat better with 12 women included among the top third of senior members and four women chairing committees in the 110th Congress. In party leadership, women are better represented, which may be due to the importance that both parties attach to women as a constituency to be acknowledged within the party hierarchy. Women comprise a quarter or more of Democratic leadership, including the whip teams. On the Republican side, women fare less well but still have proportionately more leadership slots than their membership in the caucuses would predict.

The road to leadership has not been an easy one, and for the most part women in leadership have been exceptions to the rule. Senator Margaret Chase Smith (R-ME) was the first woman to be elected by her peers to a Senate leadership position—Senate Republican Conference chair. Between

Table 11.1   110th Congressional Leadership

US Senate

Democrats

Majority leader	Harry Reid (NV)
President protempore	Robert Byrd (WV)
Assistant majority leader/majority whip	Richard Durbin (IL)
Conference vice chair/DSCC chairman	Charles E. Schumer (NY)
Conference secretary	*Patty Murray (WA)*
Policy committee chairman	Byron L. Dorgan (ND)
Steering and outreach committee chair[a]	*Debbie Stabenow (MI)*

Republicans

Minority leader	Mitch McConnell (KY)
Assistant minority leader/minority whip	Jon Kyl (AZ)
Conference chairman	Lamar Alexander (TN)
Conference vice chairman	John Cornyn (TX)
Policy committee chairman	*Kay Bailey Hutchison (TX)*
NRSC chairman	John Ensign (NV)

US House of Representatives

Democrats

Speaker of the House	*Nancy Pelosi (CA-8)*
Majority leader	Steny Hoyer (MD-5)
Majority whip	James Clyburn (SC-6)
Caucus chairman	Rahm Emanuel (IL-5)
Caucus vice chairman	John Larson (CT-1)
Steering committee co-chair[a]	*Rosa DeLauro (CT-3)*
Steering committee co-chair[a]	George Miller (CA-7)
Chairman, committee on rules[a]	*Louise Slaughter (NY-28)*
DCCC chairman	Chris Van Hollen (MD-8)
Senior chief deputy whip[a]	John Lewis (GA-5)
Chief deputy whip[a]	G.K. Butterfield (NC-1)
Chief deputy whip[a]	Joseph Crowley (NY-7)
Chief deputy whip[a]	*Diana DeGette (CO-1)*
Chief deputy whip[a]	Ed Pastor (AZ-4)
Chief deputy whip[a]	*Jan Schakowsky (IL-9)*
Chief deputy whip[a]	John Tanner (TN-8)
Chief deputy whip[a]	*Maxine Waters (CA-35)*
Chief deputy whip[a]	*Debbie Wasserman Schultz (FL-20)*

Republicans

Minority leader	John Boehner (OH-8)
Minority whip	Roy Blunt (MO-7)
Chief deputy minority whip[a]	Eric Cantor (VA-7)
Conference chairman	Adam Putnam (FL-12)
Conference vice chairman	*Kay Granger (TX-12)*
Conference secretary	John Carter (TX-31)
Policy committee chairman	Thaddeus McCotter (MI-11)
NRCC chairman	Tom Cole (OK-4)

Source: Almanac of American Politics (Washington, DC: National Journal, 2008).
Notes: Italics indicate female representatives.
a. Denotes appointed leadership position.

Table 11.2   Percentage of Women in Party Leadership by Caucus/Conference and Chamber in 110th Congress

	% Women in Conference Membership	% Women in Top Third of Party Seniority	% Women on Party Steering Committee	% Women in Party Leadership[a]	% Women as Chairs and Ranking Minority Members
House Democrats	21.1	15.4	30	38.9	19
	(49 of 232)	(12 of 78)	(15 of 50)	(7 of 18)	(4 of 21)
House Republicans	10.4	6	7.1	12.5	4.8
	(21 of 202)	(4 of 67)	(2 of 28)	(1 of 8)	(1 of 21)
Senate Democrats	22.4	6.3	n.a.	28.6	10
	(11 of 49)	(1 of 16)		(2 of 7)	(2 of 20)
Senate Republicans	10.2	0	n.a.	16.7	10
	(5 of 49)	(0 of 16)		(1 of 6)	(2 of 20)

Sources: CAWP, "Women in Elective Office 2007," Fact Sheet (New Brunswick, NJ: Center for American Women in Politics, 2007); Barone and Cohen, *The Almanac of American Politics 2008* (Washington, DC: National Journal, 2007); and Koszczuk and Angle, *CQ Politics in America 2008* (Washington, DC: CQ Press, 2007).

Note: a. Party leadership includes the elected leaders and deputy whips. Since regional whips are not consistently reported by the caucuses, they are not included.

that 1967 milestone and the 2001 election of Pelosi as House Democratic whip, women generally ran only for lower-level leadership positions such as secretary or vice-chair of their party conference. In the 1970s and 1980s, women ran without opposition for the positions of conference vice chair or secretary but were unsuccessful in attempts to move up to conference chair or higher office, a pattern evident, for example, with representatives Mary Rose Oakar (D-OH), Lynn Martin (R-IL), and Shirley Chisholm (D-NY) (Amer 2005). Women have served as appointed leaders, for example deputy whips, assistant floor leaders, or chairs of party policy or outreach committees. Neither party has ever had more than two women in elected leadership positions simultaneously.

Beginning with the 1990s, the number and success of women in congressional leadership began to change. Between the 104th Congress (1994–1995) and the 109th Congress (2005–2006), the number of women seeking elected leadership posts in the House totaled 16, compared to only 9 women who sought elected leadership posts from the 94th (1971–1972) through the 103rd (1993–1994). In 1998, Representative Jennifer Dunn (R-WA) became the first woman to run for a senior leadership post in her unsuccessful bid for majority leader. Also in 1998, Representative Rosa de Lauro (D-CT) ran for and lost a contest for Democratic Caucus chair but Democratic leader Richard Gephardt (D-MO) named her to a newly created post of assistant to the Democratic leader. In 2003, Representative Deborah

Pryce (R-OH) became the first woman since Senator Smith to be elected chair of her party's conference, though she stepped down in 2006 amidst speculation of an intraparty challenge.

In the Senate, Senator Barbara Mikulski (D-MD) broke into the all-male Democratic leadership team in 1992 as an assistant floor leader and moved up the ranks to conference secretary in 1995, a post she held until Senator Debbie Stabenow (D-MI) succeeded her in 2005. Across the aisle, Senator Kay Bailey Hutchison (R-TX) similarly broke into the all-male party leadership ranks in 2001 as GOP Conference vice chairwoman.

While few leaders rise to party leadership through the committee system, women have also not fared well in securing committee posts until the 110th Congress. During the recent era of Republican rule of the House (1995–2006), women did not benefit from the conference policy of term limits on committee chairs and the declining importance of seniority (Herrick 2000). The only Republican woman to chair a full committee during 12 years of GOP rule was Representative Jan Meyers (R-KS), who oversaw the unheralded Committee on Small Business in the 104th Congress (1995–1996). While seniority earned former representative Nancy Johnson (R-CT) clout as Ways and Means Health Subcommittee chair, her moderate politics limited her influence in the caucus. Former representative Marge Roukema (R-NJ) fell short in her bid to become the first woman to chair a major House committee at the start of the 107th Congress, even though GOP term limits created the opportunity for her to secure a committee chair based on her seniority. Representative Roukema, a moderate who is fiercely independent, lost out to Representative Michael Oxley (R-OH) when the new Financial Services Committee was created. In subsequent congresses, no GOP women were selected to chair a full committee even though term limits created 14 openings on the 19 major House committees in the 107th Congress and more openings thereafter.

With the 110th Congress, House Democratic women gained an unprecedented number of committee chairs. Four women now preside over House committees, including Representative Louise Slaughter's (D-NY) seat at the head of the powerful Rules Committee.

In the Senate, an institution that still values and rewards length of service, women have been able to secure committee and leadership posts by virtue of their seniority. In the 109th Congress, Senator Hutchison was the senior Republican woman ranking 18th on the GOP seniority list and securing a place on the Policy Committee. Senator Olympia Snowe (R-ME) at 20th and Senator Susan Collins (R-ME) at 32nd on the seniority list chaired full committees in the 109th. On the Democratic side, Senator Mikulski enjoys the greatest seniority, which translated into her decade-long stint as secretary of the caucus. In the 110th, Senator Patty Murray (D-WA) succeeded Senator Stabenow as caucus secretary and the next highest women in seniority, Senators Barbara Boxer (D-CA) and Dianne Feinstein (D-CA), became committee chairs.

The only women of color to serve in congressional leadership have been in the Democratic Party. They include Representative Patsy Mink (D-HI) as caucus secretary in the 94th Congress and Shirley Chisholm (D-NY) as caucus secretary in the 95th and 96th congresses.

Nancy Pelosi's rise to the pinnacle of congressional leadership both fits and contradicts the pattern other women faced. Speaker Pelosi did not pursue the step-by-step climb through the lower-level rungs of leadership but rather built her reputation and winning coalition in the committee system and as an appropriator. Raised in a family steeped in Baltimore city politics and celebrated as a talented political fund-raiser for the California Democratic Party, Speaker Pelosi grounded her successful leadership coalition in the large California delegation, among women, Hispanics, and African American members, and from colleagues on the defense appropriation subcommittee (especially John Murtha of Pennsylvania who managed her campaign). In shattering the "marble ceiling," her election has redefined congressional leadership.

A Review of the Literature

The relative novelty of women in congressional leadership has produced a literature in political science that has taken little note of the role of gender. Indeed, the literature has long been dominated by a focus on leadership embodied in the stories of great men and by theoretical perspectives that embrace an unspoken masculine perspective and a general failure to acknowledge women's invisibility.

The absence of gender from the literature is certainly understandable, but the persistence of masculine imagery in even recent literature is odd. For example, it may have been understandable that Frank Mackaman (1980), at a time when women were exceedingly rare in leadership, employed a football metaphor to describe leaders as "the would-be quarterbacks of Congress" (6). It is oddly jarring, however, to hear a similar metaphor—"sack the quarterback"—used in 2004 to describe the electoral strategy of trying to defeat congressional party leaders like former senator Tom Daschle (D-SD) at the polls.[3]

Barbara Sinclair's (1990) definitive review essay on congressional research makes little note of women's absence in congressional leadership, understandably reflecting the historical scarcity of women at the time. She employs gender-neutral language in the essay and writes, "The potential challenger must persuade his or her colleagues not just that he or she is preferable to the heir apparent, but that the heir apparent is so lacking. . . ."

(1990, 122). But the discussion of heirs-apparent seems to beg for some mention of representatives Oakar, Chisholm, or Martin, who went from heirs-apparent to victims of intraparty challenges as they sought to assert their claim on the next rung of the leadership ladder.

Three more contemporary analyses of leadership suggest the persistent invisibility of gender and women from the congressional research agenda. Bernard Grofman, William Koetzle, and Anthony McGann (2002) revive a controversy over what drives the selection of leaders. They test what David Truman (1959) first called the "middleman" hypothesis (i.e., that leaders are most likely to be drawn from the ideological middle of their parties) against what Aage Clausen and Clyde Wilcox (1987) suggest is a preference of members of Congress to turn to leaders from more partisan extremes. Grofman and his co-authors present their evidence, which includes many lower-level leadership races where women can be found, and conclude that party leaders are not "middlemen" but rather are more likely to come from "the area beyond the median toward the party mode" in terms of ideology (2002, 98). While the authors control for regional party leaders, they do not include sex as a relevant variable. The analysis ignores the intersection of gender and ideology, where women in both parties on average occupy the more moderate to liberal wing.

Sinclair (1999) contributes an important insight that leaders in both caucuses—beginning with the House Democrats and continued by Speaker Newt Gingrich (R-GA)—developed inclusive strategies to promote member "buy-in" through expanded leadership structures, particularly in the whip system and special task forces (428–429). She argues that the goal of the strategy is to "involve a larger proportion of the membership in leadership and thereby give them a stake in their success" (432). A gendered analysis of the same period would note the parallel trends of increasing numbers of women as members of Congress (MCs), expanding lower-level leadership opportunities for women in the 1990s and the emerging leadership strategies described by Sinclair (1999).

Updating her analysis, Sinclair (2006) notes that inclusion as a strategy has the paradoxical consequence of taming the membership: "The top leaders benefit from such members becoming a part of the leadership in a number of ways; they bring their efforts and skills to the leadership enterprise, they often provide links to important party subgroups, and they are less likely to cause problems when they are inside the tent" (133). Increasingly, the need to impose intraparty discipline has accentuated the pressures on members to be loyal, particularly within the Republican Conference where "meetings tend to take on a 'locker room' atmosphere, especially before a big vote" (Sinclair 2006, 135). Since women are perhaps the most obvious subgroup to emerge in more significant numbers in the 1990s, the dynamic of inclusion, buy-in, and party discipline raises interesting questions about gender and congressional leadership—none of which is acknowledged in the extant literature.

Finally, Douglas Harris (2006) examines the strategic choices of members as they select leaders. Most of Harris's analysis centers around a case study of Representative Gingrich's whip election. However, Harris also suggests a longer historical trend toward contested leadership elections in the House. He argues that we should see "leadership selection as political choices that parties make to adapt to broader contextual factors and to chart the party's strategic course" (192). He concludes that leadership selection has become increasingly contested and conflictual since the post-reform era of the 1970s. Again, an obvious but neglected question might be to consider what role women have played in those contests.

This literature, when linked to observations from gender analyses, suggests four important and testable hypotheses. First, "intrusiveness theory" posits that when newcomers to an organization or institution begin to increase in number, the dominant group often responds by resisting or excluding the intruders (Yoder 1991; Kathlene 1994). I hypothesize that contested elections might be more common for women as outsiders or newcomers than for men who have been the traditional insiders or dominants in Congress. Second, the theory of "tokenism" suggests that an underrepresented group may be granted some special status and visibility within an organization but often only in a limited and organizationally constrained space (Kanter 1977). In congressional leadership, I hypothesize that we might find forms of incorporation of women that do not convey equal power or opportunity—such as relegating women to low-level leadership jobs befitting of their "token" status.

Third, recent research suggests that women in Congress may be poorly situated to compete for leadership positions as "middlemen." For both party caucuses in the House, Barbara Palmer and Dennis Simon (2006) identify factors that make some districts more "women friendly" than others and thus more likely to send women to Washington, DC. The most women-friendly districts for Republican women tend to be less conservative, more urban, and more diverse than those electing their male counterparts (Palmer and Simon 2006), thus Republican women are likely to be outside the mainstream of their party in terms of ideology and neither in the middle or at the conservative extreme of the party. Similarly, Palmer and Simon (2006) point out that Democratic women are most likely to win in districts that are more liberal, more urban, more diverse, and wealthier than seats won by their male colleagues. Democratic women are more likely to be ideologically positioned beyond the median rather than close to the mean. The work of Palmer and Simon suggests two possible hypotheses: (1) women may have more difficulty qualifying as "middlemen" in leadership elections, but (2) if Clausen and Wilcox (1987) are correct, then being at the partisan extreme may work to the advantage of Democratic women in contrast with Republican women.

Exploring Hypotheses: Resistance or Something Else?

In House leadership elections between 1975 and 2007, 307 leadership candidates vied in 78 contested (thus drawing multiple candidates) and 140 uncontested races. In total, these leadership elections drew the candidacies of 260 men and 47 women. Since leadership often involves moving up the ladder, it is important to note that the elections over these 32 years involved only 137 different individuals—112 men and 25 women.

Not surprisingly, contested races occur more often when there is leadership change at the top of the party, prompting a series of leadership changes down the ladder. In nine congresses where the Speaker or minority leader left office, an average of seven leadership contests ensued. In the other eight congresses covered by this time period, most leadership elections were unchallenged, with an average of two contests occurring with each new session. I use this data set of leadership elections to explore further the gendered dynamics of congressional leadership contests. The unit of analysis is the individual candidate; thus, a total of 307 cases are analyzed. For each candidate, several pieces of information were recorded and analyzed—the number of other candidates in the race, the gender composition of the race, the member's DW-Nominate score[4] and the difference between each candidate's score and his or her party's mean and median, the position sought, party, sex, year, and the particular Congress in which the election contest occurred. These characteristics of individual candidates and the leadership contests in which they participated (the independent variables) are the most likely determinants of whether an individual won a leadership election (the dependent variable). Data for most of the leadership contests came from the Congressional Research Service (Amer 2005) supplemented by the author's data from more recent elections.

Is there evidence to support the aforementioned hypotheses? I begin with a statistical profile of men and women competing for leadership elections in their parties. Table 11.3 shows the basic descriptive statistics of congressional elections from 1975 to 2007 by sex. Reflecting the overall membership of the House, men outnumber women in seeking congressional leadership posts. Plus, Republican candidates for leadership have been more numerous than Democratic contestants because the party has many more elected leadership positions. Table 11.3 shows some significant sex differences among leadership contestants. For example, Republican women have been significantly more likely than Republican men to run in contested elections and to face more candidates in those races. A greater percentage of

Table 11.3 Characteristics of Leadership Candidates, by Party and Sex

	Men	Women
Democratic candidates/winners	$N = 81/56$	$N = 20/12$
% in contested races	54.3	55.0
% who won	69.0	60.0
Average number of opponents	1.95	1.75
Average difference between		
Candidates' DW score and party mean	.060**	.123**
Candidates' DW score and party median	.047**	.109**
Winners' DW score and party mean	.081**	.141**
Winners' DW score and party median	.069**	.124**
Republican candidates/winners	$N = 179/124$	$N = 27/17$
% in contested races	52.5*	66.7*
% who won races	69.3	63.0
Average number of opponents	1.80**	2.26**
Average difference between		
Candidates' DW score and party mean	−.059**	−.008**
Candidates' DW score and party median	−.063**	−.015**
Winners' DW score and party mean	−.058 ****	.013****
Winners' DW score and party median	−.058 ***	.019***

Note: * $p <.10$, ** $p <.05$, *** $p <.01$, **** $p <.001$ for sex differences based on means in t-tests for independent samples or crosstabs where appropriate.

men have won their leadership races than have women, but that pattern does not reach statistical significance and can be explained, in part, by the greater number of men who have run for leadership posts uncontested. In both parties, women come into leadership elections with significantly different and generally more liberal ideological voting records than do the men in their parties. What of the specific hypotheses?

Hypothesis 1: Intrusiveness and Contested Elections

As noted earlier, the literature suggests that as women become more numerous in an organization, their presence is more likely to precipitate opposition. Applied to congressional elections, we might expect to see reactions to the growing proportion of women in the membership to be manifested in opposition to their candidacy for leadership. Table 11.4 and Figure 11.1 offer three distinct gender insights. First, since the 1990s, women have been more likely than men to face contested elections. The disproportionate involvement of women in contested leadership races fits the expectations of intrusiveness theory. Second, women in the decade of the 1990s also faced a more crowded field of rivals than did men, providing more evidence in support of the intrusiveness theory. Third, the frequency of contested leadership races by decade shows no particular upward pattern, contradicting the

Table 11.4   Gender Patterns of Competition in Congressional Leadership Races over Time

	1975–1980		1981–1990		1991–2000		2001–2007	
	% in Contested Races	Average No. of Opponents	% in Contested Races	Average No. of Opponents	% in Contested Races	Average No. of Opponents	% in Contested Races	Average No. of Opponents
Men	55.3	1.89	51.2	1.82	54.1	1.78	52.6	1.95
Women	40	1.4	45.5	1.82	75	2.5	66.7	1.93
All	53.8	1.85	50.5	1.82	57.8	1.91	55.6	1.95

Figure 11.1 Gender Patterns of Competition in Congressional Leadership Races, by Decade

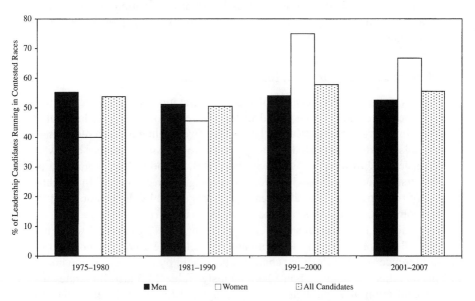

observation of Harris (2006). Indeed slight fluctuations up and down are the more obvious pattern.

Over the entire period from 1975 to 2007, 61.7 percent of women candidates have run in contested races compared with 46.6 percent of men. Looking more closely at the period from 1991 until the present when the number of women in Congress began to increase steadily (particularly in the Democratic Party), women were much more likely to run in contested races than men. For example, 77.8 percent of Democratic women ran in contested races compared with 44.2 percent of the men, and among

Republicans, 68.2 percent of women faced opponents compared with 58.0 percent of the GOP male leadership aspirants. In those contested races, Table 11.4 shows women during the 1990s faced more opponents, and more opponents reduces a candidate's likelihood of success.

What might explain the disproportionate representation of women among contested leadership elections? Perhaps women are perceived as weaker or more vulnerable. Alternatively, the opportunity structure may be gendered. The expansion of leadership positions since the mid-1990s has been mostly in lower-level positions where entry is to be expected by more junior members (where women are more numerous). Meanwhile, higher-level positions are already held by more established male members whose rise in leadership is no longer contested. In other words, first entry into leadership may produce more contested races than reselection in office or succession contests to move up the leadership ladder. The gendered pattern in contested races does not necessarily imply discrimination or bias against women, but it does suggest a gendered dynamic for women pursuing a leadership post.

Hypothesis 2: Tokenism and Less Powerful Roles

Theory suggests that because of their token status and numbers, women may be more likely to be found in less powerful or specially designated roles in an organization (Kanter 1977). Thus we might expect to see women more isolated or ghettoized in less powerful roles. As the number of lower-level leadership posts expanded in the 1990s, so too did the frequency of leadership contests involving women running against women. In the data set of races from 1975 to 2007, each race was coded by the position and by the composition of the race. Table 11.5 reports these results.

Table 11.5 provides evidence of informally reserved "women's posts," especially among Republicans. In fact since 1993, the position of conference secretary or vice chair has been held by a woman in one house or the other (sometimes both) continuously. Table 11.5 also illustrates the concentration of Republican women competing for lower-level leadership posts in mostly female-dominated races. Interestingly, in the House Republican conference since the 108th Congress, the pattern of predominantly female candidates for secretary or vice chair has changed, and none of the GOP contests for these positions drew more than one woman. While it is too early to draw a definitive conclusion, the conference secretary and vice chair positions may be evolving from the reputation as women's spots and becoming positions open to all comers. This may signal a change such that no leadership position is reserved on the basis of sex or that the need to insure a woman's place in the leadership hierarchy has disappeared.

Table 11.5   Gender Composition of Party Leadership Races, 1975–2007

Leadership Position	All Male		Mostly Male		Balanced Male/Female		Mostly Female		All Female	
	Democratic	Republican	Democratic	Republican	Democratic	Republican	Democratic	Republican	Democratic	Republican
Floor leader	11	8	0	4	2	0	0	0	0	0
Whip	10	15	0	0	2	0	0	0	0	0
Conference/caucus chair	7	13	3	10	8	0	0	0	0	0
Conference/caucus secretary/vice chair	3	7	7	0	0	10	0	8	2	2
All other elected positions	0	33	0	0	0	4	0	8	0	0
Total	31	76	10	14	12	14	0	8	2	2

Hypothesis 3: Middlewomen and Unequal Opportunities

Prior research focused on whether leaders possess voting records at the ideological middle or the extreme of their parties. As Table 11.3 illustrated, women candidates for leadership positions in both parties on average are likely to be more liberal than male leadership candidates as measured by the difference between their DW-Nominate score and the party mean or median scores.

Certainly the claim that she was too liberal to represent the mainstream of the Democratic Party haunted Nancy Pelosi in her rise to party leader. Supporters of her main opponent in 2001, Representative Steny Hoyer (D-MD), framed her as "too liberal" and him as "better able to woo centrist voters and win back the swing districts."[5] Representative Charles S. Stenholm said: "The only way we can take the House back is by getting the swing districts. We cannot do it by going to the left."[6] When she sought to ascend to party leader in 2002, challengers Representative Martin Frost (D-TX) and Representative Harold Ford (D-TN) made similar claims. Frost described himself as "an outspoken advocate for the mainstream, centrist views that will lead us to the majority."[7] Ford stated, "I am not running for Democratic leader to move our party left or right. I want to move us forward."[8]

Adding gender to the "middleman" debate suggests new questions and possible insights. Depending on whether leaders are drawn from the middle or the extremes of their party, we might expect to see a difference between the DW-Nominate scores of the candidate pool compared with the winners. If winners are more likely to be drawn from the middle of their party, then any gender difference in ideology among male and female leadership contestants should disappear or narrow among male and female winners and move closer to the party median or mean. If winners are more likely to be drawn from the extreme of their party, then any gender difference in ideology should disappear or narrow among winners but move farther from the middle of the party. Neither of these patterns holds for either party in Table 11.3.

The gender differences in DW scores do not disappear among winners. In the Democratic Party, winning leadership candidates are more liberal on average than the candidate pool, and the significant gender differences among candidates remain among winners. This finding suggests support for the Grofman, Koetzle, and McGann (2002) claim. On the GOP side, no difference is evident among male candidates and male winners in terms of their ideological record vis-à-vis the party. Paradoxically, the successful Republican women are more liberal than both the candidate pool of women and both means of the male candidates and male winners. The pattern may be the result of an anomaly in the 1990s, which had both the largest number of GOP women leadership candidates and the most striking differences in ideology, and perhaps the use of aggregate data masks differences and dynamics in actual individual races. It would seem that women running for leadership are not disadvantaged by their more liberal policy preferences or that some other leadership qualification or trait may militate against ideology in leadership selection.

Whatever the explanation, the addition of gender to the longstanding "middleman" debate suggests the need to consider whether some factor other than ideological position within the party may be at work. Two variables warrant future investigation. First, congressional leaders currently play a key role in helping raise money for their colleagues; thus a prospective leader's fund-raising acumen (e.g., Speaker Pelosi's well-known talents come to mind) may trump any ideological distance between the leader and his or her party. Second, a leader's own electoral insecurity might be a consideration that overshadows ideology. The rank-and-file may be understandably concerned about choosing an electorally vulnerable leader, as in the case of Representative Deborah Pryce (R-OH), who stepped down as chair of the GOP House caucus rather than face simultaneously an intraparty leadership challenge and a formidable reelection race in her district. To the extent that more liberal districts are "safer" or "friendlier" for women in Congress (Palmer and Simon 2006), liberal Democratic women may reap certain advantages in their leadership aspirations, while conservative Republican women with similar aspirations face a distinct gender hurdle.

Challenges in Studying Gender in Leadership Elections

Because the number of cases remains relatively small, gender in leadership elections remains difficult to study. Moreover, much of what transpires in individual contests occurs behind the scenes, where informal processes may present obstacles (and opportunities) for women in leadership. Denise Baer (2006) argues that advancement in congressional party leadership turns on informal processes, which in the past worked against women. She cites the example of Representative Oakar, caucus vice chair in the 99th and 100th congresses and acting caucus chair when Representative Richard Gephardt (D-MO) stepped aside to pursue his presidential aspirations. Baer writes:

> Shockingly Oakar was not a shoo-in for the chair post in the 101st Congress when Gephardt stepped up to the Majority Leader post. In a three-way election, Bill Gray (PA) won with 146 votes, defeating Oakar (80 votes) and Mike Synar (OK) (33 votes). [These] facts are noteworthy: the usual recruitment ladder from Vice Chair to Chair was not respected in the three-way race, and Gephardt pointedly opposed Oakar. (2006, 20)

Informal processes may have worked to the advantage of Representative Pelosi in the race for party whip. First, 35 of the 44 House Democratic

women backed Pelosi in the 2001 race for Democratic minority whip, attest-
ing to the possibility of an emerging "girls' network" in the caucus. Second,
her closest advisor and campaign manager was Representative John Murtha
(D-PA), an undisputed member of the party "old guard." When then-leader
Gephardt delayed in setting an election date, some saw his reluctance as giving Representative Hoyer a chance to "peel away votes from Pelosi."
Murtha, however, intervened with Gephardt to level the playing field.[9]

That's not to say that Representative Hoyer did not have his own
behind-the-scenes assets: "'This is an insider's game,' says a Democratic
lawmaker, who explains that Hoyer is better positioned because of his seniority and his status within the 'old boys' club' to win over the ranking
Democrats on the committees and subcommittees. They, in turn can then
influence other members."[10] In the same year that Pelosi rose to the minority leader's position, informal insider maneuvering is thought to have ultimately blocked Representative Rosa DeLauro's (D-CT) bid for caucus
chair. Whispers of "too many women" in leadership may have contributed
to her loss by one vote to Representative Robert Menendez (D-NJ) in the
108th Congress.

Is there resistance to women's leadership? One detects a lack of deference toward Representative Pelosi in the repeated doubts raised about her
skills. Generally, routine and unchallenged leadership advancement from
party leader to Speaker has been the norm (Amer 2005), though it is not
unusual for parties to acknowledge an alternate leader waiting in the wings.
Baer (2006) suggests that Representative Hoyer used his status of "Speaker-
in-waiting" to engage in very public disagreements with Pelosi in the
months before her ascendancy to the speakership. Even more unusual,
Pelosi's appointee to the Democratic Congressional Campaign Committee,
Representative Rahm Emanuel (D-IL), confronted Pelosi on policy and
strategy in the 2006 elections and thus deviated from the respect normally
accorded the party leader (Baer 2006, 20).

Another indicator of resistance is heard in the persistent doubts about
Pelosi's leadership from members of her own conference. They ask whether
she is up to the task of meting out party discipline in the way that her
Republican counterpart Tom DeLay did. Though she "systematically adopted many of the bare-knuckle tactics" to sanction members who defied party
leadership and imposed fund-raising quotas on members to help the party,
the doubts got reported: "Many Democrats told us privately that they
believe Pelosi lacks precisely that killer instinct to place her in the tradition
of DeLay or Cannon: She is not seen as menacing enough to scare members
into action."[11] Certainly the caucus leadership rivalries, which she faces, are
not new (e.g., witness the reign of Speaker Newt Gingrich in the 104th and
105th congresses). But the informal processes make the influence of gender
complicated to discern.

Applying a Gendered Analysis to Recent Leadership Choice

Notwithstanding its challenges, gender analysis can yield new insight into understanding congressional leadership. To further illustrate this point, I turn to an analysis of media coverage of recent elections involving contested Democratic and Republican Party congressional leadership elections. Specifically, I analyzed 99 articles pulled from LexisNexis using the major newspaper file and major news magazines including *Newsweek, CQ Weekly,* and *National Journal.* First, I identified 46 articles through searches that included the terms "Pelosi," "leadership," and "election" for the period between 1 January 1999 and 31 December 2002. Of these, 16 relate to the Democratic whip election in October 2001, and 30 pertain to the subsequent Democratic leader election in November 2002. Second, I identified 53 articles using the search terms "House," "majority leader," and "election" for the period between 1 January 2005 and 3 February 2006. The period covers the resignation of then–majority leader Tom DeLay and the subsequent leadership race between representatives John Boehner (R-OH), Roy Blunt (R-MO), and John Shadegg (R-AZ).

The analysis is principally descriptive and exploratory in an effort to pose some questions and implications for the study of women in congressional leadership. The analysis is limited by its reliance on print media coverage, which admittedly is a filtered representation of the event, and its focus on two fairly unique leadership elections, from which it may be difficult to generalize. The coverage and the sentiments quoted may not reflect the ultimate calculus made by members and cannot be definitively shown to be causally linked. Story framing, however, is often acknowledged to provide insight on how political leaders attempt to frame public messages and how the media "evince the power and point of view of the political and economic elites who operate and focus it" (Gamson et al. 1992, 374).

Content analysis included several coding decisions with respect to gender references, quotes from news source, story framing, leadership appeals to the rank and file, and references to leadership style.[12] Lawrence Dodd's (2001) three theoretical perspectives on the member-leader relationship provide a template for determining the story frame of member-leader choice. While Dodd did not use these perspectives to understand leadership elections, I believe that they have relevance to the choices members make in selecting new leaders. Dodd's perspectives include:[13]

- *Social choice theory:* members will choose a leader based on the congruence of their goals and who they think is best able to help achieve members' goals.
- *Social structure theory:* members will choose an institutional leader based on a need to respond to larger external forces in society.

- *Social learning theory:* members will choose a leader who they believe is best able to respond to an immediate crisis.

The content analysis yields interesting results with striking contrasts between the coverage associated with Representative Pelosi's two contests and the most recent Republican leadership election. Table 11.6 illustrates the exceptional role of gender in the contrasting coverage.

Clearly, the novelty of Representative Pelosi's ascendancy to be the first woman elected party whip for either party drives the much higher number of references to gender. While the number of gender references drops when she runs in 2002 for party leader, the coverage of her second race for minority leader still stands in stark contrast to the total absence of any references to gender in the 2006 election to replace Representative Tom DeLay. In 53 articles about the race to succeed DeLay, not one includes a gender reference. By comparison, each article about the Democratic leadership races averaged more than three references. The references are both predictable and varied. For example, from one article the reader confronted the following: "The first woman in congressional history. . . . support from many women lawmakers, while some ol' boy conservatives. . . . Hoyer was a boy wonder in the state Legislature. . . . Democrats need to 'walk the walk' when they are presented with a qualified woman candidate."[14] Hoyer is credited with being a "member's member," a construction that is seemingly ungendered but echoes the characterization of a "man's man."[15]

Similarly those quoted in the articles show a distinct gender pattern. Women were almost three times more likely to be quoted in the articles about Representative Pelosi than in the articles about representatives Boehner, Blunt, Shadegg, and DeLay. In fact, in 31 of the 53 articles

Table 11.6 Voices and Gender Coverage in Recent House Leadership Elections, Mean Counts (standard deviation)

	Gender References	Total Women Quoted	Total Men Quoted	Female Members of Congress Quoted	Male Members of Congress Quoted
Pelosi's whip race	5.31	1.31	2.88	1.25	2.56
(*n* = 16)	(4.71)	(1.35)	(3.14)	(1.24)	(2.94)
Pelosi's leader race	2.10	1.60	2.80	1.20	1.83
(*n* = 30)	(2.47)	(1.35)	(2.46)	(1.00)	(1.95)
Race to succeed DeLay	.00	.51	4.11	.32	3.11
(*n* = 53)	(.00)	(.70)	(2.42)	(.50)	(2.25)
Mean for all articles	1.50	.97	3.52	.73	2.64
(n = 99)	(2.98)	(1.16)	(2.61)	(.94)	(2.34)

(58.5%) about the Republican leadership race, no women were quoted compared with at least two male voices being heard in 43 of 53 articles (81.2%). Among the members of Congress quoted in the coverage, women are barely visible in the Republican leadership race but quoted on average in proportion to their share of the conference membership. Women MCs are quoted more often in the Democratic leadership races, and in numbers greater than their share of caucus membership. Perhaps, reporters see male MCs as less authoritative sources to comment on a woman leader.

In terms of leadership style, the most striking aspect of the coverage is the lack of characterizations of the different representatives' leadership style. The leadership styles of Shadegg, Frost, Ford, and Blunt get little or no comment. Only representatives Pelosi's and DeLay's leadership styles garnered much attention. In 15 articles, Pelosi's style was variously characterized as "unfailingly gracious,"[16] "relentless fighter,"[17] "politically shrewd" with "collaborative skills,"[18] and having "the ability to make merry while reaching for the jugular."[19] By contrast, 10 articles characterized DeLay's well-known, take-no-prisoners aggressive style, which earned him the nickname "The Hammer." Four articles made reference to Representative Hoyer's leadership style, and five made reference to Representative Boehner's style.

The greater attention to Representative Pelosi's style and the multiple perspectives taken suggest two possible explanations. First, the men running for leadership may presumptively be credited with having a leadership style that is so congruent with the norms of leadership that no description was needed. Alternatively, the perspectives on her style may reflect an effort to reconcile her femininity with the unspoken masculinity of congressional leadership. Attention to DeLay may in turn reflect a fascination with the iconic aggressiveness and hyper-masculine style, which contributed to his notoriety and demise. As a *Washington Post* article noted: "Every generation has one: the tough-as-nails leader with the pugnacity to demand the discipline, money or power to control Congress. With Tom DeLay's dramatic rise and fall, the job's now open."[20]

Finally, I turn to the issue of story frames. My interest is in understanding the meaning attached to different leadership contests and the extent to which they might be seen in a gendered context. Table 11.7 presents the coverage both in terms of the primary story frame as well as the combined primary and secondary frames identified with a particular article. In both instances there are substantively interesting and statistically significant differences.

In terms of primary story frames, Representative Pelosi's races can be seen principally in terms of the social choice frame and her ability to fulfill members' goals. This is the essence of principal-agent theory where the members' expectations will shape leaders' responses and strategies to meet

Table 11.7 Primary and Combined Frames Associated with Leadership Elections

	Pelosi's Whip Race	Pelosi's Leader Race	Race to Succeed Delay
Primary Story Frame[a]			
No primary frame	0 (0%)	4 (13.3%)	1 (1.9%)
Social choice	13 (81.3%)	20 (66.7%)	18 (34.0%)
Social structure	3 (18.8%)	2 (6.7%)	1 (1.9%)
Social learning	0 (0%)	4 (13.3%)	33 (62.3%)
$N = 99$	16	30	53
Combined Primary and Secondary Frames[b]			
No frame	0 (.0%)	4 (13.3%)	0 (.0%)
Social choice only	4 (25%)	8 (26.7%)	5 (9.4%)
Social structure only	0 (0%)	1 (3.3%)	1 (1.9%)
Social learning only	0 (0%)	4 (13.3%)	6 (11.3%)
Social choice + social structure	11 (68.6%)	8 (26.7%)	2 (3.8%)
Social choice + social learning	1 (6.3%)	5 (16.7%)	37 (69.8%)
Social learning + social structure	0 (0%)	0 (0%)	2 (3.8%)
$N = 99$	16	30	53

Notes: a. Pearson Chi-Square = 38.384, df = 6, p = .000.
b. Pearson Chi-Square = 61.12, df = 12, p = .000.

those expectations. The coverage of her ability to meet those goals is consistently paradoxical, however. More than half of the articles mention her significant fund-raising and campaign organizational prowess, but in the same stories, doubts in the tradition of the "middleman" theory are prominent. Two examples:

> Many are nervous that House Democrats under Ms. Pelosi's leadership will exacerbate the broader struggle between conservatives and traditional liberals.[21]

> The competition was being framed as a choice between a woman from one of the party's anchor states who could reinvigorate House Democrats with new ideas and leadership style and a man [Martin Frost] who has tangled successfully with tough Texas conservatives. . . . It presents lawmakers with a crucial decision on which candidate they think can shape a message and an agenda that can broaden the party's appeal to voters.[22]

The paradoxical language used to frame Pelosi's elections in terms of social choice theory typically acknowledges her skills in helping members on the campaign trail while simultaneously casting doubts on her ability to lead the party to majority status. No one described the gender ambiguities more colorfully than former Representative Patricia Schroeder (D-CO):

"'Male, female, purple, whatever, she's the best candidate,' says Schroeder. 'The only negative is that she's a woman.' Asked to explain, Schroeder says the undercurrent in this race is what she calls 'the Bubba beat—the Bubba tom-toms—that the party needs somebody who can talk to Bubba.'"[23]

By contrast, the more recent Republican Party election took on the social learning frame that focused primarily on how party leaders would respond to the scandals surrounding Tom DeLay. More than 62 percent of the stories emphasized (at least for public consumption) how the candidates viewed the ethics crisis and proposed to lead the party away from a "culture of corruption." Two examples:

> Republicans seek to assemble a new team that can better weather the storms developing around the Abramoff scandal and the recent bribery guilt plea and resignation of Rep. Randy "Duke" Cunningham.[24]

> Republicans in the House of Representatives have sought to put a "fresh face" on their leadership with the surprise choice of Ohio's John Boehner to replace Tom DeLay as majority leader. . . . Mr. Boehner campaigned as a candidate of reform.[25]

An examination of the secondary frames provides further insight. The historical significance of the first woman to achieve new heights of leadership was not lost in the coverage. Thus the combined dominant frames of the Pelosi elections tapped both the social choice and the social structure perspectives. Again for Pelosi, however, gender presented a kind of double-bind for her to navigate (Jamieson 1995). The comments of Pelosi and Hoyer themselves illustrate the conflicting messages sent.

> Hoyer: Members need to decide whether to have a symbol, or someone who represents a different kind of district, holds centrist views, backs a strong defense, and believes that we can compete in the world.
> Pelosi: I didn't run because I'm a woman, but because I can help us win the majority. . . . But the idea of a woman as whip is very powerful. It is an important signal to women that there is infinite opportunity.[26]

Navigating the shoals of gender, Pelosi sometimes asserted that geography (and the sheer size of the voting power of the California delegation) played a role in her rise to power as much as gender. About gender, she noted, "I'm not running as a woman, but we should understand who elects Democrats. I have the credentials. Being a woman is sort of a bonus."[27] Interestingly, Pelosi's gender disappeared as a rationale in Representative John Lewis's (D-GA) brief flirtation to join the race for Democratic whip. Making a pitch for needing a minority face among the party leaders, Lewis noted: "The leadership should be a reflection of the makeup of the Democratic Party and the country. Right now, the . . . leadership is all white."[28]

The secondary frame for the House Republican majority leader's race was not surprisingly the social choice perspective. One article, making little note of the shadow of scandal against which the race played out, summed up the dynamics:

> Part of the concentrated lawmaker-to-lawmaker campaigning typical of party elections, members of the exclusive electorate [try] to gauge how a candidate might do the job, and perhaps more important, calculate what might be in it for them. . . . And the candidates are not shy about reminding their colleagues what they have done for them in the past and could do in the future—or not.[29]

Notably, unlike Pelosi, none of the GOP candidates were questioned about their ability to deliver the goods to their congressional colleagues.

Implications and Questions

What should we take away from this exploration of gender in congressional leadership? First and foremost, I have tried to show the relevance of a gender lens to illuminate leadership elections. Gender plays out unevenly as a factor, even though both men and women have gender and perform gender (Duerst-Lahti 2002). The unspoken masculinity of Congress and its past leaders creates the conditions of women's exceptionalism. Even though Speaker Pelosi and other women have shattered glass ceilings and made history, women face challenges as they deviate from the norm and are measured against entrenched gender standards.

Second, congressional leadership research would benefit from reconsideration of ostensibly gender-neutral theories. For example, because of distinctive districts (Palmer and Simon 2006) that elect women, the concept of a "middleman" might need to be redefined. Principal-agent theory yields powerful insights into legislative behavior, but the theory must be understood within a distinctive social demography of token women and a hitherto masculine institution. In theory, principals select an agent based on skill and expertise, but in real life such selections may also be clouded by trust, familiarity, fear, and prejudice. The doubts about Speaker Pelosi's ability to help her members achieve their goals reflect the range of factors.

Third, gender analysis would enrich our scholarly understanding of the institutional changes that have taken place in the US Congress over the past two decades. The changes—more women among the membership and lower-level leadership, changes in seniority norms in the House, leadership strategies that are both inclusive and pacifying, and the increase in contested elections involving women—need to be considered as a piece. Yoder's "intrusiveness hypothesis" (1991) posits that male-dominated institutions respond to increasing numbers of women as "intruders" by adopting strategies of resistance. As we consider future research, scholars need to ask whether and how more women in Congress affect institutional change and how changing structures affect women's prospects for leadership. A rich set of questions lies ahead for both gender and congressional scholars.

Notes

1. This phrase, suggesting the glacial pace of change, is thought to originate from the French novelist Alphonse Karr (1808–1990). The phrase appears in George Bernard Shaw's *Revolutionist's Handbook* (1903) and was listed in the *Dictionary of American Proverbs* by Wolfgang Mieder et al. (New York: Oxford University Press, 1992).

2. Seniority and leadership data were calculated from Jackie Koszczuk and Martha Angle, eds., *CQ's Politics in America 2008: the 110th Congress* (Washington, DC: Congressional Quarterly Press, 2007), pp. 1207–1211. Because there are few women in Congress, the presence of one woman more or less in a leadership role makes the percentages quite variable, which argues for caution in making claims about women being "overrepresented" or "underrepresented" in the party hierarchy.

3. John Pitney, a distinguished scholar of congressional leadership, used the metaphor at the Princeton University conference, "The Polarization of American Politics: Myth or Reality?" 4 December 2004, Princeton, New Jersey.

4. Poole and Rosenthal's DW-Nominate scores estimate the position of individual legislators, using roll-call voting records. The score is based on two dimensions: the first dimension is based on government intervention in the economy or liberal-conservative issues in the modern era, and the second picks up the slavery conflict and later issues related to civil rights for African Americans. The difference between an individual member's score and the mean or median of his or her party provides a way of calculating a member's ideological position within his or her party.

5. Eleanor Clift, "Capitol Letter: Pelosi Power," *Newsweek*, 5 October 2001.

6. As quoted in Karen Foerstel, "Democrats Pelosi and Hoyer Stress Party-Building Ability in House Whip Contest," *CQ Weekly*, 8 September 2001, p. 2061.

7. Patty Reinert, "Texan Out, but Tennessean Ford Eyes House Post," *Houston Chronicle*, 9 November 2002, p. 6A.

8. Harold Ford Jr., "Why I Should Be Minority Leader," *Washington Post*, 13 November 2002, p. A27.

9. Eleanor Clift, "Capitol Letter: Old Boys Club," *Newsweek*, 26 July 2001, web exclusive.

10. Ibid.

11. Jim VandeHei and Juliet Eilperin, "After DeLay, Enforcers-to-Be," *The Washington Post*, 9 April 2006, p. B01.

12. Two readers coded, discussed, and recoded the articles in an effort to achieve a high degree of reliability. The coding involved several objective counts as well as subjective judgments. The coders counted the number of explicit gender references (i.e., reference to roles as father, man, female, mother) made in the article and tallied quotes by male and female members of Congress as well as other male and female voices. The three key subjective judgments included: (1) identifying

leadership appeals made by the candidates and their supporters; (2) coding leadership style using one of five styles—accommodative, competitive, avoidance, compromising, and collaborative (Thomas 1975, Rosenthal 1998); and (3) assigning a primary and secondary story frame for the article based on the leadership appeals and members' decisionmaking.

13. Each of these three perspectives parallel other work on leadership selection and all have been applied to understand the career of Speaker Newt Gingrich. The social choice perspective comes closest to principal-agent theory in leadership choice and informs Sinclair's analysis of Gingrich (1999). Social learning theory places greater emphasis on institutional context, which is a perspective emphasized by Peters (1998), and social structure theory looks beyond the members and the institution to place emphasis on political and social forces writ large, a perspective adopted by Strahan (1996) to understand Gingrich's speakership.

14. Richard Cohen, "The Race for No. 2," *National Journal* 33, no. 38 (22 September 2001), p. 2923.

15. Spencer S. Hsu, "Once More, Hoyer Aims for the Top," *Washington Post*, 7 October 2001, p. C1.

16. Marc Sandalow, "Pelosi Steps into History as New Democratic Whip,"*San Francisco Chronicle*, 15 January 2002, p. A1.

17. Karen Foerstal, "A Tireless Fundraiser Sees Herself as a 'Fresh' Face," *CQ Weekly*, 6 October 2001, p. 2324.

18. Gebe Martinez, "Solidly Backed by Her Colleagues, Pelosi Faces GOPs Sharpened Barbs," *CQ Weekly*, 16 November 2002, p. 3008.

19. David Firestone, "The 2002 Election: Woman in the News; Getting Closer to the Top, and Smiling All the Way," *The New York Times*, 9 November 2002, p. 30.

20. VandeHei and Eilperin, "After DeLay, Enforcers-to-Be."

21. Deborah McGregor, "Formidable Legislator to Become First Woman to Reach Top in Congress," *Financial Times*, 14 November 2002, p. 12.

22. Carl Hulse, "House Democrats Seeking Leader to End Losing Trend," *The New York Times*, 8 November 2002, p. 27.

23. Clift, "Capitol Letter: Pelosi Power."

24. Jonathan Weisman, "Tide Turning Against DeLay," *Washington Post*, 7 January 2006, p. A4.

25. Denis Staunton, "'Fresh Face' Leader Chosen by Republicans," *Irish Times*, 3 February 2006, p. 13.

26. Cohen, "The Race for No. 2."

27. Martin F. Nolan, "Woman of the House," *Boston Globe*, 19 January 2000, p. A21.

28. Marc Sandalow, "Rep. Pelosi Aims to Become Top Woman in the House," *San Francisco Chronicle*, 13 October 1999, p. A1.

29. Carl Hulse, "3 in GOP Leadership Race Stump Among Conservatives," *The New York Times*, 31 January 2006, p. A16.

PART 3
Conclusion

12

Taking Stock and Setting a New Agenda

Karen O'Connor

THE PRECEDING CHAPTERS represent a comprehensive compendium of some of the best work by leading women and politics scholars. As such, each entry provides new findings as well as, perhaps more importantly, points out avenues for new research. In that, this book is a treasure trove for those contemplating work in women and politics, as well as hopefully, providing a guide for those in other subfields to employ more comprehensive research strategies by including gender as well as issues of the intersectionality of gender, race, and ethnicity in their work.

This work is especially timely given how issues of intersectionality played out in the 2008 Democratic presidential primary campaign. The unprecedented contest between senators Hillary Rodham Clinton and Barack Obama catapulted issues of race and gender onto the public agenda. At times, when issues of racism came up, public actors and the media derided (properly) their invocation. Yet, it often seemed as if Clinton's confrontations with issues of sexism were inflamed by the media or simply written off as "non issues."[1] It took pressure by leaders of several women's groups, for example, to force NBC's Chris Matthews to issue a public apology for his "quips" about Clinton and other prominent women in politics. His comments about political women included:

1. Asserting Clinton was the only viable woman presidential candidate "on the horizon," challenging his guests to name one female governor.
2. Asking if Speaker Nancy Pelosi was "going to castrate Steny Hoyer" if he were elected House majority leader.
3. Focusing so excessively on Michelle Obama's appearance that

Andrea Mitchell was forced to remind him that she is a Harvard trained lawyer.

His comments about Clinton included:

1. Suggesting Clinton was the front-runner because her husband messed around.
2. Saying she did not win the New York Senate race "on her merits."
3. Referring to Clinton as a "she-devil," comparing her to a "strip teaser," and also calling her witchy.
4. Calling Clinton's male supporters "castratos in the eunuch chorus."
5. Charging that Clinton was not "a convincing mommy."[2]

Views such as this underscore the continued validity of the findings in this volume, and, in fact, unfortunately reveal that the higher the status, the more overt and covert discrimination women candidates may encounter.

To facilitate my synthesis of the comprehensive and thought-provoking chapters in this timely volume, this chapter is divided into four parts. First, I attempt to gather the main lessons and significant findings provided by each author in the context of other work in this volume, as well as in the women and politics field more generally. Next, I take a more critical look at each chapter pointing out gaps in the women and politics literature. Third, I attempt to show how the implications of this research for other subfields add to the larger research on Congress, candidates, the media, elections, and voting among other more "traditional" fields in political science that can be faulted almost uniformly for their failure to address and integrate the study of women and gender. And finally, I point out directions for future research, sometimes reiterating calls made by the authors themselves. In other instances, I note research suggested by works in this volume as well as by the changing electoral climate at this writing with the first woman Speaker of the House and the first strong, viable woman running for the presidency.

Main Lessons

Both Parts 1 and 2 of this volume provide us with several new, major findings concerning women as candidates, their impact on voters, their ability to affect public policy, the challenges they face on committees and with the leadership within both state and national legislatures, and the complex consequences of race as well the intersectionality of race, gender, and ethnicity. Jennifer Lawless and Kathyrn Pearson's study of women in congressional primaries concludes with what we all now accept as conventional wisdom in nearly all walks of life: "Women, in other words, have to be 'better' than men in order to fare equally well." This theme is echoed in nearly every chapter in this book, as well as in popular culture today. Whether it is making a case to the voters, financial backers, or colleagues, women routinely must be "better" not only in quantifiable but also difficult-to-quantify ways.

To begin to tackle these questions, Lawless and Pearson used their own meticulously constructed data set of all of the primary candidates in all congressional elections from 1958 to 2004. Their results confirm and extend Barbara Palmer and Dennis Simon's (2006) eye-opening research on the difficulties faced by women in Congress running for reelection. According to Lawless and Pearson, *all* women running in congressional primaries—incumbents, challengers, and open-seat contestants alike—face more competitive, more crowded fields than their male counterparts do. In the end, thankfully, the women are just as successful as the men, sometimes even more successful. But the women clearly had to work harder to get there, and one wonders if the no-holds-barred approach to criticizing Hillary Clinton in 2008 will work to their advantage or disadvantage.

Like Palmer and Simon, Lawless and Pearson also find some differences in the experiences of Republican and Democratic women candidates in the primaries. Democratic women are increasingly more likely than Republican women to run in their party's primaries; and in the 1990s, at least, they were also more likely to win. While Republican women have been just as likely as Republican men to win their primaries (in every year except 1960), Democratic women have been as likely and sometimes more likely than Democratic men to win their primaries. Overall, though, each new election cycle sees more women running in congressional primaries. But they are still running at far lower rates than men, which will make it far more difficult for women to achieve anything approaching parity in Congress in the near or even distant future. This is especially true for moderate Republican women who lost at disproportional rates in the 2006 midterm elections. Moreover, both research duos find that women running in Republican and Democratic primaries face unusually large or crowded fields of competitors, thus reinforcing and expanding even further the explanations offered in prior research of the difficulties faced by women.

In examining that 2006 election, Barbara Burrell highlights one additional election cycle that was of exceptional importance to Democratic women. Not only was Nancy Pelosi (D-CA) elected the first woman Speaker of the House, Democratic women won in nearly record numbers and were energized to make it "their" House as women gained record numbers of committee and subcommittee chairships, as well as other leadership positions in the House.

Burrell's work on the 2006 election cycle demonstrates how quickly gender politics changes from year to year, and how important it is for research on women in US politics to keep up with those changes. Yet the more things change, the more things stay the same. While women occupy more leadership positions in the 110th Congress than ever before, Burrell finds that women were approximately 15 percent of the House candidates in 2006 and ultimately went on to become about 16 percent of that body—underscoring the glacial pace of progress for women in that representative body. Interestingly, Burrell also finds that in 2006 women appeared to be "better candidates" in terms of qualifications and previous office holding. Seventy percent of the newly elected women but only 59 percent of the men had prior elective experience, affirming the conventional wisdom that, to succeed in most endeavors, women need to be more qualified than men.

In examining the 2006 primary and general elections, Burrell finds a significant difference between Republican and Democratic women candidates. In looking at the open-seat primaries (where women have the best opportunities to increase their overall numbers in Congress), she found that women were candidates in 37 percent of the Republican races and 59 percent of the Democratic races. Moreover, Republican women won in 3 races; Democrats in 11. Burrell also found that Republican women in open-seat races raised less money than their male counterparts, although Republican woman incumbents raised the most money on average. This work provides a nice complement to that of R. Darcy and Sarah Slavin Schramm (1979). While women running against men in the general election may be equally successful, Republican women run in primaries in far fewer numbers, which, not surprisingly, is reflected in their overall percentages in the House.

Lawless and Pearson also find that in 1992–1996, Democratic women won their primaries at significantly higher rates than did men. This may be a reflection of the 1990s era of good feeling that disappeared in the post-9/11 climate. It may also explain Burrell's findings that even in what Palmer and Simon describe as "woman friendly districts," no Republican women even sought their party's nomination. Thus, while Burrell found that the Republican Party, like its Democratic counterpart, invested more heavily in women's than men's races in the general election, it appears that the Republican Party did little outreach to potential women candidates.

Burrell also begins to answer one question posed but not answered by Lawless and Pearson: What is the role of the Republican and Democratic Congressional Committees in supporting women candidates? She finds little evidence of Republicans seeking out women candidates, a finding underscored by the fact that there were no Republican women running in women-friendly districts.[3] Burrell does find, however, that the respective party committees were significant sources of financial assistance for women candidates in the general election both in terms of independent and coordinated expenditures and anecdotally that EMILY's List played an important role in funding some Democratic women. In fact, both parties were significantly more helpful to women than to men. She also found that support translated into votes, with Democratic women winning 50 percent of their open-seat races and Republican women winning 66 percent. Yet, some of those open seats were a result of scandals, and women traditionally do better in those races, owing to the public's belief that women are "more honest" than men.

While the research is uniform in finding that women need to be "better" than their male counterparts, ascertaining who are, indeed, better candidates is not an easy task. Dianne Bystrom attempts to point out some of the disparities that even the most highly qualified candidates suffer. After a comprehensive review of the literature on women candidates and the media, her own analysis of recent campaigns for the highest statewide offices—governor and US senator—shows that women define themselves more in terms of social issues such as education and health. But what happens when issues of war and terrorism are of primary concern to voters?

Bystrom's report that a majority of the public (51%) believed that a man could do a better job than a woman leading the nation in a crisis is cause for concern. While polls particular to Hillary Clinton reveal more trust in her as a potential leader, Bystrom's findings show us how far women must go to overcome these stereotypes. (See also Chapter 7 in this volume.) When competency is an issue and the press continues to focus on women's style (*The Washington Post* recently went so far as to devote a page 1 *Style* section piece on Clinton's cleavage), it shows how far women have to go to get the press to focus on their abilities, which seem to be of greatest concern to those still on the fence about women candidates.

Underpinning Bystrom's work is her belief that the Internet gives women more control over their message and how they are presented. That control, however, may be increasingly more difficult to maintain, given the critical role that independent expenditures—on the Web or on TV—can play in any election. One need only think back to Swift Boat Veterans for Truth and be anxious about what new group will arise to try to proverbially sink Clinton's campaign for the presidency. Sue Carroll recently pointed out the huge number of 527 organizations newly created by Republicans ready to do battle against a Democratic candidate in November 2008.[4]

Key to winning races is the ability of female candidates to mobilize voters. Atiya Stokes-Brown and Melissa Neal, like Bystrom, note that candidate campaigns and their emphasis on particular issues can be an important factor in influencing women voters' attitudes and behaviors. Stokes-Brown and Neal find that women candidates who emphasize women's issues stimulate more political discussion among women. This is especially interesting because it puts women candidates, particularly those running for the Senate, or the presidency, in a difficult position. As Michele Swers notes, women running for the Senate must emphasize their international expertise. So, a candidate's efforts to mobilize voters may have to include a tricky balancing act of stressing women's issues to mobilize women voters while at the same time stressing competency in foreign affairs to better appeal to male voters. This is a particularly daunting task for women candidates for president, although few of the male candidates in 2008 had the kind of military experience past presidents have attained.

As Swers notes, regardless of what issues women candidates stress, extensive research has found that "voters perceive women to be less capable of handling defense and foreign policy issues." Thus, Swers tackles a question raised by several scholars by analyzing the sponsorship and cosponsorship activities of men and women members of the US Senate to see if there is any basis for these beliefs. In examining senatorial activity on annual defense authorization bills, she finds little support for voter bias. Importantly, she also finds that women, especially Democratic women, adopt compensatory strategies to counter acknowledged voter bias. While Swers focuses on the Senate, where most foreign policy and defense issues are at the fore, the same might be true in the House, where Jane Harman (D-CA) is still the "go to" woman most often called on by the media to comment on the Iraq War or terrorism.[5]

Cindy Simon Rosenthal's work dovetails nicely with that of Swers. Like Swers, who notes how hard women in the Senate must work to gain credibility and visibility on issues of national defense, Rosenthal deals with the "problem of invisibility" that confronts women in Congress in the political science literature, in the institution, and, I would argue, in the media and with the public. Her work examines House and Senate leadership elections between 1975 and 2007. One problem she notes is the paucity of women who have sought leadership positions—only 25 as compared to 112 men. Still, it is important to note that during this time period women have sought leadership positions beyond their proportions in any Congress. The difficulties such women might encounter are addressed by Rosenthal as well as Wendy Smooth, who finds African American women unlikely to rise to positions of influence in state legislatures. Susan Carroll, moreover, finds that women state legislators are less likely than men to ask to be on prestigious committees that would pave their way to leadership positions within state legislatures. Still, Hispanic and African American women held an unprecedented number of committee and subcommittee chairships in the 110th Congress, perhaps indicating that women in the US Congress are no longer reluctant to claim what is rightfully theirs.

Rosenthal uses masculine-based hypotheses derived from the literature to determine if they have any applicability to the study of women leaders and finds them largely wanting. For example, what political scientists term middlemen theory seems to have little application to women. In fact, women in both the Democratic and Republican party leadership are more liberal than their colleagues, thus allowing her to reject this gendered hypothesis. Rosenthal finds a more useful theory in Palmer and Simon's (2006) analysis of women-friendly districts, which suggests Democratic women may have more opportunities than their Republican counterparts. She also finds evidence supporting other theories offered in the women and politics literature. The intrusiveness theory may help explain Rosenthal's discovery that women's leadership races are more likely to be contested and crowded; and the tokenism theory helps explain why women can be found so frequently in less prestigious leadership roles. Finally, Rosenthal independently hypothesizes that a prospective leader's fund-raising abilities may trump any ideological differences posed by the middle*person* theory. Certainly some of Nancy Pelosi's rise to power can be traced to her fund-raising prowess.

Pelosi's ascendancy to the speakership also may be affecting women, especially Democratic women, in the House. As the new Speaker left the private caucus to join current and former members in the Rayburn Room of the Capitol Building to celebrate her election as Speaker, women members were ecstatic proclaiming it to be their "house."[6] They were emboldened by what they saw as new opportunities for leadership, having been shut out of any ability to govern since the Republicans took control of the House in 1995. Despite the 110th Congress's record number of women who helped elect Speaker Pelosi, electoral vulnerability may also contribute to women's leadership problems, as Rosenthal notes. But, prior to the 110th Congress, few women faced the electoral problems faced by Republican women in 2006 such as representatives Deborah Pryce (R-OH) and Nancy Johnson (R-CN). Pryce was forced to resign her position as the Republicans' highest elected woman in the House leadership when it became clear that her race was a toss-up, and Johnson lost in 2006. (Pryce declined to run again in 2008.) Nevertheless, to the extent that Democratic women incumbents, challengers, and those running in open seats can profit from the women-friendly districts noted by Palmer and Simon, it is not surprising to see women in a record number of Democratic leadership positions in the 110th Congress. Representative Louise Slaughter (D-NY), for example, chairs the prestigious Rules Committee.

Leadership issues are also tackled by Susan Carroll, this time in the context of state legislatures. Her work offers us tantalizing insights into the importance of committees for women's potential impact on public policy. Her work is also significant because she, like Fraga and colleagues and Smooth, begins to articulate well the important "next" questions in women and politics scholarship: the role of race and ethnicity in women's policy-making, prestige within institutions, and their opportunities for leadership.

Building on a significant body of work that finds that women are more likely to be found on "women's committees," Carroll uses an extensive database of interviews conducted with women legislators in 1988 and again in 2001 to find that women have made significant progress in obtaining committee assignments of their choosing. Still, she finds that women are far more likely to be on committees dealing with what we still often term as "women's issues," such as education and health. But, very importantly, she finds that such placement is often at women's request and not a product of discrimination within the legislature. Her work also shows significant reductions in discrimination in committee assignments from 1988 to 2001. It would be interesting to see if this holds true for the US House and Senate too.

Attaining power and influence in three state legislatures is the focus of Wendy Smooth's work. She finds that committee assignments along with several other factors are very important in accessing the power and influence of African American women in the Georgia, Maryland, and Mississippi state legislatures. She, like Luis Fraga and colleagues, is confronted by the problems initially faced by scholars wishing to study women in any legislative body—the numbers of women are simply too small to allow us to draw definitive answers to our research questions. Still, although Fraga and colleagues' as well as Smooth's findings are often suggestive, they are informative and provide significant food for thought. Smooth finds that African American women are largely missing from any leadership positions in state legislatures. Indications point to some intentional exclusion, yet there are so few women in the bodies that she studies that definitive findings are impossible. She does find, however, that while African American women are not often power brokers, they do have the ability to influence the policy process in a positive direction. This work, like that of Carroll's, cries out for at least some preliminary testing at the federal level where the role of the Congressional Black Caucus—dominated by women—could also be explored.

Closely allied with Smooth's work is that of Luis Fraga and colleagues on what they term strategic intersectionality. As such, it is the most comprehensive work to date on Latina legislators in the United States. Like the initial research on women in state legislatures, the numbers are so small within individual states that aggregated data make it difficult to gauge the impact of women, especially Latina women, in state legislatures. Still, Fraga and colleagues give us a first cut and produce several sophisticated hypotheses that will produce more insight as the numbers of Latina women in individual states increase to the point that simple cross-tabular analyses will allow us to observe trends in policymaking, influence, and prestige.

Perhaps Fraga and colleagues' most interesting finding is what I call, for want of a better term, the "mom thing." They find that Latina legislators are more likely to be able to build coalitions within the legislative body as well as without based on their multiple identities of ethnicity and gender. I would add to that intersectionality the fact that these women also are able to appeal to voters and their colleagues based on their status as mothers, com-

munity leaders, and experts allowing them to be (in Edmund Burke's termi-
nology) delegates, trustees, and/or politicos at will, and helping them to
negotiate the lawmaking process on behalf of their constituents.

Like Carroll, Fraga et al. find that Latina legislators are more likely to
sit on education committees (and probably pursue such issues). In contrast,
Swers finds women US senators trying to emphasize their national security
expertise. (Hillary Clinton's position on the Senate Foreign Affairs
Committee was not a fluke.) Had Bystrom analyzed gubernatorial and senatorial campaign communication separately, she undoubtedly would have
found similar differences in issue emphasis, with the more state-centered
gubernatorial women candidates running on domestic issues and those
vying for the Senate emphasizing their competence on foreign policy. Taken
together, then, the research in this volume finds that at the state level
women's issues reign supreme. And, not surprisingly, none of the committees dealing with women's issues can be identified as prestige committees
that pave the way to leadership positions and prestige in state (or the national) legislatures.

While Swers focuses on the efforts of women in the US Senate to build
and showcase expertise in "manly" issues such as defense and foreign
affairs, Carroll's examination of state legislators brings us back to where
much of the research on women began: the expectation that women are
more likely to advocate on behalf of women's issues. While, undoubtedly,
women in the US Senate also advocate for women's issues, especially
issues concerning women's health (O'Connor 2001), Carroll finds that committee assignments allow women the opportunity to become key players in
the policy process. She also finds that cosponsorship—a factor of importance to Swers—is a key way for women legislators to advance their policy
interests.

The last two chapters in Part 1 move from the problems women candidates face to a discussion of the impact of women candidates on voters.
Using data from the National Election Studies (NES) from 1990 to 2004,
Kathleen Dolan reviews the literature on women's symbolic representation
and hypothesizes that women candidates at the Senate as well as House
level—especially in competitive races—should act to bring out more
women to the polls. Interestingly, she does not find a lot of support for earlier work that concludes that women candidates positively affect women's
interest in politics and participation in a range of political activities, an area
that will need reexamination after the 2008 election cycle. Similarly,
Stokes-Brown and Neal find that while female House candidates stimulate
more political discussion among women (especially when they run on
women's issues), they have very little discernible impact on other dimensions of women's political engagement.

Both studies, however, uncover some evidence suggesting that female candidates can have a negative impact on men's political involvement. Dolan, for example, finds that the presence of Democratic women in competitive Senate races tends to depress male voting. Stokes-Brown and Neal also find that female candidates who run on women's issues have a negative effect on men's political engagement. Men in districts with female candidates "running as women" talk about and debate politics less. This too suggests that "running as a woman" is a double-edged sword, as was evidenced during the Democratic presidential primary process.

Dolan also hypothesizes that, given the gender gap in partisanship, one might expect that female Democratic candidates would be more likely to energize women voters. She finds minimal support for that hypothesis. These are major counterintuitive findings that Dolan notes and properly calls out for more research and theorizing. Still, one is left wondering two things: would or could Democratic women be mobilized by a Democratic woman running for president? And, one is left to ponder whether the largely Republican "soccer moms" of 1992 who contributed to the election of Bill Clinton could have made a resurgence had Hillary Clinton ended up being the Democratic candidate for president. What does seem clear is that she could not have won without those voters; indeed, her campaign, under the direction of Ann Lewis, former Clinton White House director of communications, made engaging women voters a top priority. So, Dolan's research is important in that its implications for the Clinton campaign point to the necessity of reaching out to Democratic, Republican, and Independent women.

Both Burrell's and Bystrom's work in this volume, in particular, complement that of Stokes-Brown and Neal. Stokes-Brown and Neal note that the presence of women running on women's issues in congressional races increases how much women in the electorate discuss politics. As Bystrom points out, the press often does not focus on women candidates' issue positions, preferring to devote more attention to style. So, when candidates are allowed to shape their message (as in those women candidates for whom Stokes-Brown and Neal were forced to look to candidate web pages because they could find no press stories about them), or are able to get the press to focus on their messages, which are often women-centered, women voters become more engaged. This finding is important given the work of others in Part 1 that note how difficult it still is for some women candidates to get adequate or appropriate press coverage. In essence, if Stokes-Brown and Neal's research is combined with Bystrom's, we can come up with a testable hypothesis that the media may exert a more powerful than expected influence on political participation simply by how they report on women candidates. Additionally, when the media reports the general surge in participation, for example, the record-high primary turnout rate of Democratic women voters in the early primaries, it may move women in other, upcoming primaries also to participate.

Gaps in the Women and Politics Literature

Although this volume is the most inclusive to date and fills many of the voids in the women and politics literature, by being so comprehensive, it necessarily cannot and does not address every issue of importance. For example, while not covered in this volume, we still need to know more about who runs for office at all levels. Jennifer Lawless and Richard Fox (2005) have made major contributions in this area, but more still needs to be done. In particular, we need to know more about Latina and other minority candidates. And, since participation on school boards and in city and local government is generally higher for women than at the federal level, we need to go back and mine that data to add to our knowledge and see if a pipeline of women poised to run for higher office exists.

Toward that end, Bystrom's work provides us with fertile ground for additional research on women as candidates and elected officials. Future studies of women as statewide candidates, however, need to treat gubernatorial and senatorial candidates differently, even though the low number of women in each category causes problems for systematic analysis. Candidates for governor and the US Senate must run different races on different issues. As the other chapters in this volume suggest, social issues such as education and health will most likely be the top concerns of gubernatorial candidates, especially the women. In contrast, senatorial candidates—male or female—must focus on issues of war, national security, and foreign policy, especially in recent years.

The might of cartoonists' pens must also be considered. From the 1870s when Thomas Nast first pilloried Victoria Woodhull—the first woman to run for president—as a "Terrible Siren" advocating free love, to Elizabeth Dole's problems with her husband being a spokesman for Viagra, to Bill Clinton's interjection of himself into Hillary Clinton's campaign, women candidates have suffered more in press than have men. And, any analysis of women as presidential candidates must at least mention Shirley Chisholm and Carol Moseley Braun, who had to confront issues of racism and sexism (see Smooth 2006). Further examinations of intersectionality are particularly needed to understand better voter choice between Barack Obama and Hillary Clinton in the Democratic primaries and caucuses.

As the Internet becomes an increasingly important tool for candidates (witness the development of YouTube presidential candidate debates) we need to learn more about how gendered—if at all—these new media are. Are blogs better used by women candidates? Are bloggers more likely to attack or support women? What proportion of women are bloggers of note such as Arianna Huffington? These are all questions that need to be addressed by women and politics scholars as well as by those who study campaigns more generally.

Similarly, the role of PACs and 527s in the campaigns of women calls out for examination. Burrell and Bystrom provide us with several hypotheses that can be tested concerning possible differences between men and women, and there is increasing urgency that we as political scientists examine these issues and find answers to these questions. Bystrom also tantalizingly notes in passing the role of surrogates—another issue that begs for more research. Most scholars credit Michael J. Fox's stem cell intercession in Claire McCaskill's Missouri race (along with that of EMILY's List money and volunteers) with her narrow victory in 2006.

By 2008 a huge number of 527s created by Republicans stand ready to fight the Democratic nominee. Research also will be needed about EMILY's List and whether formerly supported EMILY's List candidates such as McCaskill who vocally supported Obama will be penalized in the future for not supporting EMILY's List–supported Clinton.

Stokes-Brown and Neal's work on the effect of issue-driven campaigns also provides us with avenues to address gaps in the women and politics literature. They utilize press reports on the issues mentioned by the candidates. The literature, however, indicates that the press often overreports on style issues over substance as noted above. Thus, relying on how newspaper accounts frame how a woman candidate advocates for particular issues may not capture fully women's real emphasis on issues. It is unclear, therefore, whether Stokes-Brown and Neal are gauging how women portray themselves or how the media portrays them, a distinction that could have important implications according to Bystrom's work.

Future research should also be wary of relying exclusively on LexisNexis for news media analysis. Stokes-Brown and Neal discovered that some congressional candidates simply were not mentioned in any LexisNexis news articles. Furthermore, for most congressional races, the LexisNexis database underreports actual stories on candidates. Most local weekly and daily papers not included in LexisNexis are awash with stories of candidates' campaigns, local debates, and attendance at a variety of local meetings. Many media consultants point out the importance of "good" stories in local papers—most of which are not included in LexisNexis. Thus, some women candidates may be getting great local press on "their" issues and we would not know it.

Future research such as Stokes-Brown and Neal's and Dolan's may need to expand the concept and measurement of political participation. As Nancy Burns, Kay Lehman Schlozman, and Sidney Verba (2001) note, for many women, political participation comes from involvement and engagement in church-based religious activities. It may be that women and politics scholars will need to look at church-going as a surrogate measure of political engagement, at least for some women. Did Republican women evangelicals, for example, disproportionately support Governor Mike Huckabee, an ordained Southern Baptist Minister?

The two chapters on symbolic mobilization point toward other avenues for more inquiry. Both note the need for more and better studies on the effect of women candidates on male voters. This is especially noteworthy in light of research by David King and Richard Matland (2003) that notes it is men who affect the gender gap the most, especially white men. In the same vein, Dolan's work reinforces the need for more party-specific research on women candidates. Although their work does not explore differences between Democratic and Republican candidates per se, Stokes-Brown and Neal do aim to fill in some of the gaps noted by Dolan by examining press accounts of how women portray themselves.

Carroll's work on committee assignments is particularly interesting in her finding that women state senators are less likely to request assignments to prestige committees. The question this begs us to answer is: Why? Are women legislators less likely to put themselves out there where success is less likely? What effects does this have on women entering leadership positions? As former vice presidential candidate Geraldine Ferraro often says: "If you don't run, you can't win." Lawless and Fox's (2005) work on potential candidates may give us a starting point for testing theories that might explain women's reticence. But at the low rate women are seeking office in spite of efforts of groups such as EMILY's List, Wish List, and the Women's Campaign Forum (formerly the Women's Campaign Fund) and with research affirming their disinclination to seek positions of authority, these may be difficult albeit all the more important questions to address.

Swers's work on women senators in the post-9/11 107th and 108th congresses makes the study of additional congresses even more important. As Burrell's analysis of the 110th Congress underscores, an apparent sea changed occurred in 2007 that will bear watching, especially in that votes against the war now are ones generally favored by a large proportion of Democrats and even a substantial proportion of Republicans. It could be that in 2008, especially if the United States is still in Iraq and the war continues to be viewed so unfavorably, women running on "peace" platforms may have a breakthrough year reminiscent of 1992's Year of the Woman. Swers' work also notes in passing that "senators who try to develop policies that overlap with the established expertise of their same-state counterparts will have greater difficulty gaining media attention and by extension voter recognition of their work," citing Schiller (2000). At a time when 6 of the 16 women in the Senate come from states represented by two women in the Senate—California, Washington, and Maine—one immediately wonders if women in those states face more or less difficulty carving out their fields of expertise.

Burrell's findings of the uniqueness of the 110th Congress also under-score the need to extend Rosenthal's analysis of House and Senate leader-ship elections. Seven of the 16 women now in the Senate hold leadership positions or committee chairships—an unprecedented number. Researchers may want to pay special attention to leadership of the respective party's political campaign arms. In the recent past, senators Patti Murray (D-WA) and Elizabeth Dole (R-NC) and Representative Nita Lowey (D-NY) have headed their party's influential campaign committees. As work in this vol-ume notes, these committees are enormously influential and it would be interesting to see if women chairs give more money to women candidates than their male counterparts.

Also of interest, and noted by Smooth, is the role of seniority and the concurrent impact of professionalization and term limits on state legislators and their bids for leadership positions and committee assignments. While increasing professionalization may benefit women, especially women of color, as Smooth's research suggests, many have speculated that term limits have actually hurt women (Hawkesworth and Kleeman 2001).[7] Thus, it would be interesting to gauge the simultaneous impact of these factors on women's advancement in state legislatures.

In the context of leadership, Rosenthal's discussion of Representative Rosa DeLauro's unsuccessful bid for Democratic Caucus chair deserves more study. Rosenthal and others believe that DeLauro's situation happened because men viewed a Caucus whip (at that time Pelosi) and potential chair (DeLauro) as having just too many women in power. Interviews with key players, such as those conducted by Swers, could bring important insights into the limits on women's leadership in either party.

This is especially true when we look to the works of Fraga and col-leagues and by Smooth in this volume. Their work highlights the need to study more women of color in different contexts, but that cannot occur until more Latina and African American women are elected to office. Thus, an important first step might be to access the career patterns and influence of women in city or county legislatures where their numbers would allow, at least in some cases, for more robust analysis. Still, Mary Hawkesworth's (2003) work on problems and disrespect reported by African American women in the House needs to be updated in light of the Democratic change-over in Congress and the presence of a woman Speaker. We can also hope that better 2008 polling data will allow for more nuanced intersectional analysis.

Implications of This Research for Other Subfields

Several of the works in this volume have important implications for the research done in related subfields. While one would think that by 2008, all political scientists would routinely and automatically include the role of gender in any of their analyses of institutions or political behavior, this often is not the case. Thus, it is important to point out where work contained here could instruct the research of others who have yet to see gender as a variable worthy of inquiry. For example, Lawless and Pearson's work begs for the attention of those who study congressional elections, especially primaries. All too often the canon simply refuses to include gender as a variable when discussing candidate recruitment, national congressional campaign committee support, and a host of other campaign phenomena, providing a less than comprehensive analysis of the primary and the resultant general election campaign processes. What happens in campaigns matters—especially for women as is pointed out by Lawless and Pearson. Women face more challengers in their primaries—regardless of party—which in turn makes their overall battle for office more expensive, exhausting, and difficult. And with women turning out in record numbers in presidential primaries, we need to know if this is a Clinton, Obama, or Clinton/Obama effect.

Burrell's work complements the work of political scientists on campaign finance reform. It would be interesting to extend her work to a study of gender gaps in the actual votes on campaign finance reform as well as pitting "newer" women against those more entrenched in the system. This is work that has been largely neglected by those who study elections and policymaking and could provide important insights on whether or not differences between men and women legislators are apparent. It is suggestive, for example, that, as House whip, Nancy Pelosi proposed a minority bill of rights and, as Speaker, far tougher ethics rules than any man before her.

Swers's work adroitly points out that no congressional scholars have examined the legislative activity of women senators on defense issues. Swers's body of work on women in the House and Senate is pushing the field to recognize that women's initiatives need to be considered. Hopefully, we will soon see more political scientists addressing women senators as desirable foci of study as more women enter that body. With only 16 women in the Senate, split by political party, it is very difficult to make broad generalizations. Thus, Swers's work, which combines quantitative data with in-depth interviews, sets out a model that others in the Congress field should emulate.

Carroll's work on committee assignments begs for more research on the role of party leaders in these assignments. Of particular interest would be a study of Nancy Pelosi's committee assignments. Her removal of Jane Harman, the ranking member of the House Select Intelligence Committee slated to become the chair of that prestigious committee, as well as some of her other committee and subcommittee assignments, would be very interesting and tell us more about the leadership styles studied by Rosenthal.

Carroll's work also provides other directions for other subfields in political science. Particularly overdue are studies of the continued viability of Daniel Elazar's (1984) theory concerning political culture. With political scientists' preoccupation with red and blue states, urban vs. suburban vs. rural trends, and the decline of the rustbelt in electoral politics, it may be time to put Elazar to rest and find new ways to describe the political culture of the various states.

Rosenthal's work on House and Senate leadership could not more clearly point out the gendered nature of political scientists' study of leadership and the invisibility of any women in leadership positions. As she notes, the field's "focus on leadership embodied in the stories of great men" give us no frame of reference with which to study great women, although Rosenthal herself (1998) has been one of the pioneers advancing the need for, as well as theoretical constructs to begin, such analysis.

Directions for New Research

As noted above, Lawless and Pearson find that women face more challengers in their primaries—regardless of party—which in turn makes their overall battle for office more expensive, exhausting, and difficult. This is a subject that begs for additional inquiry. So, too, does the neglected role of party congressional campaign committees in the primary process. Representative Loretta Sanchez (D-CA) often recounts a story of her first visit to meet the powers that be at the Democratic Congressional Campaign Committee to ask for funds when she announced her entrance into the primary. She left empty-handed but was able to get the support of EMILY's List, the largest Democratic, women-only, pro-choice political action committee. Sanchez, like all other Democratic incumbents in 2008 except Marcy Kaptur and Nancy Pelosi, has been the recipient of considerable EMILY's List money, and many candidates credit EMILY's List with their victories at both the primary and national level. Although Jamie Pimlott (2007) recently has completed a comprehensive study of EMILY's List, the funding of women candidates—Democratic and Republican—calls out for more research of the kind Barbara Burrell provides in this volume.

While Burrell here, and in a significant body of work, has contributed much to our knowledge and understanding of how women's campaigns are funded, much more work needs to be done on funding opportunities for Republican and Democratic women. The WISH List, for example, the Republican counterpart of EMILY's List, is suffering as more and more Republican women winning in the primaries have moved to the right. Thus, the majority of Republican women now in the House are pro-life candidates supported by the pro-life Susan B. Anthony's List. These three groups also have played important roles in seeking out potential women candidates. For instance, EMILY's List unsuccessfully tried to recruit popular Atlanta mayor Shirley Franklin to run for an open Senate seat and former Women's Sports Foundation president and former captain of the Olympic gold medal winning soccer team Julie Foudy to run for an open House seat in southern California.

Also unexplored and calling out for more work is the role of the Democratic Party's outreach efforts to candidates under 40—an effort cochaired by Tim Ryan (D-OH) and Debbie Wasserman Schultz (D-FL) and heavily supported by Nancy Pelosi as the House whip and now as Speaker. Wasserman Schultz was under 40 in her first successful bid for a House seat and was also heavily supported by the Democratic Party, EMILY'S List, and the Women Under Forty PAC (WUF PAC), as was Stephanie Herseth Sandlin (D-SD) in her first (unsuccessful) and second (successful) runs. These outreach actions appear to have borne fruit in 2006, and we will need to see if they continue in 2008 and beyond as such efforts become more well established.

Research also needs to be done on what kind of PACs contribute to Republican and Democratic women in primaries and in the general elections. Do they differ, for example? These efforts are also worthy of study and would help us answer some of the thoughtful questions about candidate recruitment posed by Burrell. While Burrell suggests several reasons why women opt not to run—including low status of state legislative office, distance from home and family, constant searching for campaigns contributions, and the incivility in many elective bodies, especially Congress—further research needs to be done to determine if differences in party control affect a woman's decision to run. It could be, for example, that women may be more likely to run for Congress now that it is controlled by Democrats where they now are in the majority and able to better affect public policy. The record retirements of Republicans in 2008, for example, may lead to more Democratic women running.

More research also needs to be done on women lawyers. Burrell finds that more women in Congress are lawyers than are men. But, research by Fox and Lawless suggests that women may be opting out of the legislative pipeline by preferring to run for judgeships or simply becoming judges through appointment processes at the state and local level where jobs are closer to home, pay more, and greater anonymity and family privacy are possible.

Also of interest for future researchers is more work on women versus women primary and general election campaigns. Lawless and Pearson note that there are not many of them; still a more detailed analysis including quantitative and qualitative assessments would be useful and shed more light on the process without focusing on journalists' tendencies to focus on the "cat fight" aspect of such races.

Another important question that begs for analysis in the context of the 2006 election is what happened to Republican women incumbents? Five of the 21 women lost their races—three in races where they had formerly won with over 70 percent of the vote—Nancy Johnson (R-CN), the dean of Republican women and the most moderate Republican woman in the House, Sue Kelly (R-NY), and Anne Northup (R-KY).

Dolan's work using the National Election Studies also drives home the need for better data on individual House districts as well as at the state level. The relatively low number of NES respondents makes analysis at the state and district levels tricky; it may be time for political scientists to forge better bonds with professional pollsters hired at the district or state level by candidates, PACs, or the parties. Access to such data, especially when women are candidates, could be very helpful in expanding our knowledge.

All of the work in Part 1, especially that of Stokes-Brown and Neal, points to the validity of former House Speaker Thomas (Tip) O'Neill's famous adage: "All politics is local." The authors of each chapter in Part 1 note how important context is in each of these elections; whether it is local conditions, or media coverage, a woman candidate often finds herself up against odds difficult to control.

Swers's work also offers important directions for further research in addition to those noted above. Her research, for example, could be expanded by the inclusion of a more detailed study of strategies adopted by women to showcase their foreign policy expertise. Including the number of "fact-finding" trips taken by women versus men to foreign nations, as well as the inclusion of evidence of women seeking out photo opportunities with foreign leaders or the president, might offer additional insights. The role of seniority might also be examined as well as that of military service. While no women senators have served in the military, it might be interesting to see if there are differences among men who served in the military. (Representative Heather Wilson [R-NM], a former Air Force Academy graduate and the only congresswoman to have served in the military, resigned to run for the US Senate in 2008.) It would also be interesting for women and politics scholars to study each political party's efforts to seek out women veterans to run for Congress as the Democrats did in the case of Tammy Duckworth, who ultimately was unsuccessful in her bid to win an open House seat in Illinois.

Swers's efforts could also be expanded to a larger discussion of the political environment facing women in the 1990s versus 2000s. While the fall of the Soviet Union resulted in a national sentiment focused more on domestic issues, after 9/11, the entire political environment changed. With terror and war at the forefront of the political agenda, many women opted not to run, fearing that their gender would prove an insurmountable barrier. Even Lieutenant General Claudia J. Kennedy (Ret.), who was seriously contemplating a run for the US Senate from Virginia with the backing of EMILY's List and the Women's Campaign Fund, opted not to run.[8]

Carroll's work also provides us with many possible avenues of new research as noted above. Her research and that of others dealing with committee assignments could be enriched by a discussion of the role of the absence of any women on the Senate Judiciary Committee during the 1991 hearings of the nomination of Clarence Thomas to the Supreme Court of the United States. Women around the country were outraged by the questions posed to Anita Hill by the all-male committee, and it was not surprising that a woman was appointed to that committee immediately after the next national election—the Year of the Woman election.

Rosenthal helpfully directs us to several fruitful areas of new inquiry. Relevant to her work, as well as most of the findings in this volume, is her plea that male-centered theories be reconsidered. As her work and others underscore, these gendered theories often are not useful in explaining how women lead, vote, or run for office. Doing so, as she notes, would better help us to understand institutional changes in Congress, which would also apply to studies of state legislatures and local government.

While this volume commendably contains preliminary analyses of Latina women's political incorporation, we desperately need more data on race and ethnicity and their intersectionality. Additionally, through no fault of the editor, this volume contains no analyses of Asian American or Native American women. Granted, their numbers in state legislative bodies are too small to allow for any meaningful systematic analysis. Still, it may be incumbent on the subfield to shift its attention to lower units of institutional analysis and, if necessary, the use of more case studies modeled after Wendy Smooth's work on state legislative women and Mary Hawkesworth's work on women in the US Congress. With these tools, we can begin new, exciting analyses of women's growing political engagement in all levels of politics.

Together, these chapters offer some of the finest scholarship on women and politics. The authors individually and collectively provide us not only with rich and important insights, but also with years of new research in which to engage. As the numerous suggestions for further research noted above underscore, the study of women and politics remains an exciting, dynamic field. As the number of women in elective office grows, we will be able to come to more definitive answers to questions about women in politics generally as well as about the intersectionalities of race, gender, and ethnicity.

Notes

1. Gloria Steinem, "Women Are Never Front Runners," *New York Times*, 8 January 2008.

2. National Council of Women's Organizations (NCWO) letter to Steve Capus, 18 January 2008. Available from the author, who was a signatory.

3. Not discussed, however, is the role of the Democratic Senatorial Committee in going head to head with EMILY's List over whom to endorse in the open seat primary in the Pennsylvania senate race. The Democrats endorsed pro-life Robert Casey Jr., who went on to win the seat handily from incumbent Rick Santorum, who had become the face of the pro-life movement in the Senate.

4. Personal correspondence with author, 25 January 2008.

5. Interestingly, Rep. Harman was removed from her position on the House Select Intelligence Committee by Speaker Pelosi and there is no love lost between these two women. At the first tea honoring the new Speaker, for example, as all of the Democratic women joined Pelosi onstage, Harman stood alone to the right of stage as far as she possibly could (author personal observation).

6. Author observation and discussion with several women members in attendance.

7. Peter Slevin, "After Adopting Term Limits, States Lose Female Legislators," *Washington Post*, 22 April 2007, p. A4.

8. Author conversation with the lieutenant general.

References

Abzug, Bella. 1972. *Bella! Ms. Abzug Goes to Washington.* New York: Saturday Review Press.

Acker, Joan. 1990. "Hierarchies, Jobs, Bodies: A Theory of Gendered Organizations." *Gender & Society* 4, no. 2: 139–158.

Acker, Joan. 1992. "From Sex Roles to Gendered Institutions." *Contemporary Sociology* 21, no. 5: 565–569.

Aday, Sean, and James Devitt. 2001. *Style over Substance. Newspaper Coverage of Female Candidates: Spotlight on Elizabeth Dole.* Washington, DC: The Women's Leadership Fund.

Aldrich, John H., and Forrest D. Nelson. 1984. *Linear Probability, Logit, and Probit Models.* Beverly Hills, CA: Sage.

Alexander, Deborah, and Kristi Andersen. 1993. "Gender as a Factor in the Attributions of Leadership Traits." *Political Research Quarterly* 46, no. 3: 527–545.

Amer, Mildred. 2005. "Major Leadership Election Contests in the House of Representatives, 94th–109th Congresses." Washington, DC: Congressional Research Service.

Arnold, Laura W., and Barbara M. King. 2002. "Women, Committees, and Institutional Change in the Senate." In *Women Transforming Congress*, ed. Cindy Simon Rosenthal. Norman: University of Oklahoma Press.

Atkeson, Lonna Rae. 2003. "Not All Cues Are Created Equal: The Conditional Impact of Female Candidates on Political Engagement." *Journal of Politics* 65, no. 4: 1040–1061.

Atkeson, Lonna Rae, and Ronald B. Rapoport. 2003. "The More Things Change, the More They Stay the Same: Examining Differences in Political Communication 1952–2000." *Public Opinion Quarterly* 67, no. 4: 495–521.

Baer, Denise. 2006. "Party-Based Leadership and Gender: Beyond the Chinese Box Puzzle of Women's Recruitment to Political Office." Paper presented at the Women and Leadership Conference, American University, Washington, DC, 7–9 April.

Baker, Ross K. 2001. *House and Senate,* 3rd edition. New York: W. W. Norton.

243

Banwart, Mary C. 2002. "Videostyle and Webstyle in 2000: Comparing the Gender Differences of Candidate Presentations in Political Advertising and on the Internet." Ph.D. diss. University of Oklahoma, Norman.

Banwart, Mary C., and Diana B. Carlin. 2001. "The Effects of Negative Political Advertising on Gendered Image Perception and Voter Intent: A Longitudinal Study." Paper presented at the meeting of the National Communication Association, Atlanta, GA, 1–4 November.

Barbara Lee Family Foundation. 2007. *Positioning Women to Win: New Strategies for Turning Gender Stereotypes into Competitive Advantages*. Cambridge, MA: The Barbara Lee Family Foundation.

Barone, Michael, and Richard Cohen. 2007. *The Almanac of American Politics 2008*. Washington, DC: National Journal.

Barreto, Matt A., Mario Villerreal, and Nathan D. Woods. 2005. "Metropolitan Latino Political Behavior: Voter Turnout and Candidate Preference in Los Angeles." *Journal of Urban Affairs* 27, no. 1: 71–91.

Barrett, Edith J. 1995. "The Policy Priorities of African American Women in State Legislatures." *Legislative Studies Quarterly* 20, no. 2: 223–247.

———. 1997. "Gender and Race in the State House: The Legislative Experience." *Social Science Journal* 34, no. 2: 131–144.

———. 2001. "Black Women in State Legislatures: The Relationship of Race and Gender to the Legislative Experience." In *The Impact of Women in Public Office*, ed. Susan J. Carroll, 185–204. Bloomington: Indiana University Press.

Bartels, Larry M. 1996. "Uninformed Voters: Information Effects in Presidential Elections." *American Journal of Political Science* 40, no. 1: 194–230.

Beckwith, Karen. 1986. *American Women and Political Participation: The Impact of Work, Generation, and Feminism*. New York: Greenwood Press.

Beckwith, Karen, and Kimberly Cowell-Meyers. 2007. "Sheer Numbers: Critical Representation Thresholds and Women's Representation." *Perspectives on Politics* 5, no. 3: 553–565.

Benenson, Bob, and Jonathan Allen. 2007. "It's Looking Like Blue Skies All Over Again." *CQ Weekly* (26 November): 3536–3541.

Benze, James G., and Eugene R. DeClercq. 1985. "Content of Television Political Spot Ads for Female Candidates." *Journalism Quarterly* 62, no. 2: 278–283, 288.

Best, James J. 1971. "Influence in the Washington House of Representatives." *Midwest Journal of Political Science* 15, no. 3: 547–562.

Binder, Sarah A., and Steven Smith. 1997. *Politics or Principle: Filibustering in the United States Senate*. Washington, DC: Brookings Institution Press.

Blair, Diane D., and Jeanie R. Stanley. 1991. "Personal Relationships and Legislative Power: Male and Female Perceptions." *Legislative Studies Quarterly* 16, no. 4: 495–507.

Bledsoe, Timothy, and Mary Herring. 1990. "Victims of Circumstances: Women in Pursuit of Political Office." *American Political Science Review* 84, no. 1: 213–223.

Bobo, Lawrence, and Frank D. Gilliam. 1990. "Race, Sociopolitical Participation, and Black Empowerment." *American Political Science Review* 84, no. 2: 377–393.

Bositis, David A. 1999. "Trendletter: Black Elected Officials, 1998." *Focus Magazine*. Washington, DC: Joint Center for Political and Economic Studies.

———. 2001. *Black Elected Officials: A Statistical Summary, 2001*. Washington, DC: Joint Center for Political and Economic Studies.

Boxer, Barbara. 1994. *Politics and the New Revolution of Women in America.* Washington, DC: National Press Books.

Bratton, Kathleen A. 2006. "The Behavior and Success of Latino Legislators: Evidence from the States." *Social Science Quarterly* 87, no. 5: 1136–1157.

Bratton, Kathleen A., and Kerry L. Haynie. 1999. "Agenda Setting and Legislative Success in State Legislatures: The Effects of Gender and Race." *Journal of Politics* 61, no. 3: 658–679.

Bratton, Kathleen A., Kerry L. Haynie, and Beth Reingold. 2006. "Agenda Setting and African American Women in State Legislatures." *Journal of Women, Politics, & Policy* 28, no. 3/4: 71–96.

———. 2008. "Gender, Race, Ethnicity and Representation: The Changing Landscape of Legislative Diversity." In *The Book of the States*, volume 40. Lexington, KY: Council of State Governments.

Brians, Craig Leonard. 2005. "Women for Women? Gender and Party Bias in Voting for Female Candidates." *American Politics Research* 33, no. 1: 357–375.

Burns, Nancy, Kay Lehman Schlozman, and Sidney Verba. 2001. *The Private Roots of Public Action: Gender, Equality, and Political Participation.* Cambridge, MA: Harvard University Press.

Burrell, Barbara. 1985. "Women and Men's Campaigns for the U.S. House of Representatives, 1972–1982: A Finance Gap?" *American Politics Quarterly* 13, no. 3: 251–272.

———. 1994. *A Woman's Place Is in the House: Campaigning for Congress in the Feminist Era.* Ann Arbor, MI: University of Michigan Press.

———. 1998. "Campaign Finance: Women's Experience in the Modern Era." In *Women and Elective Office*, eds. Sue Thomas and Clyde Wilcox. New York: Oxford University Press.

———. 2005. "Campaign Financing: Women's Experience in the Modern Era." In *Women and Elective Office: Past, Present, and Future*, 2nd edition, eds. Sue Thomas and Clyde Wilcox. New York: Oxford University Press.

———. Forthcoming. *Gender in Campaigns for the U.S. Congress at the Millennium.* Ann Arbor: University of Michigan Press.

Burrell, Barbara, and Brian Frederick. 2007. "Windows of Opportunity." Paper presented at the Southern Political Science Association Annual Meeting, New Orleans, LA, 3 January.

Bystrom, Dianne. 1994. "Gender Differences and Similarities in the Presentation of Self: The Videostyles of Female vs. Male U.S. Senate Candidates in 1992." Paper presented at the meeting of the Speech Communication Association, New Orleans, LA, 19–22 November.

———. 2003. "Winning Strategies: Viewer Reactions to Female and Male Videostyles." Paper presented at the meeting of the National Communication Association, Miami, FL, 19–23 November.

———. 2006. "Media Content and Candidate Viability: The Case of Elizabeth Dole." In *Communicating Politics: Engaging the Public in Democratic Life*, eds. Mitchell S. McKinney, Dianne G. Bystrom, Lynda Lee Kaid, and Diana B. Carlin. New York: Peter Lang Publishing.

Bystrom, Dianne, Mary C. Banwart, Lynda Lee Kaid, and Terry Robertson. 2004. *Gender and Campaign Communication: Video Style, Web Style, and News Style.* New York: Routledge.

Bystrom, Dianne, and Lynda Lee Kaid. 2002. "Are Women Candidates Transforming Campaign Communication? A Comparison of Advertising

Videostyles in the 1990s." In *Women Transforming Congress*, ed. Cindy Simon Rosenthal. Norman: University of Oklahoma Press.

Cammisa, Anne Marie, and Beth Reingold. 2004. "Women in State Legislatures and State Legislative Research: Beyond Sameness and Difference." *State Politics and Policy Quarterly* 4, no. 2: 181–210.

Campbell, Angus, Philip E. Converse, Warren E. Miller, and Donald E. Stokes. 1960. *The American Voter.* New York: John Wiley and Sons.

Canon, David T. 1999. *Race, Redistricting, and Representation: The Unintended Consequences of Black Majority Districts.* Chicago: University of Chicago Press.

Carey, John M., Richard G. Niemi, and Lynda W. Powell. 1998. "Are Women State Legislators Different?" In *Women and Elective Office: Past, Present, and Future*, eds. Sue Thomas and Clyde Wilcox. New York: Oxford University Press.

Carroll, Susan J. 1985. *Women as Candidates in American Politics.* Bloomington: Indiana University Press.

——— (ed.). 1991. *Women, Black, and Hispanic Elected Leaders.* New Brunswick, NJ: Eagleton Institute of Politics, Rutgers University.

———. 1994. *Women as Candidates in American Politics.* Bloomington: Indiana University Press.

———. 2001. "Representing Women: Women State Legislators as Agents of Policy-Related Change." In *The Impact of Women in Public Office*, ed. Susan J. Carroll. Bloomington: Indiana University Press.

———. 2002. "Representing Women: Congresswomen's Perceptions of Their Representational Roles." In *Women Transforming Congress*, ed. Cindy Simon Rosenthal. Norman: University of Oklahoma Press.

Carroll, Susan J., Debra Dodson, and Ruth Mandel. 1991. *The Impact of Women in Office: An Overview.* New Brunswick, NY: Center for American Women and Politics.

Carroll, Susan J., and Krista Jenkins. 2001. "Unrealized Opportunity? Term Limits and the Representation of Women in State Legislatures." *Women & Politics* 23, no. 4: 1–30.

Carsey, Thomas M., and Barry Rundquist. 1999. "Party and Committee in Distributive Politics: Evidence from Defense Spending." *Journal of Politics* 61, no. 4: 1156–1169.

Carter, Ralph. 1989. "Senate Defense Budgeting, 1981–88. The Impacts of Ideology, Party, and Constituency Benefit on the Decision to Support the President." *American Politics Quarterly* 17: 332–347.

CAWP (Center for American Women and Politics). 2005. "Record Number of Women Seek Seats in U.S. House; Candidate Numbers at Other Levels Don't Match Record Highs." New Brunswick, NJ: Center for American Women and Politics.

———. 2006a. "Election 2006: Many New Women Expected in U.S. House." Press release. www.cawp.rutgers.edu (27 September 2006).

———. 2006b. "Women in the U.S. Congress 2006." Fact sheet. New Brunswick, NJ: Center for American Women and Politics.

———. 2007. "Women in Elective Office 2007." Fact sheet. New Brunswick, NJ: Center for American Women and Politics.

Chisholm, Shirley. 1970. *Unbought and Unbossed.* New York: Avon Books.

Clark, Janet. 1994. "Getting There: Women in Political Office." In *Different Roles, Different Voices: Women and Politics in the United States and Europe*, eds.

Marianne Githens, Pippa Norris, and Joni Lovenduski. New York: HarperCollins.

Clausen, Aage, and Clyde Wilcox. 1987. "Policy Partisanship in Legislative Recruitment and Behavior." *Legislative Studies Quarterly* 12, no. 2: 243–263.

Considine, Mark, and Iva Ellen Deutchman. 1994. "The Gendering of Political Institutions: A Comparison of American and Australian State Legislators." *Social Science Quarterly* 75, no. 4: 854–866.

Cook, Elizabeth Adell. 1998. "Voter Reaction to Women Candidates." In *Women and Elective Office*, eds. Sue Thomas and Clyde Wilcox. New York: Oxford University Press.

Cook, Elizabeth Adell, Sue Thomas, and Clyde Wilcox (eds.). 1994. *The Year of the Woman: Myths and Realities*. Boulder, CO: Westview Press.

Crenshaw, Kimberlè. 1989. "Demarginalizing the Intersection of Race and Sex: A Black Feminist Critique of Antidiscrimination Doctrine, Feminist Theory and Antiracist Politics." *University of Chicago Legal Forum* 139: 139–167.

———. 1997. "Beyond Racism and Misogyny: Black Feminism and 2 Live Crew." In *Women Transforming Politics*, eds. Cathy Cohen, Kathy Jones, and Joan Tronto. New York: New York University Press.

Dabelko, Kirsten LaCour, and Paul Herrnson. 1997. "Women's and Men's Campaigns for the US House of Representatives." *Political Research Quarterly* 50, no. 1: 121–135.

Darcy, R., and James R. Choike. 1986. "A Formal Analysis of Legislative Turnover: Women Candidates and Legislative Representation." *American Journal of Political Science* 30, no. 1: 237–255.

Darcy, R., and Charles D. Hadley. 1988. "Black Women in Politics: The Puzzle of Success." *Social Science Quarterly* 69: 629–645.

Darcy, R., Charles D. Hadley, and Jason F. Kirksey. 1993. "Electoral Systems and the Representation of Black Women in American State Legislatures." *Women & Politics* 13, no. 2: 73–89.

Darcy, R., and Sarah Slavin Schramm. 1979. "When Women Run Against Men." *Public Opinion Quarterly* 41, no. 1: 1–12.

Darcy, R., Susan Welch, and Janet Clark. 1994. *Women, Elections, and Representation*, 2nd ed. Lincoln: University of Nebraska Press.

Darling, Marsha J. 1998. "African-American Women in State Elective Office in the South." In *Women and Elective Office: Past, Present, and Future*, eds. Sue Thomas and Clyde Wilcox, 150–162. New York: Oxford University Press.

Davis, Rebecca Howard. 1997. *Women and Power in Parliamentary Democracies: Cabinet Appointments in Western Europe*. Lincoln: University of Nebraska Press.

Deering, Christopher J. 2005. "Foreign Affairs and War." In *The Legislative Branch*, eds. Paul J. Quirk and Sarah A. Binder. New York: Oxford University Press.

Delli Carpini, Michael, and Ester R. Fuchs. 1993. "The Year of the Woman? Candidates, Voters, and the 1992 Elections." *Political Science Quarterly* 108, no. 1: 29–36.

Delli Carpini, Michael X., and Scott Keeter. 1996. *What Americans Know About Politics and Why It Matters*. New Haven, CT: Yale University Press.

Deloitte and Touche, LLP. 2000. "Women in Elected Office Survey Identifies Obstacles for Women as Political Leaders." www.us.deloitte.com.

Devitt, James. 1999. *Framing Gender on the Campaign Trail: Women's Executive Leadership and the Press*. Washington, DC: The Women's Leadership Fund.

Diamond, Irene. 1977. *Sex Roles in the State House*. New Haven, CT: Yale University Press.

Dodd, Lawrence C. 2001. "Re-Envisioning Congress: Theoretical Perspectives on Congressional Change." In *Congress Reconsidered,* 7th edition, eds. Lawrence C. Dodd and Bruce I. Oppenheimer. Washington, DC: Congressional Quarterly Press.

Dodson, Debra L. 1998."Representing Women's Interests in the U.S. House of Representatives." In *Women and Elective Office: Past, Present, and Future,* eds. Sue Thomas and Clyde Wilcox. New York: Oxford University Press.

————. 2006. *The Impact of Women in Congress*. New York: Oxford University Press.

Dodson, Debra L., and Susan J. Carroll. 1991. *Reshaping the Agenda: Women in State Legislatures*. New Brunswick, NJ: Center for the American Woman and Politics.

Dolan, Julie. 1997. "Support for Women's Interests in the 103rd Congress: The Distinct Impact of Congressional Women." *Women & Politics* 18, no. 4: 81–92.

Dolan, Kathleen. 1998. "Voting for Women in the 'Year of the Woman.'" *American Journal of Political Science* 42, no. 1: 272–293.

————. 2001. "Electoral Context, Issues, and Voting for Women in the 1990s." *Women & Politics* 23, no. 1/2: 21–36.

————. 2004. *Voting for Women: How the Public Evaluates Women Candidates*. Boulder, CO: Westview Press.

————. 2005. "Do Women Candidates Play to Gender Stereotypes? Do Men Candidates Play to Women? Candidate Sex and Issues Priorities on Campaign Websites." *Political Research Quarterly* 58, no. 1: 31–44.

————. 2006. "Symbolic Mobilization? The Impact of Candidate Sex in American Elections." *American Politics Research* 34, no. 6: 687–704.

————. 2008. "Women as Candidates in American Politics: The Continuing Impact of Sex and Gender." In *Political Women and American Democracy,* eds. Christina Wolbrecht, Karen Beckwith, and Lisa Baldez. New York: Cambridge University Press.

Dolan, Kathleen, and Lynne E. Ford. 1997. "Change and Continuity Among Women State Legislators: Evidence from Three Decades." *Political Research Quarterly* 50, no. 1: 137–151.

Dominguez, Casey Byrne Knudsen. 2005. "Before the Primary: Party Elite Involvement in Congressional Nominations." Ph.D. diss. University of California, Berkeley.

Donnelly, John. 2005. "No Roadblocks for Defense Authorization Bill." *CQ Weekly* 22 (December): 3390.

Downs, Anthony. 1957. *An Economic Theory of Democracy*. New York: Harper and Row.

Duerst-Lahti, Georgia. 1998. "The Bottleneck, Women Candidates." In *Women and Elective Office: Past, Present, and Future,* eds. Sue Thomas and Clyde Wilcox. New York: Oxford University Press.

————. 2002. "Knowing Congress as a Gendered Institution: Manliness and the Implications of Women in Congress." In *Women Transforming Congress,* ed. Cindy Simon Rosenthal. Norman: University of Oklahoma Press.

Duverger, Maurice. 1955. *The Political Role of Women*. Paris: UNESCO.

Dwyre, Diana, and Robin Kolodny. 2006. "The Parties' Congressional Campaign Committees in 2004." In *The Election After Reform,* ed. Michael Malbin. Lanham, MD: Rowman & Littlefield Publishers.

Elazar, Daniel J. 1984. *American Federalism: A View from the States*, 3rd ed. New York: Harper & Row.

Ellickson, Mark C., and Donald E. Whistler. 2000. "A Path Analysis of Legislative Success in Professional and Citizen Legislatures: A Gender Comparison." *Women & Politics* 21, no. 4: 77–103.

Evans, Jocelyn Jones. 2005. *Women, Partisanship, and the Congress.* New York: Palgrave Macmillan.

Evans, C. Lawrence. 1991. *Leadership in Committee: A Comparative Analysis of Leadership Behavior in the U.S. Senate.* Ann Arbor: University of Michigan Press.

Evans, C. Lawrence, and Daniel Lipinski. 2005. "Obstruction and Leadership in the U.S. Senate." In *Congress Reconsidered Eighth Edition,* eds. Lawrence C. Dodd and Bruce I. Oppenheimer. Washington, DC: CQ Press.

Falk, Erika, and Kate Kenski. 2006. "Issue Saliency and Gender Stereotypes: Support for Women as Presidents in Times of War and Terrorism." *Social Science Quarterly* 87, no. 1: 1–18.

Fenno, Richard F., Jr. 1973. *Congressmen in Committees.* Boston: Little, Brown.

Fiber, Pamela, and Richard Fox. 2005. "A Tougher Road for Women? Assessing the Role of Gender in Congressional Elections." In *Gender and American Politics,* eds. Sue Tolleson-Rinehart and Jyl J. Josephson. Armonk, NY: M. E. Sharpe.

Fleischmann, A., and Carol Pierannunzi. 1997. *Politics in Georgia.* Athens: The University of Georgia Press.

Fox, Richard L. 2000. "Gender and Congressional Elections." In *Gender and American Politics,* eds. Sue Tolleson-Rinehart and Jyl J. Josephson. Armonk, NY: M. E. Sharpe.

———. 2006. "Congressional Elections: Where Are We on the Road to Gender Parity?" In *Gender and Elections: Shaping the Future of American Politics,* eds. Susan J. Carroll and Richard L. Fox. New York: Cambridge University Press.

Fox, Richard L., and Jennifer L. Lawless. 2004. "Entering the Arena? Gender and the Decision to Run for Office." *American Journal of Political Science* 48, no. 2: 264–280.

Fox, Richard L., and Zoe M. Oxley. 2003. "Gender Stereotyping in State Executive Elections: Candidate Selection and Success." *Journal of Politics* 65, no. 3: 833–850.

Fraga, Luis Ricardo, Valerie Martinez-Ebers, Linda Lopez, and Ricardo Ramírez. 2006. "Gender and Ethnicity: Patterns of Electoral Success and Legislative Advocacy Among Latina and Latino State Officials in Four States." *Journal of Women, Politics, & Policy* 28, no. 3/4: 121–145.

Fraga, Luis Ricardo, and Ricardo Ramírez. 2003. "Latino Political Incorporation in California, 1990–2000." In *Latinos and Public Policy in California: An Agenda for Opportunity,* eds. David Lopez and Andrés Jiménez. Berkeley: Berkeley Public Policy Press, Institute for Governmental Studies, University of California.

Francis, Wayne L. 1962. "Influence and Interaction in a State Legislative Body." *American Political Science Review* 56, no. 4: 953–960.

Frantzich, Stephen. 1979. "Who Makes Our Laws? The Legislative Effectiveness of Members of the U.S. Congress." *Legislative Studies Quarterly* 4, no. 3: 409–428.

Freeman, Jo. 2000. *A Room at a Time: How Women Entered Party Politics.* Lanham, MD: Rowman & Littlefield.

Friedman, Sally. 1996. "House Committee Assignments of Women and Minority Newcomers, 1965–1994." *Legislative Studies Quarterly* 21, no. 1: 73–81.

Frisch, Scott A., and Sean Q. Kelly. 2003. "A Place at the Table: Women's Committee Requests and Women's Committee Assignments in the U.S. House." *Women & Politics* 25, no. 3: 1–26.

Gaddie, Ronald Keith, and Charles S. Bullock III. 2000. *Elections to Open Seats in the U.S. House*. Lanham, MD: Rowman & Littlefield Publishers.

Gamson, William A., David Croteau, William Hoynes, and Theodore Sasson. 1992. "Media Images and the Social Construction of Reality." *Annual Review of Sociology* 18: 373–393.

Garcia Bedolla, Lisa, Katherine Tate, and Janelle Wong. 2005. "Indelible Effects: The Impact of Women of Color in the U.S. Congress." In *Women and Elective Office: Past, Present, and Future*, 2nd edition, eds. Sue Thomas and Clyde Wilcox. New York: Oxford University Press.

Gertzog, Irwin. 1995. *Congressional Women: Their Recruitment, Integration, and Behavior*, 2nd edition. Westport, CT: Praeger.

Gilliam, Franklin D., Jr., and Karen M. Kaufmann. 1998. "Is There an Empowerment Life Cycle? Long-Term Black Empowerment and Its Influence on Voter Participation." *Urban Affairs Review* 33, no. 6: 741–766.

Githens, Marianne, and Jewel L. Prestage. 1977. *A Portrait of Marginality: The Political Behavior of the American Woman*. New York: Longman.

Green, Joanne Connor. 2003. "The Times . . . Are They A-Changing? An Examination of the Impact of the Value of Campaign Resources for Women and Men Candidates for the US House of Representatives." *Women & Politics* 25, no. 4: 1–29.

Greene, William H. 1997. *Economic Analysis,* 3rd ed. Saddle River, NJ: Prentice Hall.

Grofman, Bernard, William Koetzle, and Anthony McGann. 2002. "Congressional Leadership 1965–96: A New Look at the Extremism Versus Centrality Debate." *Legislative Studies Quarterly* 27, no. 1: 87–105.

Hamm, Keith E., Robert Harmel, and Robert Thompson. 1983. "Ethnic and Partisan Minorities in Two Southern State Legislatures." *Legislative Studies Quarterly* 8, no. 2: 177–189.

Hansen, Susan B. 1997. "Talking About Politics: Gender and Contextual Effects on Political Proselytizing." *Journal of Politics* 59, no. 1: 73–103.

Harris, Douglas B. 2006. "Legislative Parties and Leadership Choice: Confrontation or Accommodation in the 1989 Gingrich-Madigan Whip Race." *American Politics Research* 34, no. 2: 189–222.

Hawkesworth, Mary. 2003. "Congressional Enactments of Race-Gender: Toward a Theory of Raced-Gendered Institutions." *American Political Science Review* 97, no. 4: 529–550.

Hawkesworth, Mary, Kathleen J. Casey, Krista Jenkins, and Katherine E. Kleeman. 2001. *Legislating by and for Women: A Comparison of the 103rd and 104th Congresses*. New Brunswick, NJ: Center for American Women and Politics.

Hawkesworth, Mary, and Katherine E. Kleeman. 2001. "Term Limits and the Representation of Women." New Brunswick, NJ: Center for American Women and Politics, May. www.cawp.rutgers.edu/Research/reportslist.html (8 February 2008).

Haynie, Kerry. 2001. *African American Legislators in the American States*. New York: Columbia University Press.

———. 2002. "The Color of Their Skin or the Content of Their Behavior? Race and

Perceptions of African American Legislators." *Legislative Studies Quarterly* 27, no. 2: 295–313.

Hedge, David, James Button, and Mary Spear. 1996. "Accounting for the Quality of Black Legislative Life: The View from the States." *American Journal of Political Science* 40, no. 1: 82–98.

Heldman, Caroline, Susan J. Carroll, and Stephanie Olson. 2005. "'She Brought Only a Skirt': Print Media Coverage of Elizabeth Dole's Bid for the Republican Nomination." *Political Communication* 22, no. 3: 315–335.

Herrick, Rebekah. 2000. "Seniority and the Lost Power of Female House Members." Paper presented at the Midwest Political Science Association annual meeting, Chicago, 27–30 April.

Herrnson, Paul S., J. Celeste Lay, and Atiya Kai Stokes. 2003. "Women Running 'as Women': Candidate Gender, Campaign Issues, and Voter Targeting Strategies." *Journal of Politics* 65, no. 1: 244–255.

Huckfeldt, Robert, and John Sprague. 1995. *Citizens, Politics and Social Communication*. New York: Cambridge University Press.

Huddy, Leonie, and Nayda Terkildsen. 1993a. "Gender Stereotypes and the Perception of Male and Female Candidates." *American Journal of Political Science* 37, no. 1: 119–147.

———. 1993b. "The Consequences of Gender Stereotypes for Women Candidates at Different Levels and Types of Offices." *Political Research Quarterly* 46: 503–525.

Hurtado, Aída. 1996. *The Color of Privilege: Three Blasphemies on Race and Feminism*. Ann Arbor: The University of Michigan Press.

Inter-Parliamentary Union. 2008. "Women in National Parliaments." www.ipu.org/wmn-e/classif.htm (16 June 2008).

"Iowa Poll of 500 Likely Democratic Caucus Participants, November 25–28, 2007," *Des Moines Register*, 2 December 2007, p. 2.

Iyengar, Shanto, Nicholas A. Valentino, Stephen Ansolabehere, and Adam F. Simon. 1997. "Running as a Woman: Gender Stereotyping in Political Campaigns." In *Women, Media and Politics*, ed. Pippa Norris. New York: Oxford University Press.

Jacobson, Gary. 2004. *The Politics of Congressional Elections,* 6th ed. New York: Longman.

Jamieson, Kathleen Hall. 1995. *Beyond the Double Bind*. New York: Oxford University Press.

Jewell, Malcolm E., and Marcia Lynn Whicker. 1994. *Legislative Leadership in the American States*. Ann Arbor: University of Michigan Press.

Jeydel, Alana, and Andrew J. Taylor. 2003. "Are Women Legislators Less Effective? Evidence from the U.S. House in the 103rd–105th Congress." *Political Research Quarterly* 56, no. 1: 19–27.

Johnston, Anne, and Anne Barton White. 1994. "Communication Styles and Female Candidates: A Study of Political Advertisements of Men and Women Candidates for U.S. Senate." *Political Research Quarterly* 46, no. 2: 481–501.

Jones, Jeffrey M. 2005. "Nearly Half of Americans Think U.S. Will Soon Have a Woman President: Most Say They Would Vote for a Qualified Woman." *Gallup Brain*. www.rci.rutgers.edu/~cawp/Facts/Elections/pres08_polls/Gallup_NearlyHalfofAmericans.pdf (4 October 2005).

Kahn, Kim Fridkin. 1992. "Does Being Male Help? An Investigation of the Effects of Candidate Gender and Campaign Coverage on Evaluations of U.S. Senate Candidates." *Journal of Politics* 54, no. 2: 497–517.

———. 1993. "Gender Differences in Campaign Messages: The Political Advertisements of Men and Women Candidates for U.S. Senate." *Political Research Quarterly* 46, no. 3: 481–502.

———. 1994. "Does Gender Make a Difference? An Experimental Examination of Sex Stereotypes and Press Patterns in Statewide Campaigns." *American Journal of Political Science* 38, no. 1: 162–195.

———. 1996. *The Political Consequences of Being a Woman: How Stereotypes Influence the Conduct and Consequences of Political Campaigns.* New York: Columbia University Press.

Kaid, Lynda Lee, Sandra L. Myers, Valerie Pipps, and Jan Hunter. 1984. "Sex Role Perceptions and Television Advertising: Comparing Male and Female Candidates." *Women & Politics* 4: 41–53.

Kanter, Rosabeth Moss. 1977. "Some Effects of Proportions on Group Life: Skewed Sex Ratios and Responses to Token Women." *American Journal of Sociology* 82, no. 5: 965–990.

Kathlene, Lyn. 1989. "Uncovering the Political Impacts of Gender: An Exploratory Study." *Western Political Quarterly* 42, no. 2: 397–421.

———. 1994. "Power and Influence in State Legislative Policymaking: The Interaction of Gender and Position in Committee Hearing Debates." *American Political Science Review* 88, no. 3: 560–576.

———. 1995. "Alternative Views of Crime: Legislative Policymaking in Gendered Terms." *Journal of Politics* 57, no. 3: 696–723.

Kaufmann, Karen M., and John R. Petrocik. 1999. "The Changing Politics of American Men: Understanding the Sources of the Gender Gap." *American Journal of Political Science* 43, no. 3: 864–887.

Keefe, William, and Morris Ogul. 1989. *The American Legislative Process: Congress and the States.* Englewood Cliffs, NJ: Prentice Hall.

Kelly, Rita Mae, Michelle A. Saint-Germain, and Jody D. Horn. 1991. "Female Public Officials: A Different Voice?" *Annals of the American Academy of Political and Social Science* 515: 77–87.

Kenney, Sally J. 1996. "New Research on Gendered Political Institutions." *Political Research Quarterly* 49, no. 2: 445–466.

Kenski, Kate, and Erika Falk. 2004. "Of What Is That Glass Ceiling Made? A Study of Attitudes About Women and the Oval Office." *Women & Politics* 26, no. 2: 57–80.

Kiewet, D. Roderick, and Mathew McCubbins. 1991. *The Logic of Congressional Delegation.* Chicago: University of Chicago Press.

King, David C., and Richard E. Matland. 2003. "Sex and the Grand Old Party: An Experimental Investigation of the Effect of Candidate Sex on Support for a Republican Candidate." *American Politics Research* 31, no. 6: 595–612.

King-Meadows, Tyson, and Thomas F. Schaller. 2000. "The Institutionalization of Black State Legislative Power." Paper presented at the Annual Meeting of the American Political Science Association, Washington, DC, 30 August–3 September.

———. 2006. *Devolution and Black State Legislators: Challenges and Choices in the 21st Century.* New York: SUNY Press.

Kirkpatrick, Jeanne J. 1974. *Political Woman.* New York: Basic Books.

Koch, Jeffrey W. 1997. "Candidate Gender and Women's Psychological Engagement in Politics." *American Politics Quarterly* 25, no. 1: 118–133.

———. 2000. "Do Citizens Apply Gender Stereotypes to Infer Candidates' Ideological Orientations?" *Journal of Politics* 62, no. 2: 414–429.

————. 2002. "Gender Stereotypes and Citizens' Impressions of House Candidates' Ideological Orientations." *American Journal of Political Science* 46, no. 2: 453–462.

Koszczuk, Jackie, and Martha Angle, eds. 2007. *CQ's Politics in America 2008, the 110th Congress.* Washington, DC: CQ Press.

Kroger, Gregory. 2003. "Position-Taking and Cosponsorship in the U.S. House." *Legislative Studies Quarterly* 28, no. 2: 225–246.

Larson, Stephanie Greco. 2001. "Running as Women? A Comparison of Female and Male Pennsylvania Assembly Candidates' Brochures." *Women & Politics* 22, no. 2: 107–124.

Lawless, Jennifer L. 2004a. "Politics of Presence: Congresswomen and Symbolic Representation." *Political Research Quarterly* 57, no. 1: 81–99.

————. 2004b. "Women, War, and Winning Elections: Gender Stereotyping in the Post–September 11th Era." *Political Research Quarterly* 57, no. 3: 479–490.

Lawless, Jennifer L., and Richard Fox. 2005. *It Takes a Candidate: Why Women Don't Run for Office.* New York: Cambridge University Press.

Lee, Frances E., and Bruce I. Oppenheimer. 1999. *Sizing Up the Senate: The Unequal Consequences of Equal Representation.* Chicago: University of Chicago Press.

Leeper, Mark. 1991. "The Impact of Prejudice on Female Candidates: An Experimental Look at Voter Inference." *American Politics Quarterly* 19, no. 2: 248–261.

Leighley, Jan E., and Jonathan Nagler. 1991. "Socioeconomic Class Bias in Turnout, 1972–1988: Institutions Come and Go, But the Voters Remain the Same." Presented at the annual meeting of the American Political Science Association, Washington, DC.

Lindsay, John M. 1990. "Parochialism, Policy, and Constituency Constraints: Congressional Voting on Strategic Weapons Systems." *American Journal of Political Science* 34, no. 4: 936–960.

Lublin, David, and Sarah Brewer. 2003. "The Continuing Dominance of Traditional Gender Roles in Southern Elections." *Social Science Quarterly* 84, no. 2: 379–396.

Lupia, Arthur, and Matthew D. McCubbins. 1998. *The Democratic Dilemma: Can Citizens Learn What They Need to Know?* Cambridge: Cambridge University Press.

Mackaman, Frank H. 1980. "Understanding Congressional Leadership: The State of the Art." A conference report of the Everett McKinley Dirksen Congressional Leadership Research Center, Washington, DC, 10–11 June.

Mansbridge, Jane. 1999. "Should Blacks Represent Blacks and Women Represent Women? A Contingent 'Yes.'" *Journal of Politics* 61, no. 3: 628–657.

————. 2003. "Rethinking Representation." *American Political Science Review* 97, no. 4: 515–528.

Marcedo, Stephen. 2005. *Democracy at Risk: How Political Choices Undermine Citizen Participation, and What We Can Do About It.* Washington, DC: The Brookings Institution.

Matland, Richard E. 1998. "Women's Representation in National Legislatures: Developed and Developing Countries." *Legislative Studies Quarterly* 23, no. 1: 109–125.

Matland, Richard E., and David C. King. 2002. "Women as Candidates in Congressional Elections." In *Women Transforming Congress*, ed. Cindy Simon Rosenthal. Norman: University of Oklahoma Press.

Matthews, David. 1960. *U.S. Senators and Their World.* New York: Random House Press.

Mayer, Kenneth R. 1991. *The Political Economy of Defense Contracting.* New Haven, CT: Yale University Press.

Mayhew, David. 1974. *The Electoral Connection.* New Haven, CT: Yale University.

McCutcheon, Chuck, with Donna Cassata. 2002. "Lawmakers Seek to Avoid Closures by Pumping Money Into Military Bases." *CQ Weekly,* August 8: 2190.

McDermott, Monika L. 1997. "Voting Cues in Low-Information Elections: Candidate Gender as a Social Information Variable in Contemporary U.S. Elections." *American Journal of Political Science* 41, no. 1: 270–283.

———. 1998. "Race and Gender Cues in Low-Information Elections." *Political Research Quarterly* 51, no. 4: 895–918.

Media Matters for America. 2007. "From Cleavage to 'Cackle': Media Find New Focus in Coverage of Hillary Clinton." http://mediamatters.org/items/200710040003?f=s_search (3 October 2007).

Menifield, Charles E., and Stephen Shaffer. 2000. "Voting Behavior Among African Americans in Southern State Legislatures." Paper presented at the annual meeting of the American Political Science Association, Washington, DC, 30 August–3 September.

Meyer, Katherine. 1980. "Legislative Influence: Toward Theory Development Through Causal Analysis." *Legislative Studies Quarterly* 5, no. 4: 563–585.

Miller, Cheryl M. 1990. "Agenda Setting by State Legislative Black Caucuses: Policy Priorities and Factors of Success." *Policy Studies Review* 9, no. 2: 339–354.

Mindiola, Tatcho, and Armando Gutierrez. 1988. "Chicanos and the Legislative Process: Reality and Illusion in the Politics of Change." In *Latinos and the Political System,* ed. F. Chris Garcia. Notre Dame, IN: University of Notre Dame Press.

Moncrief, Gary, Joel A. Thompson, and Karl T. Kurtz. 1996. "The Old Statehouse, It Ain't What It Used to Be." *Legislative Studies Quarterly* 21, no. 1: 57–72.

Moncrief, Gary, Joel Thompson, and Robert Schuhmann. 1991. "Gender, Race, and the State Legislature: A Research Note on the Double Disadvantage Hypothesis." *Social Science Journal* 28, no. 4: 481–487.

Montoya, Lisa J., Carol Hardy-Fanta, and Sonia Garcia. 2000. "Latina Politics: Gender, Participation, and Leadership." *PS: Political Science and Politics* 33, no. 3: 555–561.

Nelson, Candice J. 1994. "Women's PACs in the Year of the Woman." In *The Year of the Woman: Myths and Realities,* eds. Elizabeth Adell Cook, Sue Thomas, and Clyde Wilcox. Boulder, CO: Westview Press.

Niven, David. 1998. "Party Elites and Women Candidates: The Shape of Bias." *Women & Politics* 19, no. 2: 57–80.

Niven, David, and Jeremy Zilber. 2001. "Do Women and Men in Congress Cultivate Different Images? Evidence from Congressional Web Sites." *Political Communication* 18, no. 4: 395–405.

Norris, Pippa. 1994. "The Impact of the Electoral System on Election of Women to National Legislatures." In *Different Roles, Different Voices,* eds. Marianne Githens, Pippa Norris, and Joni Lovenduski. New York: HarperCollins.

Norton, Noelle. 1995. "Women, It's Not Enough to Be Elected: Committee Position Makes a Difference." In *Gender Power, Leadership, and Governance,* eds. Georgia Duerst-Lahti and Rita Mae Kelly. Ann Arbor: University of Michigan Press.

———. 2002. "Transforming Policy from the Inside: Participation in Committee." In *Women Transforming Congress*, ed. Cindy Simon Rosenthal. Norman: University of Oklahoma Press.

NWPC (National Women's Political Caucus). 1994. *Why Don't More Women Run? A Study Prepared by Mellman, Lazarus, and Lake*. Washington, DC: National Women's Political Caucus.

O'Connor, Karen. 2001. "Thirteen and Counting (and Making a Difference): Women in the U.S. Senate." *Journal of Women's Imaging* (November): 119–122.

Orey, Byron D'Andra. 2000. "Black Legislative Politics in Mississippi." *Journal of Black Studies* 30, no. 6: 791–814.

Orey, Byron D'Andra, and Wendy Smooth. 2006. "Race and Gender Matter: Refining Models of Legislative Policy Making in State Legislatures." *Journal of Women, Politics, & Policy* 28, no. 3/4: 97–119.

Owens, Chris T. 2005. "Black Substantive Representation in State Legislatures from 1971–1994." *Social Science Quarterly* 86, no. 4: 779–791.

Palmer, Barbara, and Dennis Simon. 2006. *Breaking the Political Glass Ceiling*. New York: Routledge.

Peabody, Robert. 1967. "Party Leadership in the U.S. House of Representatives." *American Political Science Review* 61, no. 3: 675–693.

Pearson, Kathryn, and Eric McGhee. 2004. "Strategic Differences: The Gender Dynamics of Congressional Candidacies, 1982–2002." Paper presented at the Midwest Political Science Association conference, Chicago, April.

Peters, Ronald M. 1998. "Institutional Context and Leadership Style: The Case of Newt Gingrich." Presented at the Florida International Conference on Republican Control of the U.S. House of Representatives, Miami, 31 January.

Petrocik, John R. 1996. "Issue Ownership in Presidential Elections, with a 1980 Case Study." *American Journal of Political Science* 40, no. 3: 825–850.

Pew Research Center for People and the Press. 2000. "Internet Election News Audience Seeks Convenience, Familiar Names." www.people-press.org.

———. 2006. "Online Papers Modestly Boost Newspaper Readership." Released July 30, 2006. http://people-press.org/reports/display.php3?ReportID=282.

Pimlott, Jamie. 2007. "This Isn't Your Mom's Tupperware Party: How EMILY's List Changed the American Political Landscape." Ph.D. diss. University of Florida, Gainesville.

Pitkin, Hannah. 1967. *The Concept of Representation*. Berkeley: University of California Press.

Plutzer, Eric, and John F. Zipp. 1996. "Identity Politics and Voting for Women Candidates." *Public Opinion Quarterly* 60, no. 1: 30–57.

Poole, Keith T., and Howard Rosenthal. 1997. *Congress: A Political-Economic History of Roll Call Voting*. New York: Oxford University Press.

Preuhs, Robert R. 2006. "The Conditional Effects of Minority Descriptive Representation: Black Legislators and Policy Influence in the American States." *Journal of Politics* 68, no. 3: 585–599.

Prinderville, Diane-Michele. 2002. "A Comparative Study of Native American and Hispanic Women in Grassroots and Electoral Politics." *Frontiers* 23, no. 1: 67–88.

Project for Excellence in Journalism. 2007. "The Invisible Primary—Invisible No Longer: A First Look at Coverage of the 2008 Presidential Campaign." www.journalism.org/node/8187.

Rahn, Wendy. 1993. "The Role of Partisan Stereotypes in Information Processing

About Political Candidates." *American Journal of Political Science* 37, no. 2: 472–496.

Rapoport, Ronald B. 1981. "The Sex Gap in Political Persuading: Where the 'Structuring Principle' Works." *American Journal of Political Science* 25, no. 1: 32–48.

Reingold, Beth. 1992. "Concepts of Representation Among Female and Male State Legislators." *Legislative Studies Quarterly* 27, no. 4: 509–537.

———. 2000. *Representing Women: Sex, Gender, and Legislative Behavior in Arizona and California.* Chapel Hill: University of North Carolina Press.

———. 2008. "Women as Officeholders: Linking Descriptive and Substantive Representation." In *Political Women and American Democracy*, eds. Christina Wolbrecht, Karen Beckwith, and Lisa Baldez. New York: Cambridge University Press.

Richardson, Lilliard E., and Patricia K. Freeman. 1995. "Gender Differences in Constituency Service Among State Legislators." *Political Research Quarterly* 48, no. 1: 169–179.

Rieck, Donald. 2007. "Election Study Finds Media Hit Hillary Hardest." Center for Media and Public Affairs. www.cmpa.com/releases/07_12_21_Election_Study .pdf.

Rosenstone, Steven J., and Mark John Hansen. 1993. *Mobilization, Participation, and Democracy in America.* New York: Macmillan.

Rosenthal, Alan. 1998. *Decline in Representative Democracy.* Washington, DC: Congressional Quarterly Press.

Rosenthal, Cindy Simon. 1998. *When Women Lead: Integrative Leadership in State Legislatures.* New York: Oxford University Press.

———. 2000. "Gender Styles in State Legislative Committees: Raising Their Voices in Resolving Conflict." *Women & Politics* 21: 21–45.

Rule, Wilma. 1987. "Electoral Systems, Contextual Factors, and Women's Opportunity for Election to Parliament in Twenty-Three Democracies." *Western Political Quarterly* 40, no. 3: 477–498.

Saint-Germain, Michelle A. 1989. "Does Their Difference Make a Difference? The Impact of Women on Public Policy in the Arizona Legislature." *Social Science Quarterly* 70, no. 4: 956–968.

Sanbonmatsu, Kira. 2002a. "Political Parties and the Recruitment of Women to State Legislatures." *Journal of Politics* 64, no. 3: 791–809.

———. 2002b. "Gender Stereotypes and Vote Choice." *American Journal of Political Science* 46, no. 1: 20–34.

———. 2006a. "State Elections: Where Do Women Run? Where Do Women Win?" In *Gender and Elections: Shaping the Future of American Politics*, eds. Susan J. Carroll and Richard L. Fox. New York: Cambridge University Press.

———. 2006b. *Where Women Run: Gender and Party in the American States.* Ann Arbor: University of Michigan.

Sapiro, Virginia. 1981. "When Are Interests Interesting? The Problem of the Representation of Women." *American Political Science Review* 75, no. 3: 701–716.

———. 1981/1982. "If U.S. Senator Baker Were a Woman: An Experimental Study of Candidate Images." *Political Psychology* 3, no. 1/2: 61–83.

Sapiro, Virginia, and Pamela Johnston Conover. 1997. "The Variable Gender Basis of Electoral Politics: Gender and Context in the 1992 U.S. Election." *British Journal of Political Science* 27, no. 4: 497–523.

Schiller, Wendy. 2000. *Partners and Rivals: Representation in U.S. Senate Delegations.* Princeton, NJ: Princeton University Press.

Schlozman, Kay Lehman, Nancy Burns, Sidney Verba, and Jesse Donahue. 1995. "Gender and Citizen Participation: Is There a Different Voice?" *American Journal of Political Science* 39, no. 2: 267–293.

Sellers, Patrick J. 2002. "Winning Media Coverage in the U.S. Congress." In *U.S. Senate Exceptionalism,* ed. Bruce I. Oppenheimer. Columbus: Ohio State University.

Seltzer, Richard A., Jody Newman, and Melissa Voorhees Leighton. 1997. *Sex as a Political Variable: Women as Candidates and Voters in U.S. Elections.* Boulder, CO: Lynne Rienner.

Shapiro, Robert Y., and Harpreet Mahajan. 1986. "Gender Differences in Policy Preferences: A Summary of Trends from the 1960s to the 1980s." *Public Opinion Quarterly* 50, no. 1: 42–61.

Sierra, Christine Marie, and Adaljiza Sosa-Riddell. 1994. "Chicanas as Political Actors: Rare Literature, Complex Practice." *National Political Science Review* 4: 297–317.

Simon, Dennis, and Barbara Palmer. 2005. "When Women Run Against Women: The Hidden Influence of Female Incumbents in Elections to the U.S. House of Representatives, 1956–2002." *Politics and Gender* 1, no. 1: 39–63.

Sinclair, Barbara. 1989. *The Transformation of the U.S. Senate.* Baltimore: Johns Hopkins University Press.

———. 1990. "Congressional Leadership: A Review Essay and a Research Agenda." In *Leading Congress: New Styles, New Strategies*, ed. John Kornacki. Washington, DC: CQ Press.

———. 1999. "Transformational Leader or Faithful Agent? Principal-Agent Theory and House Majority Party Leadership." *Legislative Studies Quarterly* 24, no. 3: 421–449.

———. 2005. "The New World of U.S. Senators." In *Congress Reconsidered*, 8th edition, eds. Lawrence C. Dodd and Bruce I. Oppenheimer. Washington, DC: CQ Press.

———. 2006. *Party Wars: Polarization and the Politics of National Policymaking.* Norman: University of Oklahoma Press.

Smith, Eric R.A.N., and Richard L. Fox. 2001. "A Research Note: The Electoral Fortunes of Women Candidates for Congress." *Political Research Quarterly* 54, no. 1: 205–221.

Smith, Kevin B. 1997. "When's All Fair: Signs of Parity in Media Coverage of Female Candidates." *Political Communication* 14: 71–82.

Smith, Steven S., and Christopher J. Deering. 1997. *Committees in Congress*, 3rd edition. Washington, DC: Congressional Quarterly.

Smooth, Wendy G. 2001. "African American Women State Legislators: The Impact of Gender and Race on Legislative Influence." Ph.D. diss. University of Maryland.

———. 2006. "African American Women and Electoral Politics: Journeying from the Shadows to the Spotlight." In *Gender and Elections: Shaping the Future of American Politics*, eds. Susan J. Carroll and Richard L. Fox. New York: Cambridge University Press.

Soherr-Hadwiger, David. 1998. "Military Construction Policy: A Test of Competing Explanations of Universalism in Congress." *Legislative Studies Quarterly* 23, no. 1: 57–78.

Sorrells, Neil. 2003. "Veterans Funding Legislation Sparks Unusually Partisan Fight." *CQ Weekly,* May 23: 1281.

Spraggins, Renee E. 2000. *Women in the United States: A Profile.* US Census Bureau, Current Population Reports.

Squire, Peveril. 1992. "Legislative Professionalization and Membership Diversity in State Legislatures." *Legislative Studies Quarterly* 17, no. 1: 69–79.

———. 2000. "Uncontested Seats in State Legislative Elections." *Legislative Studies Quarterly* 25, no. 1: 131–146.

Strahan, Randall. 1996. "Leadership in Institutional and Political Time: The Case of Newt Gingrich and the 104th Congress." Presented at the annual meeting of the American Political Science Association, San Francisco, 29 August–1 September.

Sundar, S. Shyam, Siriam Kalyanaraman, and Justin Brown. 2003. "Explicating Web Site Interactivity: Impression Formation Effects of Political Campaign Sites." *Communication Research* 30, no. 1: 30–59.

Swers, Michele L. 2002. *The Difference Women Make: The Policy Impact of Women in Congress.* Chicago: University of Chicago Press.

———. Forthcoming. *Making Policy in the New Senate Club: Women and Representation in the U.S. Senate.* Chicago: University of Chicago Press.

Takash, Paule Cruz. 1997. "Breaking Barriers to Representation: Chicana/Latina Elected Officials in California." In *Women Transforming Politics: An Alternative Reader*, eds. Cathy J. Cohen, Kathleen B. Jones, and Joan C. Tronto. New York: New York University Press.

Tate, Katherine. 1991. "Black Political Participation in the 1984 and 1988 Presidential Elections." *American Political Science Review* 85, no. 4: 1159–1176.

———. 1993. *From Protest to Politics: The New Black Voters in American Elections.* Cambridge, MA: Harvard University Press.

———. 2003. *Black Faces in the Mirror: African Americans and Their Representatives in the U.S. Congress.* Princeton, NJ: Princeton University Press.

Teixeira, Ruy A. 1992. *The Disappearing American Voter.* Washington, DC: Brookings Institution.

Thomas, Kenneth. 1975. "Conflict and Conflict Management." In *The Handbook of Industrial and Organizational Psychology*, ed. Marvin Dunnette. Chicago: Rand McNally.

Thomas, Sue. 1992. "The Effects of Race and Gender on Constituency Service." *Western Political Quarterly* 45, no. 1: 161–180.

———. 1994. *How Women Legislate.* New York: Oxford University Press.

———. 1998. "Introduction: Women and Elective Office: Past, Present, and Future." In *Women and Elective Office: Past, Present, and Future*, eds. Sue Thomas and Clyde Wilcox. New York: Oxford University Press.

Thomas, Sue, and Susan Welch. 1991. "The Impact of Gender on Activities and Priorities of State Legislators." *Western Political Quarterly* 44, no. 2: 445–456.

———. 2001. "The Impact of Women in State Legislatures: Numerical and Organizational Strength." In *The Impact of Women in Public Office*, ed. Susan J. Carroll. Bloomington: Indiana University Press.

Thomas, Sue, and Clyde Wilcox, eds. 1998. *Women and Elective Office: Past, Present, and Future.* New York: Oxford University Press.

Tolleson-Rinehart, Sue. 1992. *Gender Consciousness and Politics.* New York: Routledge.

Tomz, Michael, Jason Wittenberg, and Gary King. 2003. *CLARIFY: Software for Interpreting and Presenting Statistical Results* (version 2.1). Cambridge, MA: Harvard University.

Towell, Pat. 2002. "Defense Bill Action Could Be Delayed to Avoid Pre-Election Veto of Veterans Law." *CQ Weekly,* October 4: 2611.

————. 2003. "Chambers Agree on Funding, Not Pentagon Operations." *CQ Weekly* May 24: 1272.

Trent, Judith, and Teresa Sabourin. 1993. "Sex Still Counts: Women's Use of Televised Advertising During the Decade of the 80s." *Journal of Applied Communication Research* 21, no. 1: 21–40.

Truman, David. 1959. *The Congressional Party.* New York: Wiley.

Uhlaner, Carole Jean, and Kay Lehman Schlozman. 1986. "Candidate Gender and Congressional Campaign Receipts." *Journal of Politics* 48, no. 1: 30–50.

Vega, Arturo. 1997. "Gender and Ethnicity Effects on the Legislative Behavior and Substantive Representation of the Texas Legislature." *Texas Journal of Political Studies* 119, no. 1: 1–21.

Verba, Sidney, and Norman H. Nie. 1972. *Participation in America.* New York: Harper & Row.

Verba, Sidney, Kay Lehman Schlozman, and Henry E. Brady. 1995. *Voice and Equality: Civic Voluntarism in American Politics.* Cambridge, MA: Harvard University Press.

Wadsworth, Anne J., Phillip Patterson, Lynda Lee Kaid, Ginger Cullers, Drew Malcomb, and Linda Lamirand. 1987. "'Masculine' vs. 'Feminine' Strategies in Political Ads: Implications for Female Candidates." *Journal of Applied Communication Research* 15, no. 1/2: 77–94.

Walsh, Katherine Cramer. 2002. "Enlarging Representation: Women Bringing Marginalized Perspectives to Floor Debate in the House of Representatives." In *Women Transforming Congress*, ed. Cindy Simon Rosenthal. Norman: University of Oklahoma Press.

Weissert, Carol S. 1991. "Issue Salience and State Legislative Effectiveness." *Legislative Studies Quarterly* 16, no. 4: 509–520.

Welch, Susan. 1977. "Women as Political Animals? A Test of Some Explanations for Male-Female Political Participation Differences." *American Journal of Political Science* 21, no. 4: 711–730.

Wheeler, Winslow T. 2004. *The Wastrels of Defense: How Congress Sabotages U.S. Security.* Annapolis: Naval Institute Press.

Wilcox, Clyde. 1994. "Why Was 1992 the 'Year of the Woman'? Explaining Women's Gains in 1992." In *The Year of the Woman: Myths and Realities*, eds. Elizabeth Adell Cook, Sue Thomas, and Clyde Wilcox. Boulder, CO: Westview Press.

Williams, Leonard. 1994. "Political Advertising in the Year of the Woman: Did X Mark the Spot?" In *The Year of the Woman: Myths and Realities*, eds. Elizabeth Adell Cook, Sue Thomas, and Clyde Wilcox. Boulder, CO: Westview Press.

Wilson, Rick K., and Cheryl D. Young. 1997. "Cosponsorship in the U.S. Congress." *Legislative Studies Quarterly* 22, no. 1: 25–43.

Witt, Linda, Karen Paget, and Glenna Matthews. 1994. *Running as a Woman.* New York: Free Press.

Wolbrecht, Christina. 2002. "Female Legislators and the Women's Rights Agenda: From Feminine Mystique to Feminist Era." In *Women Transforming Congress*, ed. Cindy Simon Rosenthal. Norman: University of Oklahoma Press.

Woods, Harriet. 2000. *Stepping Up to Power: The Political Journey of American Women.* Boulder, CO: Westview Press.

Yoder, Janice D. 1991. "Rethinking Tokenism: Looking Beyond Numbers." *Gender & Society* 5, no. 2: 178–192.

The Contributors

Barbara Burrell is professor of political science at Northern Illinois University. She is the author of *Public Opinion, the First Ladyship and Hillary Rodham Clinton* and *A Woman's Place Is in the House: Campaigning for Congress in the Feminist Era*. She is currently writing an update on women's and men's campaigns for the US House from 1994 through 2008.

Dianne Bystrom is director of the Carrie Chapman Catt Center for Women and Politics at Iowa State University. A frequent commentator about political and women's issues for state and national media, she is the coauthor, coeditor, or contributor to eleven books, including *Gender and Elections* and *Gender and Candidate Communication*. She currently serves as secretary/treasurer of the Political Communication Division of the American Political Science Association, and teaches courses in leadership, women and politics, and political campaigns.

Susan J. Carroll is professor of political science and women's and gender studies at Rutgers University and senior scholar at the Center for American Women and Politics of the Eagleton Institute of Politics. She is the author of *Women as Candidates in American Politics,* and the editor of several volumes. Her recent research focuses on gender and political representation and the role of gender in elections.

Kathleen Dolan is professor of political science at the University of Wisconsin–Milwaukee. She is the author of *Voting for Women: How the Public Evaluates Women Candidates*. Her work on women candidates, elections, and voting behavior has appeared in the *American Journal of Political Science, Political Research Quarterly, American Politics Quarterly, Political Psychology, Political Behavior, Women and Politics,* and *Social Science Quarterly.* She currently serves as coeditor of the journal *Politics & Gender.*

Luis Ricardo Fraga is associate vice provost for Faculty Advancement, director of the Diversity Research Institute, Russell F. Stark University Professor, and professor of political science at the University of Washington. He was a member of the special taskforce of the American Political Science Association that wrote *Democracy at Risk: How Political Choices Undermine Citizen Participation and What We Can Do About It.* He is coauthor of *Multiethnic Moments: The Politics of Urban Education Reform* and coeditor of *Racial and Ethnic Minorities in Advanced Industrial Democracies.* He has published in the *American Political Science Review, American Journal of Political Science, Perspectives on Politics, Dubois Review, Journal of Politics, Urban Affairs Quarterly, Western Political Quarterly,* and the *Harvard Journal of Hispanic Policy.* He was secretary of the American Political Science Association and is a former president of the Western Political Science Association. He is one of the coprincipal investigators of the Latino National Survey (LNS), the first-ever state stratified survey of Latinos in the United States.

Jennifer L. Lawless is assistant professor of political science at Brown University, where she has a courtesy appointment at the Taubman Center for Public Policy. Her teaching and research focus on gender politics, electoral politics, and public opinion, topics on which she has published widely. Most notably, she is the coauthor (with Richard L. Fox) of *It Takes a Candidate: Why Women Don't Run for Office* (2005). Lawless has become a recognized speaker on the subject of women candidates, frequently discussing these issues on national and local media outlets. She also was a candidate for the US House of Representatives in the 2006 Democratic primary in the second district of Rhode Island.

Linda Lopez is a political scientist and expert on public policy and opinion. Most recently, she served as an expert consultant to the National Science Foundation (NSF), Washington, DC. Previously, she served as program director for Cross Directorate Activities in the Directorate for Social, Behavior, and Economic Sciences at the NSF. Prior to joining the NSF, she served as director of education at the American Political Science Association, Washington, DC; and was formerly assistant professor in the Department of Political Science and director of the legal studies program at Chapman University. Her recent research and publications have focused on women and politics with particular attention to women elected officials in state legislatures. She has published in *American Political Science Review*, *Political Research Quarterly*, *Journal of Women, Politics and Policy,* and other scholarly journals. She is currently examining the mediating effect of skin tone on perceptions of discrimination in the workplace and education settings across racial and ethnic groups.

Valerie Martinez-Ebers is professor of political science at the University of North Texas and vice president of the American Political Science Association. A former president of the Western Political Science Association, her teaching interests and research expertise include race, ethnicity, and politics; Latino politics; public policy; survey research; and political tolerance. Most of her publications are on the consequences of education policy for minority students, but she also has publications on Latino/a politics, aging policy, and methods of survey research. Her most recent copublications include *Politicas: Latina Public Officials in Texas* and "Su Casa Es Nuestra Casa: Latino Politics Research and the Development of American Political Science," published in the *American Political Science Review*. She has a forthcoming book entitled, *Perspectives on Race, Ethnicity and Religion: Minority Politics in the United States.*

Melissa Olivia Neal is a PhD candidate at Florida State University. She is currently associate director of the Haas Center for Business Research and Economic Development at the University of West Florida, Emerald Coast, where she is involved in economic development research, which focuses on various topics including tourism, education, military impacts, and workforce development. She is focusing her academic research on institutions, specifically Congress, as well as women in politics.

Karen O'Connor is the Jonathan N. Helfat Distinguished Professor of Political Science at American University where she also directs the Women & Politics Institute. She is the immediate past president of the American Political Science Associations's Organized Research Section on Women and Politics. She is the coauthor of *American Politics: Continuity and Change* (9th ed.), *Women, Politics, and American Society,* and *No Neutral Ground: Abortion Politics in an Age of Absolutes,* among others. She is considered an expert on abortion politics and has testified before both the House and Senate Judiciary Committees on abortion law.

Kathryn Pearson is assistant professor of political science at the University of Minnesota. She specializes in US politics, especially the US Congress, women and politics, political parties, congressional elections, and public opinion. She is currently working on a book manuscript about party discipline in the House of Representatives and on projects analyzing gender dynamics in congressional elections. Her work has been published in the *Journal of Politics* and *Perspectives on Politics*. She is a former research fellow at The Brookings Institution, and from 1993 to 1998 she worked on Capitol Hill as a legislative assistant for two congresswomen.

Ricardo Ramírez is assistant professor in the Department of Political Science and the Department of American Studies and Ethnicity at the University of Southern California. His contribution to Chapter 9 is funded by the National Science Foundation (award # 0512085). His research interests include political behavior, state and local politics, and the politics of race and ethnicity, especially as they relate to participation, mobilization, and political incorporation. He has been principal investigator of a longitudinal study of patterns of gendered career paths among Latina/o elected officials since 1990. He is coeditor (with T. Lee and K. Ramakrishnan) of *Transforming Politics, Transforming America: The Political and Civic Incorporation of Immigrants in the United States*. His most recent writing includes "Segmented Mobilization: Latino Nonpartisan Get-Out-the-Vote Efforts in the 2000 General Election"; (with M. Barreto and N. Woods) "Are Naturalized Voters Driving the California Latino Electorate? Measuring the Impact of IRCA Citizens on Latino Voting"; and "Giving Voice to Latino Voters: A Field Experiment on the Effectiveness of a National Nonpartisan Mobilization Effort."

Beth Reingold is associate professor of political science and women's studies at Emory University. Her primary research and teaching interests are in the areas of gender, race, and the politics of representation and identity in the United States. She is the author of *Representing Women: Sex, Gender, and Legislative Behavior in Arizona and California*. Her articles have appeared in the *Journal of Politics*, *Legislative Studies Quarterly*, *Social Science Quarterly*, *State Politics & Policy Quarterly*, *Women & Politics*, and other scholarly journals. Her current research examines representation and the intersections of gender, race, and ethnicity in US state legislatures.

Cindy Simon Rosenthal is director of the Carl Albert Congressional Research and Studies Center at the University of Oklahoma, and an associate professor of political science with a joint appointment to the women's studies faculty. At the Albert Center, she started the National Education for Women's Leadership in Oklahoma, part of a national network of programs to encourage and empower undergraduate women to enter public service and politics. She is the author of *When Women Lead* and editor of *Women Transforming Congress*. Her work has appeared in the *Journal of Public Administration Research and Theory*, *Political Research Quarterly*,

Legislative Studies Quarterly, Women & Politics, (with Ronald M. Peters Jr.) *Politics & Gender;* and *Social Science Quarterly.* She is currently working on a book on Speaker Nancy Pelosi. In 2007, she was elected mayor of the city of Norman, Oklahoma.

Wendy G. Smooth is assistant professor in the departments of women's studies and political science at The Ohio State University. She also holds a faculty appointment with the Kirwan Institute for the Study of Race and Ethnicity. Her research and teaching interests are in US politics with particular emphasis on gender and public policy, racial politics, and state and local government. Her work appears in several academic journals including *Politics & Gender, Journal of Women, Politics and Policy,* and in various edited volumes. Her current research focuses on the impact of gender and race in state legislatures and she is currently completing a book entitled *Power and Influence: The Impact of Race and Gender in American State Legislatures* (forthcoming 2008).

Atiya Kai Stokes-Brown is assistant professor of political science at Bucknell University. Her research and teaching interests include campaigns and elections, state politics, political behavior, gender, and race/ethnicity. Her research has appeared in the *Journal of Politics, American Politics Research, National Political Science Review, Politics and Policy, Political Research Quarterly,* and in various edited volumes. She is currently working on a book manuscript about the use of deracialization strategies in black electoral politics. Other projects include analyses of the determinants of Latinos' racial choices and the effect of racial identity on Latino political behavior.

Michele L. Swers is associate professor in the Department of Government at Georgetown University. Her research and teaching interests encompass Congress, women and politics, and issues of representation. Her publications include *The Difference Women Make: The Policy Impact of Women in Congress* and (with Julie Dolan and Melissa Deckman) *Women and Politics: Paths to Power and Political Influence.* Her work on gender differences in legislative behavior also appears in academic journals including *Legislative Studies Quarterly, PS: Political Science, Women and Politics,* and the *Japanese Journal of the International Society for Gender Studies,* as well as numerous edited volumes. She is currently writing a book on gender differences in policy participation in the US Senate in the areas of women's issues, defense, and judicial nomination politics.

Index

Abzug, Bella, 137
African American women in state legislatures: as committee and subcommittee chairs, 190–191, 228; distribution of leadership positions for, 182, 183*tab*; effectiveness ranking of, 179; exclusion from circles of power of, 177, 182, 188–189; factors in success of, 178; gender and race impacts on influence of, 178–179, 194–195; general influence of, 179, 181–188; in informal leadership groups, 186–188; and institutional response to new entrants, 178; institutional values and norms impacting on influence of, 176, 193, 195; issue-specific influence of, 179, 189–192; legislative context impacting on influence of, 177; leveraging power and influence through caucuses, 195; peer evaluation of, 176–177; power and general influence through committee chair assignments of, 182–186; power through prior knowledge and expertise of, 191–192; research on power and influence of, 178–181; and tactics to maintain existing system, 192–194; in upper tier leadership, 182–184; and women's technical competence, 180

African American women in US Congress: as committee and subcommittee chairs, 228; prestigious committee assignments of, 137
African Americans in state legislatures: committee assignments for, 139–140, 143; disadvantage of race and gender intersectionality for, 161; exclusion from leadership positions, 230; focus and success of legislation introduced by, 161; limits on influence and goal attainment of, 160–161; white colleagues' perceptions of, 160
African Americans in US Congress: dramatic electoral gains of, 8; gender diversity among, 8; political efficacy and interest in elections resulting from, 103
American National Election Studies (ANES), 105; question wording in, 112

Braun, Carol Moseley, 233

Campaign finance reform: proposed study of gender gaps in, 237; and women's presence in electoral office, 56
Campaign negativity, fund-raising's contribution to, 56–57
Candidate websites: advantages of, 67;

istics in, 47; examination of women candidates' fund-raising success in, 42; gender comparison of winners and vote obtained in, 46*tab*; and "women friendliness" index, 46–47

Congressional primaries: candidate-centered model in, 24; conventional wisdom on women's electoral success in, 34–35; data set for analyzing outcomes of, 26–27; decrease of women entering, 35; findings on aggregate bias against women candidates in, 34–35; and gender stereotyping, 25; gauges of competition in, 30–33; hypotheses to assess gender dynamics in, 24–26; obstacles to women's participation in, 24–26, 35–36; partisan gap in, 26–27; totals of women candidates in 1958–2004 races, 26; and traditional gender socialization, 24; victory rates and vote margin results in, 28–30; women challenging women in, 33–34, 35; and women's more difficult electoral environment, 25–26

Defense authorization bill: and amendment sponsorship by gender and party, 122–123; amendments to assess gender influence on senators' strategic decisions, 121–122; assessment of constituent interest in defense issues, 124; decisions on best use of legislative resources, 124; driving factors in sponsorship of amendments to, 124; gender differences in types of amendments to, 125*tab*, 126; purpose and requirements of, 120–121; and Senate women's defense-related amendments, 123; and senators' influence on defense policies, 121; and senators' participation in floor debates, 121; types of issues in, 121–122; women's cosponsorship of amendments and compensatory strategies in, 127–128, 131–132; women's overall participation in development of, 126–128

DeLauro, Rosa, 212, 236

Democratic Congressional Campaign

Committee (DCCC), fund-raising and spending in 2006 elections, 51–52

Democratic women legislators: compensatory strategies to counter voter bias, 228; and credibility on defense issues, 131; liberalism and party loyalty of, 35; historic accomplishments of, 1; and 1992 Year of the Woman, 7; primary performance of, 25; Speaker Pelosi's impact on, 229; and substantive representation, 6

Dole, Elizabeth, 59; stereotyped campaign coverage of, 64

Emanuel, Rahm, 212

EMILY's List, 2, 27, 49, 226, 235, 238, 241, 242

Fund-raising and spending, as negative factor in decision to seek office, 56

Gender stereotypes, of candidates and public officials, 6, 10–11, 12, 15, 25, 60–62, 63–64, 68, 80–81, 102, 104–105, 109, 113, 117, 119–120, 130–132, 227

Latina state legislators: analysis of legislation introduced by, 161; appeal to voters based on their status as mothers, 230–231; caucus support of, 171–172, 173; in coalitions with African American and Asian American educators, 169–170; committee assignments of, 143; dramatic electoral gains of, 7–8; gender inclusive advantage of, 158, 163; intersection of race/ethnicity and gender as leverage for, 159; intersectionality and coalition building of, 230; multiple identity advantage of, 157, 163; numbers of, 157, 165*tab*; political efficacy and interest in elections resulting from presence of, 103; and political incorporation and policy benefit in legislatures, 158; positioned for advocacy for working class minorities, 157, 158; potential coalition partners for, 172–173; propensity to identify with gender

About the Book

THIS WIDE-RANGING new study grapples with the increasingly complex array of opportunities and challenges that face women today as both legislative candidates and elected officials.

Offering cutting-edge, original research, *Legislative Women* expands our knowledge on an array of critical topics. The contributors address everything from campaign finance to the significance of race and ethnicity, from media relations to how women advance within the ranks of the elite, and more. As they examine exactly how and in what circumstances gender matters, they bring new depth to the study of women and politics.

Beth Reingold is associate professor of political science and women's studies at Emory University. She is author of *Representing Women: Sex, Gender, and Legislative Behavior in Arizona and California*.